CW00496117

"I enjoy reading Phil Moore's book
Christian life with perce
– **Nicky Gumbel** –

"In taking us straight to the heart (
magnificently. We so need to get int(
get into us. The fact that Phil writes so relevantly and with
submission to biblical revelation means that we are genuinely helped to
be shaped by the Bible's teaching."

– **Terry Virgo**

"Fresh. Solid. Simple. Really good stuff."

– **R. T. Kendall**

"Phil makes the deep truths of Scripture alive and accessible. If you want
to grow in your understanding of each book of the Bible, then buy these
books and let them change your life!"

– **P. J. Smyth** – GodFirst Church, Johannesburg, South Africa

"Most commentaries are dull. These are alive.
Most commentaries are for scholars. These are for **you**!"

– **Canon Michael Green**

"These notes are amazingly good. Phil's insights are striking, original, and
fresh, going straight to the heart of the text and the reader! Substantial
yet succinct, they bristle with amazing insights and life applications,
compelling us to read more. Bible reading will become enriched and
informed with such a scintillating guide. Teachers and preachers will find
nuggets of pure gold here!"

– **Greg Haslam**, Westminster Chapel, London, UK

"A strong combination of faithful scholarship, clear explanation and deep
insight make these an invaluable tool. I can't recommend them highly
enough."

– **Gavin Calver** – Director of Mission, Evangelical Alliance

"The Bible is living and dangerous. The ones who teach it best are those
who bear that in mind – and let the author do the talking. Phil has
written these studies with a sharp mind and a combination of creative
application and reverence."

– **Joel Virgo** – Leader of Newday Youth Festival

For more information about the Straight to the Heart series, please go to **www.philmoorebooks.com**.
You can also receive daily messages from Phil Moore on Twitter by following **@PhilMooreLondon**.

STRAIGHT TO
THE HEART OF

Joshua, Judges & Ruth

60 BITE-SIZED INSIGHTS

Phil Moore

MONARCH
BOOKS

Published by
Lion Hudson Limited
Wilkinson House, Jordan Hill Business Park,
Banbury Road, Oxford OX2 8DR, England
www.lionhudson.com

ISBN 978 0 85721 893 3
e-ISBN 978 0 85721 894 0

First edition 2018

Acknowledgments
Scripture quotations taken from the *Holy Bible, New International Version* Anglicised. Copyright © 1979, 1984, 2011 Biblica, formerly International Bible Society. Used by permission of Hodder & Stoughton Ltd, an Hachette UK company. All rights reserved. "NIV" is a registered trademark of Biblica. UK trademark number 1448790. Both 1984 and 2011 versions are quoted in this commentary.

A catalogue record for this book is available from the British Library.

This book is for my wife Ruth.
"All the people of my town know that you are
a woman of noble character."
Ruth 3:11

CONTENTS

JUDGES: GOD'S GIFT TO SINNERS

RUTH: GOD'S GIFT TO YOU

About the *"Straight to the Heart"* Series

On his eightieth birthday, Sir Winston Churchill dismissed the compliment that he was the "lion" who had defeated Nazi Germany in World War Two. He told the Houses of Parliament that *"It was a nation and race dwelling all around the globe that had the lion's heart. I had the luck to be called upon to give the roar."*

I hope that God speaks to you very powerfully through the "roar" of the books in the *Straight to the Heart* series. I hope they help you to understand the books of the Bible and the message which the Holy Spirit inspired their authors to write. I hope that they help you to hear God's voice challenging you, and that they provide you with a springboard for further journeys into each book of Scripture for yourself.

But when you hear my "roar", I want you to know that it comes from the heart of a much bigger "lion" than me. I have been shaped by a whole host of great Christian thinkers and preachers from around the world, and I want to give due credit to at least some of them here:

Terry Virgo, Dave Holden, Guy Miller, John Hosier, Adrian Holloway, Greg Haslam, Lex Loizides and all those who lead the Newfrontiers family of churches; friends and encouragers, such as Stef Liston, Joel Virgo, Stuart Gibbs, Scott Taylor, Nick Sharp, Nick Derbridge, Phil Whittall, and Kevin and Sarah Aires; Simon Cox and Jenny Muscat at Monarch books; Malcolm Kayes and all the elders of The Coign Church, Woking; my fellow elders and church members here at Everyday Church in London; my great friend Andrew Wilson – without your friendship, encouragement and example, this series would never have happened.

I would like to thank my parents, my brother Jonathan and my in-laws, Clive and Sue Jackson. Dad – your example birthed in my heart the passion which brought this series into being. I didn't listen to all you said when I was a child, but I couldn't ignore the way you got up at five o' clock every morning to pray, read the Bible and worship, because of your radical love for God and for his Word. I'd like to thank my children – Isaac, Noah, Esther and Ethan – for keeping me sane when publishing deadlines were looming. But most of all, I'm grateful to my incredible wife, Ruth – my friend, encourager, corrector and helper.

You all have the lion's heart, and you have all developed the lion's heart in me. I count it an enormous privilege to be the one who was chosen to sound the lion's roar.

So welcome to the *Straight to the Heart* series. My prayer is that you will let this roar grip your own heart too – for the glory of the great Lion of the Tribe of Judah, the Lord Jesus Christ!

Introduction: The God Who Keeps on Giving

"I will give you every place where you set your foot."
(Joshua 1:3)

If I invited you around for dinner, you wouldn't expect to eat it in the hallway. You might comment on how nice and warm it feels to step inside. You might even stop to admire one of the pictures on the wall. But you wouldn't want to stay there. You would see my hallway for what it is: a place to leave your dirty shoes before stepping into the rest of my home.

The same is true with Christianity. Forgiveness is the hallway through which we enter the palace of God's salvation. It's glorious, but it is the means to a far more glorious end. God cleans up our sin so that he can embrace us and lead us into all the riches that are ours in Jesus: deep friendship with the God who made us, adoption as his children, a profound sense of purpose, complete freedom from fear – those are just a few of the magnificent rooms in the palace. When Christians talk and sing about their faith as if it were all about forgiveness for their sins, it falls as short as you and I would if we sat down to eat our dinner between my daughter's wet coat and my son's smelly trainers.

That's why we need the books of Joshua, Judges and Ruth. They are the great antidote to "hallway Christianity" – a downsizing of what it means for us to have been saved by God. These three books were written to remind us that forgiveness is the start, not the end, of the Gospel. They restore to us a proper grasp of the grand vista of our salvation.

The first five books of the Bible are all about forgiveness and redemption. Moses writes about the God who rescued the Israelites from their slavery in Egypt and who led them across the desert as far as the border of the Promised Land. The sixth, seventh and eighth books of the Bible tell us what happened next. They take us beyond the hallway of salvation to describe what it meant for Israel to take possession of that Promised Land. They remind us that the God of Israel is not a reluctant Saviour who begrudgingly permits people to enter his palace and to sit among the coats and shoes in his hallway. He is the God who keeps on giving. He calls us sons and daughters, and he invites us to enjoy the vast delights of what has become ours through the death and resurrection of his Son.

Joshua and Judges aren't just history books. The Hebrew Old Testament groups them among the "Former Prophets". It sees them as far more than a simple record of the past. They are full of prophetic pictures of what it means to be saved by the God of Israel.[1] The apostle Paul has books like these in mind when he reflects that *"These things happened to them as examples and were written down as warnings for us, on whom the culmination of the ages has come."* So does the writer of Hebrews when he points out that *"If Joshua had given them rest, God would not have spoken later about another day... Let us, therefore, make every effort to enter that rest, so that no one will perish by following their example of disobedience."*[2] These books aren't simply a record of what God did for the nation of Israel over 3,000 years ago. They are also his call for believers in our own generation to step out of the hallway to explore all the great rooms of their salvation.

In **Joshua 1–12**, we discover the scale of **God's gift to his people**. As we watch the Lord empower a nation of former

---

[1] The other books listed among the "Former Prophets" are 1 and 2 Samuel and 1 and 2 Kings. The "Latter Prophets" are the 17 final books of the English Old Testament, from Isaiah to Malachi. The Hebrew Old Testament lists the book of Ruth separately among the "Additional Writings".

[2] 1 Corinthians 10:6, 11; Hebrews 4:8–11.

slaves to conquer with ease the most desirable portion of the Middle East, it starts to dawn on us that Christians tend to speak too much about what they have been saved *from* and too little about what they have been saved *for*. We find ourselves challenged that there are many things that belong to us in Jesus that we have yet to conquer and possess. These chapters remind us that our salvation is huge.

In **Joshua 13–24**, we discover the scale of **God's gift to each of us**. The story gets personal, focusing first on each specific tribe within the nation of Israel, and then on Joshua himself as an individual. This is even more significant if we believe the Jewish Talmud when it tells us that the book was written by Joshua himself – supported by the author's references to *"we"* and *"us"*, and by his statement in 6:25 that Rahab is still alive at the time of writing.[3] Joshua wants to stop us from treating his book as a general challenge to God's people. It is a call for each one of us to lay full hold of our salvation.

In the book of **Judges**, we are invited to marvel at **God's gift to sinners**. When the Israelites reject the God who granted them many mighty victories under Joshua, they discover that he keeps on giving. He judges them for worshipping the idols of the Canaanites, but he does so to bring them back to him. Whenever they repent and serve him, he provides them with a leader who delivers them from their oppressors and restores the broken borders of the Promised Land. He anoints those leaders with his Holy Spirit and invites his people to celebrate the way he gently restores any sinner who repents of their sins. All of this is meant to correct the idea, still pervasive among Christians, that we please God by lamenting our sin in the hallway instead

---

[3] *We* and *us* are in the Hebrew text of Joshua 5:1 and 6. The rabbis who wrote down the Jewish oral traditions in the Talmud in *c.*200 AD were convinced that Joshua wrote the last eight verses of Deuteronomy and the whole of Joshua, except its final chapter that records his death (Baba Bathra 15a). Scholars debate this, but their claim is backed up by a statement in Joshua 24:26 that he was a Scripture writer, just like Moses.

of celebrating his salvation in the palace. It encourages us to respond gladly to the Lord's command in Psalm 100:4 – *"Enter his gates with thanksgiving and his courts with praise."*

The book of **Ruth** makes this message personal again. It celebrates **God's gift to you**. It homes in on one particular family during the rule of the judges, as a way of helping you consider your own personal response to the God who keeps on giving. By charting Ruth's journey from pagan idolatry to the very heart of the Messiah's family tree, the author invites you to believe that God has opened wide to you the doors of the palace of his salvation. Ruth invites you to believe that the Lord will do great things in your own life if you resolve as firmly as she did that you will follow him.

So let's read Joshua, Judges and Ruth together, not just as history, but as a prophetic invitation to us from God. Let's see the highs and lows of Israel's early history as his call for us to step out of the hallway to enjoy the full measure of our salvation. Let's discover together what it truly means for us to know and love the God who keeps on giving.

Joshua 1–12:

God's Gift to His People

Step Forward
(Joshua 1:1–18)

After the death of Moses the servant of the Lord, the
Lord said to Joshua son of Nun, Moses' assistant...
"Get ready to cross the River Jordan."

(Joshua 1:1–2)

Nobody wants to take over leadership from a genius. Think of
David Moyes, who succeeded Sir Alex Ferguson as manager
of Manchester United. Unable to live up to his predecessor's
twenty-seven years of almost non-stop trophy winning, he was
sacked after less than ten months in the job. Or think of Philip
Arridhaeus, who succeeded Alexander the Great as ruler of the
largest empire the world had ever seen, and who destroyed it
even faster than David Moyes destroyed Manchester United's
reputation.

So imagine how Joshua must have felt when he took over
leading Israel from Moses.[1] His predecessor wasn't just a great
leader. He had created the nation he led by facing up to Pharaoh
and performing miracles that brought the mighty superpower
Egypt to its knees. Moses had spoken to the Lord face to face on
Mount Sinai, descending from the mountain with God's Law in
his hands and the plans for God's Tabernacle in his heart. Moses
had fed two million Israelites four million litres of manna every
day for forty years in the desert. He had led them to victory
against the Amalekites, the Amorites and the Midianites. The
first verse of Joshua therefore emphasizes how intimidated and

---

[1] Joshua begins where Deuteronomy ended, at the end of 30 days of mourning
for the death of Moses.

insecure he was feeling. It says that these things happened after the death of *"Moses the servant of the Lord"* to a man who knew that he was merely *"Moses' assistant"*.

Joshua was tempted to look back at Moses and to look down on himself. He was the one whose army had been defeated by the Amalekites every time Moses left him to fight them on his own. He was the one that Moses left behind in the Tabernacle whenever there was important business for him to attend to elsewhere.[2] He was the one who had failed to persuade the Israelites that they could conquer the Promised Land if they listened to him instead of the ten spies who doubted the Lord. Although he had served Moses faithfully for forty years, he had only been recognized as his successor two months before Moses died. This can't have made him feel confident. Aged eighty-four, he wasn't just older than anyone else in Israel. He was also more out of his depth.[3]

That's why Joshua needed to listen to the Lord when he commanded him to step forward in faith. *"Moses my servant is dead. Now then, you and all these people, get ready to cross the River Jordan into the land I am about to give to them – to the Israelites. I will give you every place where you set your foot, as I promised Moses."* Joshua needed to look up and to believe that the Lord is the God who keeps on giving. He needed to believe that the Lord would empower him to succeed where Moses failed, by conquering the most fertile stretch of land in the Middle East, stretching from the desert of Sinai, in modern-day Egypt up to modern-day Lebanon, and from the Mediterranean Sea to the

STEP FORWARD (JOSHUA 1:1–18)

---

[2] Exodus 17:8–16; 33:11; Numbers 27:12–23. Joshua had been leader of the tribe of Ephraim for 40 years, but even his own tribe refused to follow his lead in Numbers 13–14. This didn't bode well for him.

[3] For a timeline of the book of Joshua, see the chapter "Milk and Honey". Since Joshua died aged 110 in 1380 BC (Joshua 24:29), he must have been aged 44 when the Israelites came out of Egypt in 1446 BC. Only Caleb, five years younger than him, also survived from that generation (Numbers 26:65; Joshua 14:10).

River Euphrates, in modern-day Iraq.[4] He had to trust that the leadership genius of Moses had not originated with Moses. It had been given to him by God's Holy Spirit.[5] *"As I was with Moses, so I will be with you; I will never leave you or forsake you."*[6]

Joshua felt weak and afraid, so he needed to listen to the solemn charge that he is given four times in this opening chapter: *"Be strong and courageous, because you will lead these people to inherit the land."*[7] We are told in verse 8 that this courage comes from reading and reciting the Word of God. Joshua had only the first five books of the Bible, whereas we have it all. When the Lord tells Joshua to *"Be careful to do everything written in it. Then you will be prosperous and successful"*, he is still speaking to you and me today, reminding us that his Word raises our expectations and prevents us from settling for something less than our salvation.[8] As we study the Bible, we discover all that Jesus has won for us and we receive the courage we need to step forward to inherit our own Promised Land.

These opening verses also remind us that courage comes through surrounding ourselves with Christian friends. That's why we need to join a local church. Joshua encourages the

[4] Joshua 1:4 emphasizes the vast expanse of God's promises to us. The territory described here would not be fully conquered until the time of King David (2 Samuel 8:1–15).

[5] A change of church leader always feels like an upheaval, but there is far more continuity than change. This principle from Joshua 1:5 is restated in Hebrews 13:7–8, when many of the original apostles were dying.

[6] Joshua 1:5 is the closest the New Testament ever comes to quoting from the book of Joshua, yet even here Hebrews 13:5 may actually be quoting from Deuteronomy 31:6.

[7] Joshua 1:6 echoes the charge that Moses gave to Joshua when he commissioned him to lead Israel a few weeks earlier (Deuteronomy 31:6–8, 23). It is echoed in turn by 1 Corinthians 16:13, where Paul takes the Greek word *andrizomai*, meaning *to be manly*, from the Greek Septuagint translation of this verse. God's promises must never breed passivity. Christian leadership is always a call to courageous action.

[8] The Hebrew word *hāgāh* in 1:8 is the same word used in Psalm 1:2 for *meditating* on the Word of God. Reading the Bible isn't enough. We need to meditate on it until it drowns out the voice of fear in our minds.

eastern tribes of Israel to fight, and they encourage him by echoing God's words back to him: *"Just as we fully obeyed Moses, so we will obey you... Only be strong and courageous!"*[9]

Moses means *Drawn Out*, because his mission was to save Israel out of slavery in Egypt. Joshua had been born Hoshea, which means *Salvation*, but Moses changed his name to Joshua in Numbers 13:16, which means *The Lord Saves*, because his mission was to lead Israel into the full reality of their salvation. He was not to be a David Moyes or a Philip Arridhaeus, a pale shadow of his predecessor. He was to take Israel further than Moses ever had into an experience of the Lord as the God who keeps on giving.

The name Joshua in Hebrew is *Yehōshua'* or *Yēshūa'*. It is the same Hebrew name that the angel commanded Mary and Joseph to give to the baby boy that was born to Mary in Bethlehem. Although English Bibles try to honour the Lord by translating it as either *Joshua* or *Jesus*, we need to remember that both are *Yēshūa'* in Hebrew and *Iēsous* in Greek.[10] The life of Joshua is meant to be a prophetic promise that a better Conqueror will come after him and lead God's people into a better Promised Land. If you feel too weak to step into all that your salvation means, remember that you have a far better Joshua to lead you into your own Promised Land than the men of Israel. ❤

Don't stay in the hallway of your salvation. With Jesus leading you, if you step forward in faith you cannot fail.[11] Don't settle for anything less than the vast expanse of spiritual

19

---

[9] These 2½ tribes had settled in the land to the east of the River Jordan in Numbers 32. While Joshua models how second-generation leaders ought to take up the reins, these tribes model how they ought to be received.

[10] Matthew 1:21; Luke 1:31. Joshua calls himself *Yehōshua'* throughout the book of Joshua, but later historians shortened his name to *Yēshūa'* (Nehemiah 8:17). Jesus is called *Yēshūa'* throughout the Hebrew New Testament, and they are both called *Iēsous* throughout the Greek Bible (see Acts 7:45 and Hebrews 4:8).

[11] The Lord uses a Hebrew perfect tense in 1:3 to assure Joshua it is a done deal – literally, *"I have given you"*.

territory that is yours through his death and resurrection. The Lord encourages you:

> *Be strong and courageous. Follow your great Joshua. Step forward into your Promised Land.*

Unreasonable
(Joshua 2:1–24)

"The Lord your God is God in heaven above and on the earth below. Now then, please swear to me by the Lord that you will show kindness to my family."

(Joshua 2:11–12)

The great British playwright George Bernard Shaw argued that *"The reasonable man adapts himself to the world: the unreasonable one persists in trying to adapt the world to himself. Therefore all progress depends on the unreasonable man."*[1]

I don't know if George Bernard Shaw was right, but what I do know is that Rahab was an unreasonable woman and that the Lord loved it. She had no reason to expect favour from the God of Israel, yet she gambled everything on his mercy. She was saved from the destruction of Jericho because she trusted that he is the God who keeps on giving.

For a start, she was a Canaanite. She was part of a nation that sacrificed its babies on the altars of its false gods and had sex with close family members and even with animals. The Lord had vowed to judge her nation's sin when it *"reached its full measure"*. Rahab was living in a nation on death-row.[2]

What was more, she lived in the city of Jericho, one of the greatest strongholds of Canaanite sin. Its name means *Moon City* because its citizens worshipped the moon instead of the Lord. Her own name means *Proud*, signifying that she was part of the problem. She works as a prostitute and doesn't think twice about

---

[1] This is one of his *Maxims for Revolutionists*, published in 1903.

[2] Genesis 15:16; Leviticus 18:1–30; Deuteronomy 12:29–31; Ezra 9:11.

lying to the squad of soldiers who knock on her door.[3] On top of all this, we are told in verse 15 that her house was built into the walls of Jericho, the very structure that the spies had come to learn how to destroy![4] Putting all of this together makes one thing exceedingly clear: if Rahab expected to receive anything good from God then she was being totally unreasonable.

And yet God saves her. This account of the conquest of the land of Canaan begins with the Lord extending grace towards a Canaanite who pleads for mercy. It doesn't matter that she is so steeped in sin that she embodies everything that has provoked the Lord to judge her nation. Anyone can be saved if they lay hold of the God who keeps on giving.

Rahab proclaims her faith in the God of Israel. While the Israelites east of the River Jordan wonder whether they can trust Joshua to lead them into battle, Rahab states her own conviction unequivocally: *"I know that the Lord has given this land to you."* While Joshua fears that he may not lead Israel as well as Moses, Rahab recognizes that Israel's victories were never manmade. It was the Lord who parted the Red Sea for them in Exodus 14 and who gave them victory over the Amorites in Numbers 21. She recognizes the root cause of all their victories: *"The Lord your God is God in heaven above and on the earth below."*[5]

That's why readers miss the point when they question how Rahab could attract God's salvation despite telling a lie. Her deceit towards the soldiers is the least of her problems. Her idolatry, her prostitution and her sinful lifestyle have already

---

[3] The Greek word *pornē* in Hebrews 11:31 and James 2:25 makes it clear that Rahab was a *prostitute*, although innkeeping and prostitution were closely linked in the ancient world. She must have recognized who the spies were when they asked for a room only, and not for a girl on the side.

[4] Moses sent 12 spies to explore the land of Canaan in Numbers 13. Joshua only sends two spies because their mission is simply to inspect the city of Jericho and to come back with thoughts on how to destroy it.

[5] Compare Rahab's words of faith with the Hebrew words of unbelief in Numbers 13:33. The enemies of God often see the realities of Kingdom warfare much more clearly than believers do. See also James 2:19.

forfeited any reasonable hope of her receiving forgiveness from God. Her only hope lies in his mercy, which is why this chapter shouts so loudly about the God who keeps on giving.

In the Hebrew text of this chapter, the word that is used for the *"scarlet cord"* that Rahab hangs from her window in verses 18 and 21 is *tiqvāh*. In the thirty-two occurrences of that word elsewhere in the Old Testament, it never means *rope*; it only ever means *hope*. The word is therefore used here as a clue to explain how a prostitute whose house was built into the very walls of Jericho could be spared its destruction. Rahab didn't know that the redness of the scarlet cord pointed prophetically to the blood that Jesus would one day shed to save sinners such as her.[6] All she knew was that the spies God had sent to her from Shittim told her that hanging it from her window would express her faith in his willingness to save her.[7] Remember that the book of Joshua is listed among the "Former Prophets" in the Hebrew Old Testament. Remember also that the writers of the New Testament use Rahab as an example of how God loves to forgive the undeserving.

By faith the prostitute Rahab, because she welcomed the spies, was not killed with those who were unbelieving. (Hebrews 11:31)

Was not even Rahab the prostitute considered righteous for what she did when she gave lodging to the spies and sent them off in a different direction? (James 2:25)

---

[6] She knew a remarkable amount about the God of Israel. She refers to him four times by his covenant name *Yahweh* (2:9–12), and she uses the technical words *hāram* and *hēsēd* to describe his *destructive judgment* of sin (2:10) and his *loving mercy* towards those who repent (2:12).

[7] The Israelite campsite at Shittim, meaning *Acacia Trees*, was the place where Israel sinned by having sex with pagan women in Numbers 25:1. Don't miss the irony as men go from there to save a pagan prostitute.

There is a reason, therefore, why the book of Joshua begins with a visit to a prostitute in Jericho. The God who keeps on giving wants to teach us what it means to put our faith in him. Faith in God is seen, not by what we say we believe, but by what we actually do. If Rahab had sung songs about the God of Israel but failed to hang the scarlet cord from her window, she would have died on the Day of Judgment. If she had hung out something other than the scarlet cord that pointed to the blood of Jesus, then she would have died too. It isn't the amount of faith we have that saves us, but what we place that faith in. It didn't matter how little faith the members of Rahab's family had in her story about the scarlet cord – if they stepped inside her brothel and closed the door behind them, they were saved. A little faith unleashes an unreasonable amount of mercy.

So don't move on from this chapter without praying to the God who turned a brothel in the walls of Jericho into a centre for salvation. Tell him that you trust him for your own forgiveness too. It doesn't matter who you are or where you've been or what you've done. The blood of Jesus is powerful enough to wipe away all of your sin.

If you pray that prayer, the Lord will do far more than simply let you into the hallway of his salvation. Rahab wasn't just spared from the destruction of Jericho. We are told in 6:25 that she was admitted to the very heart of Israel, and in Matthew 1:5 that she went on to become an ancestor of the royal family of Israel, including Jesus the Messiah.

Rahab was sinful. Her faith was unreasonable. But God is even more unreasonably merciful. Tell him that you share the faith of a prostitute in the God who keeps on giving.

Believing Is Seeing
(Joshua 3:1–17)

"Tell the priests who carry the ark of the covenant: 'When you reach the edge of the Jordan's waters, go and stand in the river.'"

(Joshua 3:8)

You can tell if you have fallen for a puny view of Christianity by how you respond to the mighty promises in the Bible. Although most of us feel offended by the suggestion that we might be squatting in the hallway instead of enjoying all the rooms of our salvation, even a cursory look at how we treat those promises proves that it's true.

How do you respond when the Bible tells you that the Devil and his demons are real, and that you have full authority and power to send them packing in Jesus' name? The story of Rahab reminds us that faith is seen by what we do, not just by what we say, so how do you respond to the many Bible promises that God will heal and deliver people if you lay hands on them and pray? How do you respond to the promise of the book of Joshua that Jesus wants to lead you into many such victories today?

The truth is, many Christians never get to explore these rooms of the palace. They are too affected by the idea that seeing is believing. That's why the book of Joshua begins with a reminder that this simply isn't true. Seeing is not believing. Believing is seeing, as Jesus says in John 11:40: *"Did I not tell you that if you believe, you will see the glory of God?"*

The River Jordan was uncrossable. It protected the land of Canaan from eastern invaders, like a moat around a castle. It was now late March, so the melting snowcaps on the mountains to the north had swelled the waters and made them burst their banks.[1] There wasn't a worse time of year for Joshua to attempt a crossing of the River Jordan.

We can tell that Joshua was nervous because he hesitates. In 1:11, he told the Israelites that they would cross the river in three days' time, but then he changed his mind and sent out spies instead. They took three or four days to return, then Joshua waited three more days before telling the people to consecrate themselves to cross the following day.[2] This hesitation was quite natural. It was a make-or-break moment for Joshua's leadership and the conquest of the Promised Land. It was the moment of truth for all God's promises to Israel.

Joshua understands that, when it comes to experiencing God's promises, believing is seeing, not the other way around. He prophesies to the Israelites that *"Tomorrow the Lord will do amazing things among you"*, and he commands the priests to *"Take up the ark of the covenant and pass on ahead of the people."* This was the golden box that Moses had built in response to the Lord's promise that his glorious presence would dwell above its lid in the inner sanctuary of the Tabernacle.[3] Joshua warns the people to keep half a mile away from the ark because the time has come to bring God's presence out of the sanctuary. He reasons that only the presence of the Lord will be able to part the floodwaters of the River Jordan as it did the Red Sea forty years before under Moses.

The Lord is delighted that Joshua is willing to trust him

[1] Israel is so sunny that its fields yield multiple harvests each year. Joshua 4:19 clarifies that the *harvest* in 3:15 is the harvest of late March and early April. Normally 30 metres across, the River Jordan could be up to a mile across when it was flooded. God chose the hardest time of year for this miracle to showcase his power.

[2] Joshua 1:11; 2:1, 22; 3:1–2, 5. Consecration meant washing their clothes and abstaining from sex as an expression of their utter holiness and devotion to the Lord (Exodus 19:10–15).

[3] Exodus 30:6; Numbers 7:89.

without demanding upfront proof.[4] He assures him that *"Today I will begin to exalt you in the eyes of all Israel, so that they may know that I am with you as I was with Moses."*[5] Moses had also been willing to act first and get his proof later, since the Lord had told him in Exodus 3:12 that *"This will be the sign to you that it is I who have sent you: when you have brought the people out of Egypt, you will worship God on this mountain."* The shepherds would require the same faith when the angel told them in Luke 2:12 that *"This will be a sign to you: you will find a baby wrapped in cloths and lying in a manger."* Most of us want our proof upfront, which is why we never get to enjoy all the rooms of the palace of God's salvation. It is vital that we grasp that the God who keeps on giving gives his proof *after* we believe, and not before.

Joshua is therefore teaching us a great principle of faith here. He is speaking to us, not just to the Israelites, when he declares that this miracle will demonstrate *"which way to go, since you have never been this way before"*. Joshua believes the Lord's promise that the River Jordan will be parted when the priests who carry the ark set foot in it. He commands them to step into the river in faith, without any outward proof it will be parted as they do so. Sure enough, believing is seeing. The very moment that the priests dip their feet into the river, an invisible dam cuts off its waters twenty miles upstream, providing twenty-seven miles of dry riverbed for the Israelites to cross between the town of Adam to the north and the Dead Sea to the south.[6]

The Lord chose a town named Adam because the difficult

---

[4] Faith in God's promises isn't blind. It sees more clearly than conjecture based on what we see. That's why Numbers 13:33 and Joshua 2:8–11 encourage us to doubt our doubts rather than God's promises.

[5] Joshua 3:7 and 4:14, and Exodus 14:31 encourage us that if we step out in faith then God will perform such mighty miracles through us that the people around us will believe the words we speak in his name.

[6] This enabled 2 million Israelites to cross the river quickly, while remaining half a mile away from the ark.

floodwaters in our own lives can all be traced back to Adam's original sin.[7] As Joshua steps into the Jordan behind the presence of the Lord, he is pointing prophetically to the day when Jesus would be baptized in that same River Jordan and the Holy Spirit would descend on him like a dove to anoint him to save us. As the Israelites cross over into the Promised Land through faith in God, they therefore remind us that the Gospel is far more than the promise of forgiveness through Jesus' blood – it is also the promise of inheritance through Jesus' resurrection. It isn't just about what we have been forgiven *from*. It is about what we have been forgiven *for*. Faith in Jesus means stepping forward to lay hold of our own Promised Land.[8]

However beautiful the hymn may be that teaches us to sing of our deathbeds, *"When I tread the verge of Jordan, bid my anxious fears subside. Bear me through the swelling current, land me safe on Canaan's side"* – it is terrible theology![9] This chapter isn't talking about what awaits us in heaven. It's talking about what we ought to be experiencing right now!

What is your own Promised Land? How much have you crossed over to possess it? What Bible promises have you yet to experience day by day? Whatever they are, the example of Joshua and the instruction of Jesus remains the same to you today: *"Did I not tell you that if you believe, you will see the glory of God?"*

So don't wait for proof before you act in faith. Seeing isn't believing. Believing is seeing.

---

[7] Romans 5:14; 1 Corinthians 15:22. The dry riverbed stretching backwards and forwards from the ark proclaims that Jesus' blood saved people in BC history as well as in AD history (Romans 3:25).

[8] Hebrews 3:7–4:11 treats the Promised Land as a prophetic picture of our own inheritance in Christ.

[9] This is the last verse of the hymn by William Williams "Guide me, O Thou great Jehovah" (1745).

Stones (Joshua 4:1–24)

*"In the future when your descendants ask their
parents, 'What do these stones mean?' tell them,
'Israel crossed the Jordan on dry ground.'"*

(Joshua 4:21–22)

Stones matter a lot in the book of Joshua, and I don't just mean
the archaeology that silences scholars who cast doubt on its
story. I'm not just talking about the tablets that a Canaanite king
sent to Egypt to grovel for Pharaoh's help against Joshua and
his army: *"Thus says Yapahu, ruler of Gezer, your servant... The
Hebrews are too strong for us, so may the king, my lord, help me
to escape from the Hebrews so that the Hebrews do not destroy
us."*[1] Nor am I talking here about what John Garstang discovered
when he excavated ancient Jericho in the 1930s. Knowing that
the walls of besieged cities always topple inwards, he concluded
with surprise that *"The outer wall suffered most, its remains
falling down the slope... There remains no doubt: the walls fell
outwards so completely that the attackers would be able to
clamber up and over their ruins into the city."*[2]

No. I am talking about the stones that are mentioned in the
book of Joshua itself. He repeatedly commands the Israelites to
build piles of stones as monuments to landmark moments in
the conquest of Canaan. We will read later about a pile of stones
to mark the execution of a traitor, a pile of stones to mark the

---

[1] These *Amarna Letters* are on display in the British Museum in London. They
date from a few years after the Hebrews crossed the River Jordan in March
1406 BC. Yapahu refers to the Hebrews as *"the Hapiru"*.

[2] John Garstang says this in his account of his excavations, *The Story of
Jericho* (1940).

grave of a Canaanite king defeated in battle, a group of stones on which Joshua chiselled the words of the Law of Moses, a pile of stones to mark the grave of several more defeated Canaanite kings and a stone to mark the renewal of God's covenant with Israel.[3] Joshua was a prophet who was keenly aware of the importance of marking out the milestones on our spiritual journey. He knew how easily we forget that the Lord is the God who keeps on giving.

No sooner had the Israelites crossed the River Jordan than Joshua sent twelve men back into the riverbed to create a milestone for the people of Israel. The Lord instructed him to send one man from each of the twelve tribes of Israel to retrieve a large rock so that he could build a monument of twelve rocks to recall this moment in Israel's history.[4] God was determined that his people should never forget his power or his desire to bless their nation. He told Joshua that these stones would *"serve as a sign among you. In the future, when your children ask you, 'What do these stones mean?' tell them that the flow of the Jordan was cut off before the ark of the covenant of the Lord. When it crossed the Jordan, the waters of the Jordan were cut off. These stones are to be a memorial to the people of Israel forever."*

This poses a very natural question for us. What are the major milestones in our own spiritual journeys? Some of them we have in common. They are why a previous generation of believers decided to mark the birth of Jesus at Christmastime and the death and resurrection of Jesus on Good Friday and Easter Sunday. It is easy for us to despise these milestones, since we know that Jesus wasn't born in December and that nowadays both festivals are more about eating and drinking than reflecting on the source of our salvation, but Joshua reminds us that such festivals have value. It is not the task of the children's workers at

---

[3] Joshua 7:26; 8:29, 32; 10:27; 24:25–27.

[4] Moses and Joshua had already appointed these 12 tribal leaders (4:4). Rather than change Israel's leadership wholesale, Joshua kept in place the leaders that he and Moses had already appointed (1:10).

your church to educate your children in the truth of the Gospel. That task is primarily yours, and festivals such as Christmas and Easter pique their curiosity to enable you to do so. The same is true of all your nonbelieving friends. Don't despise traditions, monuments and ceremonies. Christmas presents and Easter eggs are your chance to tell people around you about the God who keeps on giving.[5]

Many of the other milestones in our spiritual journeys are unique to ourselves. That's why I have a little journal in which I record the key locations of my own faith in God. There's the roof of a building in Cambridge which I climbed while drunk and suddenly felt God warning me that I was playing with fire. There's the bench by a river in the Czech Republic where I finally surrendered my life to him after reading the Bible while backpacking the following summer. There's the little church where I was baptized a few weeks later. There's the history library where I found answers to my first major crisis of faith and where a chance conversation two years later led me to go abroad as a missionary. The list goes on, but right now I'm more interested in your own list. What are the major milestones on your own walk with God? I strongly encourage you to take some time to write a list of your own spiritual milestones. Forgetting is easy and remembering is hard, so don't miss the important lesson that Joshua teaches us here.

Joshua spurs us on by telling us in verse 9 that this particular pile of rocks was still there when the book was written. This is the first of twelve occasions when Joshua tells us that a spiritual marker is still *"there to this day"*.[6] Reflecting and recording the milestones in our journey with God takes time, but it is always worth the effort. The Lord chisels their memory so deeply into our hearts that they shape the way we view ourselves and what it means for us to follow him. Joshua also spurs us on by telling

---

[5] We see this principle again in Exodus 12:26–27; 13:7–9; 13:14–16 and in Deuteronomy 6:6–9; 11:18–21.

[6] Joshua 4:9; 5:9; 6:25; 7:26; 8:28, 29; 9:27; 10:27; 13:13; 15:63; 16:10; 23:9.

us in verse 19 that Israel crossed the River Jordan on the tenth day of the first month of the Jewish calendar, the day on which Passover lambs were selected for sacrifice and the day on which Jesus would later ride into Jerusalem on a donkey to die. This little detail emphasizes that each of our milestones is more significant than we realize.[7]

That's why Joshua warns us in verses 12–13 that such milestones are far too easily forgotten. Moses had pleaded with men of Reuben, Gad and Manasseh not to settle for less than God had promised them by settling for land on the east side of the River Jordan. They had assured him in Numbers 32 that nothing would ever make them forget to enter the Promised Land to fight alongside the rest of Israel. However, only 40,000 of the 110,000 fighting men that were counted in the census of Numbers 26 ever made it over the River Jordan. Joshua warns us that two-thirds failed to enter the Promised Land.

So as the floodwaters rush back to cover the dry riverbed, take some time to record the major milestones in your own spiritual journey.[8] It takes time and effort to record them and to praise the Lord for them, but it is always worth the investment. It safeguards against the danger we are warned about in Hebrews 6:12: *"We do not want you to become lazy, but to imitate those who through faith and patience inherit what has been promised."*

---

[7] Compare Joshua 4:19 with Exodus 12:1–6. Joshua's arrival in Canaan prefigures Jesus' arrival in Jerusalem.

[8] Joshua 4:15–16 and 18 prevent us from explaining away this miracle as a purely natural phenomenon caused by falling rocks upstream. The river stopped flowing at the precise moment that the priests stepped into it from the east bank, and it started flowing again at the precise moment they stepped out onto the west bank.

Whose Side Are You On?
(Joshua 5:1–15)

Joshua went up to him and asked, "Are you for us or for our enemies?" "Neither," he replied.

(Joshua 5:13–14)

Joshua 5 is a chapter that needs to be read backwards. If that sounds odd, let's do it together and you will see what I mean. The flint knives and the foreskins are confusing until the final verses of the chapter interpret them as a question: *Which side are you on?*

In verses 13–15, Joshua leaves the Israelite camp to scout out Jericho. His troops are camped at Gilgal, three miles west of the River Jordan and two miles north-east of Jericho, so this means travelling through enemy territory. Suddenly Joshua is ambushed, not by the soldiers of Jericho (we are told in 6:1 that they are all hiding in fear), but by the same Angel of the Lord who appears to the patriarchs in the book of Genesis. Their encounters are known as theophanies, and many readers see them as appearances of the Son of God to people long before his incarnation as a human baby in Bethlehem.[1] Joshua is so scared at the sight of him that he blurts out in fear, *"Are you for us or for our enemies?"*

The Angel of the Lord is blunt in his reply: *"Neither, but as commander of the army of the Lord I have now come."* He hasn't come to take sides in a human battle. <u>He has come down from heaven to enlist Joshua and the Israelites in the army of the Lord!</u> It is crucial we remember this when we see them slaughtering

---

[1] That's why this mysterious *Angel of the Lord* is revealed to be the Lord himself in Genesis 16:7–13; 22:11–18; 32:24–30, in Exodus 3:2–6, and in Judges 6:11–24; 13:3–23. See also Revelation 19:11–16.

people later. The Lord tells Joshua that he is living at a solemn moment in history: it's Judgment Day for the land of Canaan.

In case Joshua is in any doubt as to who he is, the Angel of the Lord repeats his command to Moses at the burning bush: *"Take off your sandals, for the place where you are standing is holy."* He calls Joshua to confess his weakness and his sin and his desire to enlist God's help in his own plans. He needs to line up instead with whatever God is doing. When verse 14 tells us literally that *"he fell on his face to the ground and worshipped"*, it is meant to act as a punchline to the whole of chapter 5. Salvation must always lead to service. Forgiveness must always lead to fruitfulness through surrender to the Lord.

With that in mind, let's go back and read the start of the chapter. Up until this moment, the Israelites have been far more focused on what they have been saved *from* than on what they have been saved *for*. It is shocking to hear that they have disobeyed the Lord by failing to be circumcised during forty years in the desert, but it's no more shocking than somebody today who prays for God to forgive them yet fails to obey his command that new believers be baptized. The Israelites loved the promises in the Torah that God would forgive their sins. They loved the statement in Leviticus 17:11 that *"it is the blood that makes atonement for one's life."* But they had remained in the hallway of forgiveness. They hadn't explored the rooms of what it meant to devote their lives to serving God.[2]

That all changes with the crossing of the River Jordan. Joshua commands them in 3:5 to *"Consecrate yourselves"* – in other words, to respond to God's forgiveness by pledging to live as his holy people in a sinful world. Having done so, Joshua leads them through the River Jordan, as Moses led their parents through the Red Sea, which 1 Corinthians 10:2 explains is a

---

[2] Ironically, when our own desires become the Lord's desires he is very happy to fight for us (10:14, 42; 23:3, 10). He just insists that we get the order right before he is willing to make us fruitful.

prophetic pointer to baptism in water.[3] Joshua explains to them in 4:24 that their baptism is to be a visual aid that helps them make a clear decision as a nation about whose side they are on. It was given *"so that you might always fear the Lord your God"*.[4]

Joshua hasn't finished his lesson. At the start of chapter 5, he circumcises the Israelites. This was necessary for them to eat the Passover meal four days after crossing the River Jordan, but it was still an act of madness for an army deep inside enemy territory.[5] The pain was so incapacitating that two lone fighters had been able to slaughter an entire city after its men were circumcised in Genesis 34, so this left Israel in a vulnerable position. Joshua doesn't care. He trusts the Lord to make the Canaanites too afraid to venture out of their cities (5:1). Despite the fact that there are plenty of metal swords to use, Joshua circumcises the Israelites using flint knives to emphasize that they are returning to the devotion of Abraham. Pledging ourselves to live in holiness is always painful, but it is always worth it. The name Gibeath Haaraloth means *Hill of Foreskins* and speaks of Israel's pain, but the name Gilgal means *Rolled Away* and speaks of the fruit of their pain. The Lord sees this as the end of their sinfulness in the desert and the start of their conquest of the Land. He celebrates, *"Today I have rolled away the reproach of Egypt from you."* He has led them out of the hallway of their salvation and into the Promised Land.[6]

---

[3] This is also emphasized by the floodwaters piling up and "baptizing" the town of *Adam* in 3:16. Romans 2:28–29 and Colossians 2:11–12 treat circumcision and baptism as pictures of dying and being raised in Christ.

[4] This is still why the Lord performs miracles today. It helps nonbelievers to put their faith in him for forgiveness (4:24a) and it helps believers to embrace a life of holiness (4:24b). See also Exodus 20:20.

[5] Since Exodus 12:43–49 says men had to be circumcised to eat the Passover meal, this must have been the first time they had celebrated the Feast for 39 years, since Numbers 9:1–5.

[6] It was a reproach to Israel that they had been redeemed but still lived in the desert. It is a reproach to a Christian to be forgiven but unfruitful. The Lord wants to lead you to your own Gilgal today.

In the midst of their Passover celebrations, the Lord stops providing them with manna for the first time in forty years.[7] This may not sound like good news, but it is. It forces them to stop focusing on what they have been saved *from* and to start focusing on what they have been saved *for*. No more manna means that they now have no choice but to press forward to conquer the Promised Land. They will starve if they remain in the hallway of their salvation. Sometimes Christians hark back to the early days of their conversion when it seemed so easy to walk with God, so we need to understand what is happening here. The Lord props up our faith in its early days but then he tends to kick away those props to keep us pressing forward into all he has in store for us to discover.

The stopping of manna after forty years also reassures the Israelites that God is serious about helping them to conquer the Promised Land. It reinforces the notion that there is no backup plan. It is now do-or-die. The blood of their Passover lambs promised forgiveness. Their avoidance of yeast during the week-long Feast of Unleavened Bread which followed it pledged their repentance from sin and consecration to the Lord. The appearance of the Angel of the Lord to Joshua at the end of the chapter is therefore the final nail in the coffin of their old lives. They are now on the Lord's side. They have moved out of the hallway of forgiveness and into the vast palace of what it means to be devoted to God.

Joshua wants us to go on this journey ourselves. He asks us the same question that the Angel of the Lord asked him: *Whose side are you on?* It's great to celebrate that Jesus died for your sake, but can you also say gladly that you have died with him for his sake? Joshua wants this chapter to teach you to say with the apostle Paul in Galatians 2:20:

> *I have been crucified with Christ and I no longer live, but Christ lives in me.*

---

[7] Exodus 16:35. The New Testament explains the true significance of this feast in 1 Corinthians 5:6–8.

Blood on the Walls
(Joshua 6:1–20)

When the priests sounded the trumpet blast, Joshua commanded the army, "Shout! For the Lord has given you the city!"

(Joshua 6:16)

There is an old joke about a school teacher who was too quick to hand out punishments. He terrified the children in his class whenever he asked them questions. One particular morning he demanded that they tell him who knocked down the walls of Jericho. After an awkward pause, one worried boy raised his hand: "Please sir, it wasn't me!"

That schoolboy missed the point, but make sure you don't miss the point as well. This chapter emphasizes that Joshua did not topple the walls of Jericho either. The key word in the Hebrew text is *shōphar*, which means a *trumpet-made-from-a-ram's-horn*. The Battle of Jericho wasn't won by screaming and shouting. It was won by the blood on its walls.[1]

Verse 1 interrupts the words that the Angel of the Lord speaks to Joshua. It reminds us that *"the gates of Jericho were securely barred"* – in other words, there was no way Joshua and his men could capture the city on their own. When the archaeologist John Garstang excavated the ruins of Jericho in

---

[1] The word *shōphar* is used 14 times in only 20 verses in Joshua 6:1–20. Although horns can be harvested from live rams, most come from the slaughterhouse. In ancient Israel, after a sheep was slaughtered, its blood poured out on the ground and its flesh eaten, only its horns remained to bear testimony to its sacrifice.

the 1930s, he discovered that its outer and inner walls were two metres and four metres thick. The city was totally impregnable.

In verses 2–5, the Angel of the Lord therefore reveals his battle plan to Joshua.[2] He commands him to march around the city for seven days with seven priests blowing on seven ram's-horn trumpets. On the seventh day, they are to march around the city seven times. The Angel of the Lord does not explain how the ram's-horn trumpets will bring about a victory. We are left to work that out from Revelation 12:11 – *"They triumphed over the Devil by the blood of the Lamb and by the word of their testimony."* Nor does he explain what is signified by this repetition of the number seven. We are left to work that out from the book of Revelation too, where seven represents the perfection of the salvation that is ours in Jesus. The fortress of Jericho will prove no match for the blood on its walls.

In verses 6–11, Joshua goes out of his way to emphasize that the city was conquered through these ram's-horn trumpets and not by the army of Israel. *"The seven priests carrying the seven trumpets before the Lord went forwards, blowing their trumpets... All this time the trumpets were sounding. But Joshua had commanded the army, 'Do not give a war cry, do not raise your voices, do not say a word.'"* Joshua wants nothing to eclipse this powerful prophecy that the blood of Jesus carries power to conquer Satan's forces and to lead God's people to possess their Promised Land.

In verses 12–14, Joshua continues to emphasize this. For five more days the Israelite army circles the city in silence while *"the seven priests carrying the seven trumpets went forwards, marching before the ark of the Lord and blowing the trumpets... The trumpets kept sounding."*

In verses 15–20, we see what happens when we put our faith in the perfect sacrifice of Jesus. Against all odds, the

---

[2] The text is not entirely clear, but it appears that 6:2–5 is part of the same theophany as 5:13–15.

walls of Jericho fall down. Not a single weapon is fired at the Canaanite defences. Not a single voice is raised until *"the priests sounded the trumpet blast"* after circling the city seven times on the seventh day. Only then does Joshua command his men to raise a war cry of faith that the blood on the walls of Jericho will be its downfall. *"Shout! For the Lord has given you the city!"* is not a cry of self-confidence, but a cry that comes from knowing that we are called to play a small part in God's great salvation plan. Hebrews 11:30 tells us that *"By faith the walls of Jericho fell, after the army had marched round them for seven days."* With a sudden crash the walls collapse. The blood of Jesus has delivered victory on a plate to God's people.

We tend to think of Joshua as a general, but the ancient Hebrews were right to list him among the "Former Prophets".[3] His actions at the Battle of Jericho are meant to teach us how God grants us victory in our own battles too. We need these verses every time we pray for someone to be healed or delivered of a demon. We need these verses every time we share the Gospel and hope that God will use our simple words to bring about conversion. The Devil laughs at us from the walls of his fortress, mocking the idea that we can ever step into the fruitfulness that is promised us in the New Testament. He mocks the idea that we will ever see a breakthrough with nothing more than words of faith and a proclamation of the blood of Jesus. We need these words of prophecy to remind us that these were all that Joshua needed to topple the mighty walls of Jericho.[4]

Victory does not come by denying that the gates of hell are strong (verse 1). It does not come by ignoring the existence of demon warriors in the world (verse 2). It does not come by downplaying the size of the barriers that stand against us (verse 5). When the Lord uses a Hebrew perfect tense to promise

---

[3] Joshua prophesies most clearly in 3:9; 4:21–24; 6:26; 20:1–6 and 24:2–27.

[4] It's preposterous when people try to argue that the walls of Jericho must have fallen because they were weak and crumbling. The Canaanites were renowned for their mighty city walls (Deuteronomy 1:28; 9:1).

Joshua in verse 2 that *"I **have delivered** Jericho into your hands"*, he is telling us that victory comes by trusting him that heavenly realities trump earthly realities every time.

Joshua had to risk looking foolish to see victory. Had he not just parted the River Jordan for his soldiers, he might well have had a mutiny on his hands.[5] It was humiliating for his troops to be led on a four-mile march around Jericho for six days without even being permitted to raise their voices, let alone to fire an arrow, but he had to bring them to a place where they would recognize that victory had to come from the Lord. On the seventh day, with no visible fruit for their twenty-four miles of marching, they were finally ready. Isn't this the reason why we see far fewer miracles in our own day than in the days of Joshua? We get embarrassed and give up too early, then we blame the Lord for not having delivered on his Bible promises to us.[6]

These verses assure us that victory will be ours if we persevere in holding the blood of Jesus high, testifying to its power in our own lives, no matter how foolish nonbelievers make us feel. Whatever mighty stronghold stands before you today, you ought to take great comfort from these verses. Believe what Revelation 12:11 says about the way in which we overcome the Devil: *"They triumphed over him by the blood of the Lamb and by the word of their testimony; they did not love their lives so much as to shrink from death."*

---

[5] Joshua saw this problem coming and told his men from the start that they would need to keep on marching for seven days. Wise leaders trust their people by letting them in on their God-given strategy.

[6] Joshua rebukes us gently in 6:12 and 15 by telling us that he and his men kept on getting up early to obey.

Genocide (Joshua 6:21–27)

*They devoted the city to the Lord and destroyed with
the sword every living thing in it – men and women,
young and old, cattle, sheep and donkeys.*

(Joshua 6:21)

Many people don't make it past the sixth chapter of Joshua. When
they read about the systematic slaughter of the Canaanites, they
get offended and check out early. In some ways, I don't blame
them. What we read about here is horrific. But before you throw
down the book of Joshua in disgust, make sure you understand
what life was like in Canaan during the Bronze Age.[1] There are
five big factors that we need to consider here.

First, we need to recognize *we are less familiar with
genocide than Joshua*. We ought to be appalled to read in verse 21
that the Israelites killed old men, young women and even babies
in the bloodbath that accompanied the capture of Jericho, but
we mustn't imagine we are more appalled about it than Joshua.
For us, genocide is something that we studied in history lessons
about the Nazis. Ethnic cleansing is something that we see on
the TV news in lands many miles away, not a reality at home.
Joshua, however, was a genocide survivor. In his father's day,
Pharaoh tried to murder every Hebrew baby boy.

Second, we need to recognize *we are less familiar with
Bronze Age life than Joshua*. What is described here isn't
genocide. It's what the ancient world described as *devoting to*

---

[1] For a sense of how differently they thought from us, take a look at Judges
14:6. The author expects it to help us understand Samson's fight with a lion
when he says, *"You know, like when you tear apart a young goat"*!

the ban. In the "Moabite Stone", now on display in the Louvre Museum in Paris, King Mesha of Moab devotes to the ban one of the cities that he captures – in other words, he judges its people in the name of his god Chemosh. The Hebrew word *hāram* that is used throughout Joshua describes this ancient practice.[2] It conveys that this was more than manmade slaughter. God used the Israelites to bring his divine judgment to bear on the sins of the Canaanites.[3] We find it hard to stomach because we don't like the idea of God judging people, but that's precisely the point. What happened to the Canaanites points towards a far more terrible Day of Judgment. If even those who were slaughtered recognized that God was judging them, we must not deny it. We must believe the king of Canaan who confesses freely in Judges 1:7 that *"God has paid me back for what I did."*

Third, we need to recognize *we are less familiar with the sins of the Canaanites than Joshua.* Leviticus 18 describes them for us. Men had sex with their mothers, their sisters and their daughters. They had sex with one another's wives and – still not satisfied – they had sex with their farm animals and with each other too. Their wives were just as bad, presenting themselves to have sex with their farm animals. That's why the Lord explains at the end of Leviticus 18 that *"The land was defiled; so I punished it for its sin, and the land vomited out its inhabitants."* Deuteronomy 12:29–31 adds that this was merely the tip of the iceberg of their sin. The Canaanites also murdered their own children as human sacrifices on the altars of their idols. So

---

[2] The verb *hāram* and its noun *hērem* are used 90 times in the Old Testament, 15 of which are in Joshua 6–7. The word *hāram* is used by an envoy from Babylon in 2 Chronicles 32:14 to describe *devoting cities to the ban* in the name of the gods of Babylon. Though shocking, this concept was central to the Bronze Age worldview.

[3] This is why the Angel of the Lord appeared to Joshua in 5:13–6:5 to tell him he was to fight the Lord's cause, not the other way around. Deuteronomy 20 clarifies that Joshua's calling was unique to him.

before you throw the book of Joshua away in disgust, make sure you grasp the daily horrors that were happening in Jericho.[4]

Fourth, we need to recognize *we are less familiar with God's mercy than Joshua.* In the brutal Bronze Age, nobody was surprised that the God of Israel should judge sin. What surprised them was that he was willing to forgive any sinner who turned to him. One of the reasons why he commanded Joshua to circle the city of Jericho for seven days before its walls fell was so that its citizens had time to make the same choice as Rahab. This is not ethnic cleansing, but a spiritual sort-out between those who repent of their sin at the sight of God's judgment and those who continue to show contempt towards the Lord. Rahab's parents and the other hangers-on in her family have done nothing to protect the spies, yet they are saved when they put their faith in what she says about the scarlet cord. Achan, on the other hand, is a full-blooded Hebrew from the tribe of Judah, but he becomes *hērem* in chapter 7 when he decides to side with sin against the Lord.

Only the God who keeps on giving would be willing to forgive like this. If it seems surprising in our own day, it was jaw-droppingly unthinkable in the Bronze Age. It isn't wrong to be upset about the slaughter of the Canaanites, but our view of it is distorted if we miss how much this chapter is dominated by God's offer of salvation to the people of Jericho.[5] Verses 17, 22 and 25 all emphasize that Rahab is a prostitute and that absolutely anyone who seeks refuge inside her brothel will be saved. Verse 25 invites us to rejoice in the totality of their salvation. Rahab wasn't merely let over the threshold of salvation to grovel in the hallway. We are told *"she dwells **at the heart of Israel** to this day."* In our disgust at the judgment that fell upon Jericho, let's not forget we are spectators of it and the Lord is not. The scarlet cord that hangs from Rahab's window to offer salvation to the

---

[4] Given this, it's surprising God held off for 400 years until their sin *"reached its full measure"* (Genesis 15:16).

[5] 8:33–35 also emphasizes that many sinful foreigners besides Rahab chose to convert to the God of Israel too.

people of Jericho points prophetically to the blood of Jesus. He became *hērem* when he died on the cross to save anyone who repents from the greater Judgment Day to come.[6]

Fifth, we need to recognize that *we are less familiar with Israel's weaknesses than Joshua*. Like the generation of Israelites that died in the desert, we tend to underplay God's warnings that association with the Canaanites would quickly lead them into sin.[7] Sadly, we discover in the book of Judges that the Lord was right and our confidence in the Israelites is wrong. The handful of Canaanites that went unslaughtered soon persuaded God's people to follow their evil lead and to abandon the God who brought them into the Promised Land. Joshua isn't overreacting in verse 26 when he pronounces a curse on any Israelite who attempts to reconstruct this sinful city.[8] He is like a master gardener who recognizes Japanese knotweed in his garden. He roots the Canaanites out of the Promised Land because he grasps the deadliness of the sin they harbour in their hearts.

Yes, the book of Joshua is brutal, but in its context it is full of mercy. Instead of judging the Lord for not treating Bronze Age barbarians like peace-loving twenty-first-century democrats, we need to recognize these five factors underneath the story. As Rahab's family is saved from the slaughter of Jericho, and as the Gibeonites are saved from the slaughter of the other Canaanites, don't miss the fact that the book of Joshua is good news for sinners. God has set a day of reckoning for the world, but nobody will be condemned who has not chosen to side with sin against the Saviour he has given them.[9]

---

[6] The contrasting fates of Rahab and Achan show that this is not ethnic cleansing, but the cleaning up of sin.

[7] For example, in Numbers 33:55–56, in Deuteronomy 7:1–4 and 7:16, and in Joshua 23:12–13.

[8] The Lord fulfils this curse in 1 Kings 16:34 when the city is rebuilt during the rebellious reign of King Ahab.

[9] Note how unashamed the early Christians were about the slaughter described in Joshua (Acts 7:45; 13:19). They see it as Good News in the face of a far greater Judgment Day to come (Acts 17:30–31).

Trading Places
(Joshua 6:22–7:26)

When I saw in the plunder a beautiful robe from Babylonia, two hundred shekels of silver and a bar of gold weighing fifty shekels, I coveted them and took them.

(Joshua 7:21)

If you're still tempted to think that the slaughter of the Canaanites was a case of ethnic cleansing, then slow down and reflect on what happened to Rahab and to Achan. These two figures dominate the aftermath of the fall of Jericho, and their contrasting fates are meant to prove to us that this slaughter was a case of divine justice, not of genocide.

45

Rahab was as Canaanite as Canaanite could be. Her name meant Proud and she instinctively lied to get herself out of trouble. She was a sex worker whose brothel formed part of the very city walls the Lord had vowed to destroy. In other words, if God had it in for the Canaanites then she hadn't got a hope in hell.

But God hadn't got it in for the Canaanites. These chapters show us that he wanted to save them. They remind us that 2 Peter 3:9 describes him as *"patient... not wanting anyone to perish, but everyone to come to repentance"*. The example of Rahab is meant to show us that everyone in Jericho could have been spared if they had done more than tremble at the news that the God of Israel had defeated the idols of the Egyptians and the Amorites. What happened to the local prostitute might have happened to them all.

It was the grace of God that made the two spies knock on the door of her brothel. It was the grace of God that caused her to guess that they were Israelites when they asked to book a room instead of a girl. It was the grace of God that persuaded her to do more than marvel at the miracles that had accompanied their nation. It was the grace of God that made the city police force knock on her door in search of the spies, forcing her to choose sides in an instant. It was the same grace that convinced her to betray her nation to side with the God of Israel, and which permitted her to hang a scarlet cord out of her window as an expression of her faith in the God who keeps on giving.

All of this is meant to convince us that the slaughter at Jericho was not about Canaanites and race, but about confession and repentance. Joshua gives Rahab a special mention in his speech before the battle, emphasizing that the only section of the walls of Jericho that will not fall down is the section that contains her home. Recognizing the scarlet cord hanging from her window, the Israelites lead her and all the others in her brothel to a safe place outside the camp where they can commit themselves more fully to the God of Israel. Once they have consecrated themselves to the Lord like the Israelites in chapter 5, they are free to dwell at the very heart of Israel.[1] The tragedy of Jericho isn't just that its citizens were slaughtered. It's that none of them needed to have been. God would have accepted them all.

Achan, on the other hand, is a Hebrew of Hebrews. He isn't just an Israelite. He belongs to the tribe of Judah, the tribe that would give birth to King David and to Jesus the Messiah, who is hailed in Revelation 5:5 as *"the Lion of the tribe of Judah"*. Achan's sin is highlighted here to prove that the destruction of Jericho was not race-related. While Rahab betrays her city to side with the God of Israel, Achan betrays the God of Israel to plunder her city. He knows full well that everything he finds in the city is

---

[1] Most of the soldiers underwent these seven-day rites of purification with her (Numbers 31:19). Only two verses later, the end of the seven days, she is as much part of Israel as Joshua.

hērem – that is, *to be destroyed as an act of devotion to the Lord* – yet he steals from the plunder a Babylonian robe and around three kilograms of gold and silver.[2] When he hides them in a hole under his tent, he does the very opposite to what Rahab did when she hung a scarlet cord from her window.[3] He is about to find out that no amount of Jewish blood would protect him from God's judgment if he acted like a Canaanite at heart.[4]

If you are troubled by the slaughter in the book of Joshua – and to some extent, I hope you are – then be reassured. The contrasting fates of Rahab and Achan prove that it is not a case of genocide, but of divine justice. It points forward to a greater Day of Judgment, when every secret sin will be revealed and when ethnicity will save no one.[5]

If you are a church leader, be instructed. When you need to discipline someone for claiming to follow Jesus while rejecting his teaching, be as loving as Joshua, who calls Achan *"my son"* and who patiently offers him many chances to repent. When alerted to the fact that one of his soldiers has brought the sins of Jericho into the midst of Israel, he calls everyone together to warn them that the following day he will draw lots to see which of them has disobeyed the Lord. Note the tone of mercy. The Lord gives Achan time to repent and be forgiven. When he fails to confess by sunrise, he extends him further mercy by identifying him very slowly. Instead of singling him out in an

---

[2] Babylon is the great enemy of God's people throughout the rest of the Bible, represented by a prostitute in Revelation 17. It is therefore significant that Achan steals a *Babylonian* robe while a prostitute is saved.

[3] Eyes that lust quickly lead to a heart that covets and to hands that act out those desires. Therefore, guard your eyes and heart from temptation. See 2 Samuel 11:2–4; Proverbs 4:23; Matthew 6:22–23 and James 1:14–15.

[4] Because there are no equivalent words in English, *hāram* is usually translated as *to destroy* and *hērem* as *things devoted to destruction*. These two words are used 15 times in Joshua 6–7.

[5] To emphasize the way that Rahab and Achan trade places, the phrase *"to this day"* is used when calling people to choose sides (4:9; 5:9) and when describing the result of their different choices (6:25; 7:26).

instant, the Lord goes through the rigmarole of narrowing the search down to the tribe of Judah, then to the clan of Zerah, then to the family of Zimri, then to the sons of Karmi and only then to Achan himself.[6] At any point along this process Achan could have thrown himself on God's mercy and been forgiven. But he leaves it too late. Refusing to be drawn out, he is caught out and executed along with the Canaanites.[7]

If you are troubled by your own sin, be encouraged to lay hold of God's mercy. There is an epilogue to this story in Hosea 2:15. After executing Achan, Joshua uses an alternate spelling to name the valley where a mound of stones marks his grave. The *Valley of Achan* and the *Valley of Achor* both mean the *Valley of the Trouble-Maker*, so the Lord has these chapters in mind when he promises in Hosea 2:15 to *"make the Valley of Achor a door of hope"*, since the Hebrew word that he uses for *hope* is *tiqvāh*, the same word that is used for the scarlet cord that Rahab is told to hang from her window in Joshua 2:18 and 21. Even if we are as sinful as Achan, God promises to forgive us if we confess our sin.

Sin made Achan trade places with Rahab after the fall of Jericho, but the Lord prophesies that a Saviour will trade places with sinners like Achan. He pledges that the one whose blood was prefigured by Rahab's scarlet cord will still save people like you and me. It isn't about race, but about repentance, and about faith in the one who traded places with us when he died on a Roman cross for all our sin.

What an offer. What a Saviour. What a God who keeps on giving.

---

[6] Israel camped by family (Numbers 2), marched by family (Numbers 10) and fought by family within their tribes (1 Chronicles 12:24–38). Churches need similar leadership structures to be strong.

[7] Deuteronomy 24:16 ruled that children should not die for the sins of their fathers, but this was different. Achan's family must have seen him digging. Like Rahab's family, they had chosen with him.

Presumption
(Joshua 7:1–8:35)

Joshua said, "Alas, Sovereign Lord, why did you ever bring this people across the Jordan?... If only we had been content to stay on the other side of the Jordan!"
(Joshua 7:7)

If the rabbis who wrote the Talmud almost 2,000 years ago were right that Joshua wrote the book that bears his name, then we have got to admire his honesty.[1] He never sugar-coats the story to compare himself favourably with his predecessor Moses. He simply tells it how it happened. He never hesitates to tell us things that make him look bad if he thinks that they can act as a prophetic picture that will do us good.

In 7:1–5, Joshua blows it. He messes up bigtime. He grows overconfident and forgets to consult the Lord before attacking the next city. Its name Ai means *Heap of Ruins*, so it is clearly far less fortified than Jericho. Buoyed by what his spies see, Joshua forgets that the Lord is the invisible general of Israel.[2] There is no mention here of asking guidance from God or instructing the priests to blow their ram's horns as a reminder that victory belongs to the Lord. Joshua sends only 3,000 men against a city of 12,000 because he has forgotten that the fall of Jericho was a blood-bought miracle, not a measure of the prowess of his army. Unaware that someone in the Israelite camp has

49

---

[1] Their claim cannot be proven or disproven, but 6:25 suggests that it is certainly credible.

[2] The most dangerous time for a leader is often after great success, and so it proves for Joshua.

stolen forbidden treasures, he assumes that, now that Jericho has fallen, the conquest of the rest of the Promised Land is automatic. He is very wrong.

Faith and presumption are different things. Faith moves out of the hallway of forgiveness, through the corridor of consecration and into the palace of God's promises. It recognizes that all its rooms are accessed through relationship with God, not through religious formulae and remote control. Presumption tries to bypass that relationship. It isn't interested in seeking God's face, but in snatching things out of God's hand. For that reason, it always ends in disaster. Like a burglar attempting to climb in through a tiny window instead of entering through the hallway, presumption always gets us stuck. As Joshua demonstrates, it always ends in abject failure.

Joshua is honest with us about this because he wants his failed attack on Ai to speak prophetically to our own lives. How much of our failure to experience all that God has promised us can be traced back to a prior failure to pursue deep friendship with him? How much of what we call faith is in fact presumption? If we can identify with Joshua's problem in the first five verses of this chapter, then there is good news for us in what follows.

In 7:6–9, Joshua shows us what to do with all our failures. We need to bring them into the presence of God.[3] These were days when Israel's leaders were still permitted to enter the inner sanctuary of the Tabernacle, so Joshua and the elders of Israel go inside to fall face down before the Lord together.[4] They tear their clothes and sprinkle dust on their heads as an outward expression of their humility and repentance. They are honest with the Lord that this defeat at Ai spells disaster. The Canaanite rulers, whose hearts melted with fear in 2:11 and 5:1, have now

---

[3] God rebukes him for this prayer but he loves its conclusion: *"What then will you do for your own great name?"*

[4] When Joshua succeeded Moses, he did not dismantle the leadership structures that they had set up for Israel together. The *elders of Israel* are also mentioned in 8:33; 20:4; 23:2; 24:1 and 24:31.

found a fresh confidence to fight them. The Israelite soldiers, who were so confident to follow Joshua in 3:7, 4:14 and 6:27, are now in despair.[5] Knowing that an alliance of Canaanite kings is gathering against him, Joshua exclaims,

> *Alas, Sovereign Lord, why did you ever bring this people across the Jordan to deliver us into the hands of the Amorites to destroy us? If only we had been content to stay on the other side of the Jordan! The Canaanites and the other people of the country will hear about this and they will surround us and wipe out our name from the earth.*

The Lord is pleased with Joshua's honesty, but he rebukes him in 7:10–15 for focusing far too much on earthly facts and far too little on the facts of heaven.[6] *"Stand up! What are you doing down on your face?"* is what the Lord still says to us when we get discouraged by the Church's failures and start to downsize our expectations of him in our generation. There is a time for praying on our knees, but there is also a time for jumping to our feet and acting. The Lord reminds Joshua he can still access the room that has "conquering Ai" written on the door. He simply needs to go back to the hallway of forgiveness and make his way back down the corridor of consecration. The room cannot be entered any other way. Wielding God's authority requires us to submit to his authority. Seeing Gospel breakthrough requires us to respond wholeheartedly to the Gospel ourselves. There is no back door to blessing.[7] The Lord tells Joshua to go back to where he began.

---

[5] Church discipline is essential because one person's sin affects so many. Achan's sin caused the death of 36 soldiers and shattered the idea that the Canaanites were unable to stand against Israel.

[6] Honesty is good in prayer, but don't miss how much Joshua sounds like the ten spies in Numbers 13–14.

[7] We are told in 7:6 that Joshua had to wait a whole day in prayer before the Lord answered his question. How many of our own prayers go unanswered

In 8:1–29, Joshua shows us what happens whenever people repent of their presumption and pursue true faith in God. The city of Ai was built on a hilltop that towered 300 metres above Jericho. Nevertheless, Joshua manages to march thousands of men undetected fifteen miles up the hill to set an ambush behind the city.[8] He takes all his soldiers with him, staking everything on the Lord's fresh promise that *"I have **delivered** into your hands the king of Ai, his people, his city and his land."*[9] This time it is not the blowing of a ram's horn that acts as a pointer to the victory of Jesus on the cross. Instead, the Lord commands Joshua to raise the wooden shaft of his javelin, just as Moses raised his staff during the Battle of Rephidim, and to hold it in the air throughout the Battle of Ai as a sign of his faith in the Conqueror to come.[10]

In 8:30–35, Joshua shows that he has learned his lesson. In Deuteronomy 11:26–32 and 27:1–28:68, the Lord had commanded the Israelites to mark their entry into the Promised Land by chiselling a copy of the Law of Moses into stones at the top of Mount Ebal and Mount Gerizim, and by proclaiming to one another its blessings and curses across the valley. Those two mountains lay over twenty miles to the north of Jericho and Ai, deep inside hostile territory, yet Joshua wastes no time after the battle. He leads the Israelites on a brisk march north to reconsecrate their nation to the God who keeps on giving.[11]

He has learned the difference between presumption and

---

because we give up too soon? See Exodus 24:16.

[8] Receiving a promise from the Lord does not mean we can dispense with clever strategies. Prayer without action is as much presumption as action without prayer.

[9] This time the Lord allows the Israelites to keep the plunder. If only Achan had waited, he would have had a better return than at Jericho! Sin always impoverishes us by stealing God's blessing from us.

[10] Verse 26 draws a deliberate parallel between Joshua's victory prayer and that of Moses in Exodus 17:8–16.

[11] Joshua is now meticulous in his obedience to the Law. Compare 8:29 with Deuteronomy 21:22–23.

faith. He now knows there are no back doors to blessing and no shortcuts to victory. As he leads Israel back through the hallway of forgiveness and down the corridor of consecration, he reminds us that all God's blessings flow towards his people through their pursuit of friendship with him.

Too Busy for God
(Joshua 9:1–27)

*The Israelites sampled their provisions but did not
enquire of the Lord.*

(Joshua 9:14)

In the novel *Lustrum*, the private secretary of Cicero observes
that *"Problems do not queue up outside a stateman's door,
waiting to be solved in an orderly fashion, chapter by chapter, as
the books would have us believe; instead they crowd in en masse,
demanding attention."*[1]

If you are a leader, you know that this is true. The second
big mistake that Joshua makes is entirely understandable. We've
all made it ourselves. He becomes so busy making leadership
decisions that, on a crucial occasion, he fails to wait for God. He
values getting things done above pursuing friendship with the
Lord, and it spells disaster.

Capturing Jericho first had been a superb strategy. Midway
up the land of Canaan, it cut off the southern kings from the
northern kings, enabling Joshua to divide and conquer.[2] In the
short term, however, it placed the Israelites in danger. They were
surrounded by hostile armies on three sides and hemmed in to
the east by the flooded River Jordan. They had only advanced
as far as Ai, seventeen miles from their base camp at Gilgal, and
news was trickling in that the southern kings were forming

---

[1] Robert Harris in his novel *Lustrum* (2009).

[2] The seven nations that inhabited the Promised Land lived in city states, each
with its own king. Although autonomous, the ethnic ties between those cities
united them whenever they were threatened by outsiders.

a grand coalition to destroy them.[3] Joshua must have already been stressed by the time the visitors arrived.

There is a lesson here. The Devil's primary tactic for preventing believers from living in the good of all God's promises to them is *distraction*. Joshua does not spare his own blushes when he confesses freely that this was his major error here. It wasn't that he had no way of discerning the Lord's response to his sudden visitors. He was served by a high priest who bore the Urim and Thummim, the sacred dice by which the leaders of Israel drew lots to discern the Lord's will.[4] He even had access to the inner sanctuary of the Tabernacle. The problem was he felt too busy. He made a snap decision instead.[5]

The Devil's second tactic is *deception*. He finds it easy when we allow our busyness to distract us from spending proper time with the Lord. When we neglect God's Word, we invariably make decisions based on what we see. Joshua assumes from the scruffy clothes of his visitors that they must have come on a long journey. He thinks he has confirmed this when he tastes the stale food on their donkeys. When the visitors claim that *"We have come from a very distant country"* (note how vague they are!), he is too busy to see through their lies. *"The Israelites sampled their provisions but did not enquire of the Lord."*

The Devil's third tactic is to make us *doubt*. Faith is one of the first casualties when we grow too busy to spend time with God. The Lord commanded Joshua in 3:10 to wipe out seven sinful nations from the land – the Canaanites, Hittites, Hivites, Perizzites, Girgashites, Amorites and Jebusites – but Joshua starts to doubt how essential this is. He doesn't take the time

---

[3] Gilgal, Jericho and Ai were only three, five and twenty miles west of the River Jordan.

[4] Exodus 28:26–30; Leviticus 8:8; Numbers 27:18–21. *Urim* means *Lights* and begins with the first letter of the Hebrew alphabet. *Thummim* means *Perfections* and begins with the last. They are almost certainly what Joshua used to draw lots in chapter 7 to discover the perpetrator of Achan's sin.

[5] Contrast this with Moses in Numbers 9:8: *"Wait until I find out what the Lord commands concerning you."*

to ask his visitors to specify the exact location of their far-off land so that he can check whether it is inhabited by one of those seven nations. He acts like we do when we doubt the importance of God's command to spend one day a week resting as part of a local church community, attempting to disciple ourselves by downloading online sermons from around the world whenever we have time. He also acts like we do when we doubt the importance of God's command not to marry nonbelievers, fooling ourselves that we will convert them over time. Don't miss the parallels when the Gibeonites assure Joshua that they are interested in *"the fame of the Lord your God"*.[6]

The Devil's fourth tactic is division. The people of God are usually happy to follow leaders who have a track record of listening to him. When the Israelites discover three days later that Joshua didn't stop to listen, they are furious. They want to tear up the treaty he signed, since the men of Gibeon are Hivites – one of the seven sinful nations – and their city is only five miles south-west of Ai. When Joshua insists they must abide by the terms of the treaty, the Israelites begin to grumble against their leaders. It doesn't matter that Joshua curses the Gibeonites for their deception and forces them to act as slaves to the Israelites. Whenever we get distracted, deceived, doubtful and divided, it always robs us of something that the Lord has promised us.[7]

Joshua is brutally honest because he wants to teach us four big lessons. First, make it your priority to read the Bible and to pray each day. Don't let yourself become too busy for God. This chapter goes alongside Proverbs 3:5–6, which commands us to *"Trust in the Lord with all your heart and lean not on your own understanding; in all your ways submit to him, and he will make your paths straight."* Don't get rushed into making snap

---

[6] Deuteronomy 7:3–4; Joshua 23:12–13; Judges 3:6; 1 Corinthians 7:39; 2 Corinthians 6:14–18.

[7] This fulfilled Noah's prophecy in Genesis 9:25–26 that the Canaanites would become slaves to the Hebrews. It was what the Lord told Israel to do in Deuteronomy 20:11 to any conquered city beyond these seven nations.

decisions. If Joshua had only waited three days, verse 16 tells us that the Lord would have revealed their deception to him. Better a right decision next week than a wrong decision today.

Second, make it your priority to ask tough questions before making decisions. Joshua was so busy that he failed to ask the right questions and heard what he wanted to hear. He had to learn the hard way that tough questioning avoids tough consequences.

Third, make it your priority to doubt your doubts. Whenever the Devil tries to tempt you to disregard the Lord's commands, always remember what Jesus teaches in John 8:44: *"When he lies, he speaks his native language, for he is a liar and the father of lies."*

Fourth, make it your priority to do the right thing, even when it hurts. Despite their sin and his own foolishness, Joshua acts honourably towards the Gibeonites. As he does so, the Lord transforms his mistake into a great act of mercy.[8] The Lord takes their flawed confession of faith in verses 9–10 at face value, treating their ruse as the equivalent of Rahab's scarlet cord – a desperate attempt to find salvation in Joshua. As a result, he not only rescues them from the slaughter of the Canaanites, but also makes them servants in his Tabernacle and honorary members of the tribe of Benjamin.[9] When verse 26 says that *"Joshua saved them from the Israelites"*, it acts as a prophetic pointer to Jesus saving many pagans. Faith saves the lying town of Gibeon, just as it saved the lying Rahab.

Joshua was too busy for God and it spelt disaster. In this chapter, he warns us not to do the same. He also reassures us that the Lord turns even our mistakes around for good. The chapter ends in salvation. Let's marvel at the mercy of the God who keeps on giving.

---

[8] See Psalm 15:4 and the Lord's defence of Joshua's rash vow in 2 Samuel 21:1–9.

[9] Joshua 18:25; 21:17; 2 Chronicles 1:3–13.

The Day the Sun Stood Still
(Joshua 10:1–15)

The sun stopped in the middle of the sky and delayed going down about a full day. There has never been a day like it before or since.

(Joshua 10:13–14)

Joshua is a book of miracles. That offends a lot of people. They feel far more comfortable being told that manna ceased to fall from heaven than that the River Jordan parted and the walls of Jericho fell.[1] But Joshua was written to persuade us that when God speaks out a promise, all of creation has to bend to what he says.

These fifteen verses recount the greatest miracle in the book of Joshua. The sun is 1.3 million times bigger than the earth. It burns at temperatures of up to 15 million degrees Celsius and accounts for 99.86 per cent of all the mass of the entire solar system. That's why many Canaanites worshipped it. They could see it was by far the most powerful object in the universe. The Lord therefore reaches out to them by commanding the sun to stand to attention like an obedient soldier in the sky. The Lord makes one final Gospel appeal to the Canaanites through this mighty miracle. This was the day the sun stood still.

Joshua is still reeling from the fallout of the two mistakes he made. Had he not sent troops against Ai without first dealing with Achan's sin, the Canaanites would still be trembling in fear behind the walls of their cities. Joshua's failure has given them

---

[1] Joshua 5:12; 3:15–17; 6:20.

hope, emboldening five southern kings to form a coalition army ready to march against him.[2] Had he not signed a peace treaty with the Gibeonites, that coalition army might have bided its time, but the news that Gibeon has betrayed them spurs the southern kings into immediate action. Joshua has to tell his disgruntled soldiers, still smarting from his refusal to allow them to sack and slaughter Gibeon, that they now need to go one step further. They need to march to defend the city that has just deceived them.

The southern coalition army is led by King Adoni-Zedek of Jerusalem. His name means *Lord of Righteousness* and he reigns from Mount Zion, so we are meant to see him as an imposter, a false messiah, a demonic parody of all that Jesus will one day be.[3] As he sets up his siege camp outside the walls of Gibeon, we are meant to see it as a picture of what happens whenever sinners convert to Christ: their former friends frequently respond with bullying and persecution, but the Lord stands alongside them. Joshua responds kindly to the messengers from Gibeon who arrive out of breath at his camp at Gilgal to plead with him, *"Do not abandon your servants. Come up to us quickly and save us! Help us, because all the Amorite kings from the hill country have joined forces against us."* He bravely marches twenty miles up a steep mountain road to meet a foe who knows the contours of Canaan far better than he does. His tired army moves fast to obtain the element of surprise.

The Lord performs three separate miracles in these verses to defeat the southern coalition. All of them do more than simply

---

[2] Jerusalem, Hebron, Jarmuth, Lachish and Eglon were all cities south of Jericho. The people of Jerusalem were actually Jebusites (15:63), but the Bible refers to any of these seven nations as *Canaanites* or *Amorites*. The Gibeonites were Hivites (9:7) but they are similarly called Amorites in 2 Samuel 21:2.

[3] His predecessor Melchizedek, whose name means *King of Righteousness*, acts as a much more positive prophetic picture of Jesus in Genesis 14:18–20. However, Joshua 10 emphasizes that Adoni-Zedek had rejected the Lord and was therefore counted among the Amorites whose sin had reached its full measure.

turn the battle in Israel's favour. They also demonstrate that Israel's God is far greater than the idols of the Canaanites.

The Canaanites worshipped the violent war-goddess Anath, who is celebrated in city names such as Beth Anath and Anathoth.[4] The Lord therefore proves he is the true war God by enabling Joshua and his men to pull off a military miracle. They manage to march undetected up the mountain road from Gilgal to Gibeon, falling from nowhere on the coalition soldiers as the sun begins to rise. The Israelites show no signs of exhaustion from their all-night climb, but are energized by the Lord to fight and slaughter for the next twenty-four hours. As the Lord throws the Canaanites into confusion, there can be no doubt about it. The score is the God of Israel one and the gods of Canaan nil.

The Canaanites also worshipped the storm-god Baal, whose name means *lord* and who is mentioned over forty times in Joshua and Judges. The Lord therefore finds a clever way to demonstrate that he is the true Lord and the real storm God. The Israelite army cannot cut down all the troops fleeing thirty miles south-west along the Aijalon Valley – the trade route to the sea – so he lends them a helping hand. He sends a hailstorm on the Canaanites – something they thought only Baal had power to do – with hailstones large enough to kill them. The storm is localized, affecting the fleeing Canaanites but not their Israelite pursuers, and more coalition soldiers die from the Lord's hailstones than from Israel's swords. The score is now the God of Israel two and the gods of Canaan nil.

The Canaanites worshipped the sun-goddess Shemesh and the moon-god Yarikh, who are celebrated in names such as Samson and Jericho. Seeing that the Israelite soldiers need more time to finish off the coalition army, the Lord therefore performs an even greater miracle: he holds the sun up in the sky and keeps the moon at bay so that Joshua's troops can press

---

[4] Joshua 19:38; 21:18. She also features in the name of Joseph's Egyptian wife Asenath (Genesis 41:45).

home their victory for the entire night under a sky of blazing sunshine. Joshua cannot explain to us how this happened any more than he can explain the parting of the River Jordan or the collapse of the walls of Jericho. He simply tells us that it happened and that contemporary writers also hailed it as one of the mightiest miracles they had ever seen.[5] There was no doubt about it: the score was the God of Israel three and the gods of Canaan nil. *"There has never been a day like it before or since, a day when the Lord listened to a human being. Surely the Lord was fighting for Israel!"*[6]

We do not know enough about the sun or about the workings of the universe to deny that this happened or to explain how it did. Joshua simply tells us that this is the kind of thing that happens when we trust the promises of God. When the Lord speaks, even the most powerful objects in the universe are forced to fall into line with what he says.

Martin Luther encourages us to believe that God still speaks words of such great power today: *"When Jesus Christ utters a word, He opens His mouth so wide that it embraces all heaven and earth, even though that word be but in a whisper. The word of the Emperor is powerful, but that of Jesus Christ governs the universe."*[7]

61

---

[5] *The Book of Jashar* is better translated *The Book of the Upright* because 2 Samuel 1:18 says new sections were still being added to the book many centuries later. Joshua's quote from the book helps clarify that the miracle in chapter 10 was not an extra-long night for marching, but an extra-long day for fighting.

[6] The Lord refused to support any human army in 5:13–15. But as soon as Joshua pledged to fight for the Lord's glory instead, we are told in 10:14 and 42 that the Lord was willing to fight on behalf of Israel.

[7] Point 230 in Martin Luther's *Table Talk* (1566).

Things Go South
(Joshua 10:16–43)

Joshua subdued them from Kadesh Barnea to Gaza
and from the whole region of Goshen to Gibeon.

(Joshua 10:41)

The best laid plans of generals have a habit of quickly going south on the battlefield. Joshua must have thought his own plans had been ruined by the mistakes he made against Ai and Gibeon. When he heard that these failures had emboldened the kings of the south to form a coalition army against him, he must have been tempted to run away and hide. He therefore isn't bragging when he lists his follow-up victories after the Battle of Gibeon. He wants to use what happened in his own life to reassure us that God can make things all right even when they all go wrong.

The kings of southern Canaan had in fact played unwittingly into Joshua's hands. By gathering their forces into one single army, they enabled him to conquer their land in a single campaign. Much of this was due to Joshua's determination to make the most of the opportunity that the Lord had handed him. Recognizing that his troops were beginning to tire after an all-night march and a twenty-four-hour slaughter, he commanded them not to waver and allow the defeated coalition soldiers to get away. Winston Churchill gave a similar command to an exhausted general after a hard-fought victory in North Africa: *"It is at the moment when the victor is most exhausted that the greatest forfeit can be exacted from the vanquished.*"[1] Joshua understands this principle. His stubborn perseverance prevents most of the Canaanites from making it home to defend their cities. When he musters the Israelite army at its new camp at Makkedah, thirty miles south-west of where it started, he finds that not a single one of them is missing. The kings of southern Canaan have spent their forces all for nothing.

The kings are holed up in a cave nearby, so Joshua turns them into a training exercise for his senior officers. These commanders were men whose fathers had been too scared to enter the Promised Land under Moses and who had died in the desert due to their fear. Joshua therefore orders them to place their feet on the necks of these five kings so that they can graduate to a new level of courage in the Lord. Joshua issues them with the same charge that the Lord gave to him at the start of chapter 1: *"Do not be afraid; do not be discouraged. Be strong and courageous. This is what the Lord will do to all the enemies you are going to fight."*[2] This deliberate echo celebrates the fact that God has turned what looked like a disaster into a springboard for fresh victory. These commanders now have an even bigger stomach for a fight than before, and once the Canaanites hear that Joshua has impaled their kings on poles as food for the vultures they have even less stomach for a fight than they did before Ai.[3] Joshua therefore throws the corpses of the kings back inside the cave and builds a pile of rocks over its

---

[1] Churchill wrote this to General Archibald Wavell on 13th December 1940.

[2] This is a great example of 2 Corinthians 1:3–4 in action. We are to encourage others with similar encouragement to that which we ourselves have received from God.

[3] This is what Joshua means when he tells us in 10:21 that *"no one uttered a word against the Israelites."* When these five kings were defeated, the remaining southern kings lost all courage to ally against them. The Lord placed such dread in their hearts that all resistance to the Israelite army melted away.

entrance as another spiritual milestone for Israel.[4] It proclaims that whenever our plans go south, the Lord remains in control.

Most of the cities listed by Joshua in verses 28–39 mean very little to modern readers, but a map of ancient Canaan shows them to be his route south from the battlefield to conquer the entire region in the weeks that followed. Conquering each of these mighty fortresses would have required a lengthy siege had not their defenders been decimated as part of the coalition army.[5] As it was, these walled cities quickly fell to Joshua and its inhabitants were swiftly slaughtered.[6] Even the arrival of troops from the powerful Philistine city of Gezer could not slow him down.[7] The city of Lachish fell in just two days. The city of Eglon fell in a single day. This astonishing speed of conquest was only made possible by the gathering of a coalition army that had at first seemed to spell disaster for Israel.

Verses 40–42 form the great crescendo of the chapter. Kadesh Barnea, on the southern frontier of the Promised Land, was where Joshua and Caleb had failed to persuade the Israelites that God would enable them to conquer the Canaanites if they trusted him (Numbers 13:26). It is therefore very poignant that Joshua should use it to describe the vast expanse of land they conquered in a very short campaign.[8] The entire south of Canaan was now suddenly theirs. The Lord had turned seeming disaster into the very means by which his promises towards them were

---

[4] Note Joshua's careful attention not to disobey the Lord a third time. See Deuteronomy 21:22–23.

[5] A replacement king had evidently been crowned in Eglon, but too few men survived to defend his city.

[6] Once again Joshua presents this slaughter as God's righteous judgment on sinful cities that defiled the land with their idolatry. He uses the verb *hāram*, meaning *to inflict destructive judgment*, ten times in Joshua 10–11.

[7] Gezer was so powerful it resisted conquest for many centuries to come (Judges 1:29; 1 Kings 9:16).

[8] This entire campaign took only a few weeks in late 1406 BC. For more on this dating, see the chapter "Milk and Honey". The *Goshen* mentioned in 10:41 is a city in southern Canaan. It is not the Goshen in far-off Egypt.

fulfilled. *"All these kings and their lands Joshua conquered in one campaign, because the Lord, the God of Israel, fought for Israel."*

Think about your own life. How many times has the Lord turned even your sins into sources of blessing? How often has he turned your failures into fruitfulness? How many times has he used your backsliding to renew your appreciation of his forgiveness and to enable you to share the Gospel in language that nonbelievers can understand? How many times have you stared defeat in the face, only to discover that the death-and-resurrection pathway is the believer's route to victory? How many times have you been terrified by the Devil's onslaught, only to discover that the Lord allowed his attack to break his teeth on your defences so that you can advance faster against him? How many times have things gone south in your own life, only to be turned to sudden victory?

If you can think of examples of this, then follow Joshua in verse 43 back to Gilgal, the place of worship and consecration. Having been too busy for God, he now takes time out of his campaigning to enjoy some downtime with the Lord. Let's do the same.

Let's make time to praise the God who keeps on giving that he turns even the bitterest attacks of our enemy into ways to fulfil his promises: *"Whoever attacks you will surrender to you... When enemies come in like a flood, the Spirit of the Lord will put them to flight."*[9]

---

[9] Isaiah 54:15; 59:19.

Hard Northerners
(Joshua 11:1–20)

It was the Lord himself who hardened their hearts
to wage war against Israel, so that he might destroy
them totally, exterminating them without mercy.

(Joshua 11:20)

Joshua appears to have suspected that people like you and me would be tempted to skim-read his chapters listing the many kings he defeated in Canaan. That's why he throws in the occasional shocking verse to stop us in our tracks. How about this one? *"It was the Lord himself who hardened their hearts to wage war against Israel, so that he might destroy them totally, exterminating them without mercy."* Joshua expects verse 20 to make us do a double-take and read a bit more carefully. What on earth can it mean?

First, it means that God remains in control even when people defy him. Joshua wants us to understand that, even when people reject the Lord, they play into his hands. Like the demons that pleaded with Jesus for permission to enter a herd of pigs, allowing him to kill two birds with one stone by ridding the region of both demons and non-kosher food, Joshua reassures us that God's enemies can never thwart his promises. Even as the northern kings form a fresh coalition against God's people, he is in complete control.

Second, it means that God's offer to forgive the Canaanites was genuine. When he extended grace to individuals such as Rahab and to towns such as Gibeon, he was truly offering to save all seven nations of Canaan. He made Joshua cross the River

Jordan in the centre of the country so that the news of the fall of Jericho would reverberate throughout the entire land. Joshua spent the whole of his first year in Canaan campaigning in the centre and south of the land, giving the cities of the north plenty of time to renounce their empty idols and to embrace the God of Israel. It was only after they rejected his Gospel invitation for a whole year that Joshua tells us literally in verse 20 that the Lord hardened their hearts *"so that they would have no share in his grace"*.[1]

Third, it also means that there is a time limit on God's call to repent and be saved. When Paul pleads with his readers in 2 Corinthians 6:2, *"I tell you, now is the time of God's favour, now is the day of salvation"*, he teaches that there is a shelf life on the Gospel message. If we ignore it today, we have no guarantee that we will be able to respond to it tomorrow. If we harden our hearts towards the Lord, he will eventually harden our hearts towards him too. Like so much of the book of Joshua, verse 20 echoes the book of Exodus, which tells us interchangeably that *"Pharaoh hardened his heart"* (four times), that *"Pharaoh's heart hardened itself"* (four times) and that "*the Lord hardened Pharaoh's heart*" (nine times). The Hebrew word that Joshua uses in verse 20 is *hāzaq*, which means either *to harden* or *to confirm*. When the northern cities of Canaan refused to accept the Lord, even after witnessing the defeat of the southern cities, the Lord actively confirmed them in the hardness of their hearts. What happened to these northerners is very sobering: even the God who keeps on giving eventually calls time on his offer of salvation.[2]

In verses 1–5, we find that hardening their hearts brought great glory to the Lord. A literal translation of Psalm 76:10

---

[1] I am not being anachronistic by referring to "the Gospel" before the arrival of Jesus. Hebrews 4:2 and 6 tell us that *"We also have had the gospel preached to us, just as they did."* See also Galatians 3:8.

[2] Paul warns us that God still does this today. See Romans 1:24–28 and 2 Thessalonians 2:10–12.

exclaims that *"Surely the anger of man brings you praise!"*, and that is what the Lord does through these hard northerners.[3] The city of Hazor was the greatest fortress city in the land of Canaan, so its King Jabin forms a far stronger coalition than the southern kings.[4] It has so many infantrymen that Joshua cannot even estimate their number, and it is reinforced with chariots, the superweapon of the Bronze Age. In the first leg of his contest with the gods of Canaan, the Lord had won three–nil. Travelling north for a much harder second leg would settle the result once and for all.[5]

In verses 6–9, we find that hardening the hearts of the northern Canaanites brought the Israelites into a place of even deeper consecration. They had no charioteers in their own army, so they were scared. For a sense of how much difference these ancient war machines could make on a battlefield, just look at the excuse that the men of Ephraim and Manasseh give in 17:16 for not having laid hold of all their Promised Land: *"The Canaanites who live in the plain have chariots fitted with iron."* It was therefore a massive act of faith and consecration to the Lord when Joshua and the Israelites obeyed his command to hamstring all the horses and burn all the chariots they captured on the northern battlefields. They must have been tempted to hang on to them, like Achan at Jericho, to use them in their next campaign, but they passed this test of their devotion. During this campaign, they learned to trust entirely in the Lord, like the

---

[3] *Kinnereth* in 11:2 means *Harp* and was the ancient name for the harp-shaped *Sea of Galilee*. If some of the city names in this chapter are unfamiliar, it helps to understand that they were all in the region around Galilee.

[4] Hazor was ten miles north of Lake Galilee. It took about five years to defeat this coalition, from 1405 to 1400 BC.

[5] One of the big themes of Judges is that the Israelites threw away many of the victories they scored under Joshua. Many years later, in Judges 4, a new King Jabin of Hazor emerges to oppress the Israelites.

writer of Psalm 20:7: *"Some trust in chariots and some in horses, but we trust in the name of the Lord our God."*[6]

In verses 10–20, we find that hardening the hearts of the northern Canaanites brought about a spiritual spring clean of their land. Four times in these verses Joshua uses the Hebrew word *hāram* to emphasize that his slaughter is *divine destructive judgment* on the people of Canaan. Three times he says that he did simply *"as the Lord had directed"*.[7] This campaign serves as a prophetic picture of what will happen at the Final Judgment, when Jesus rids the earth entirely of sin. King Jabin and his coalition did not thwart God's purposes for the world. He merely pointed to its glorious conclusion.

So be encouraged. When you see God-haters forming alliances in your own day, devising schemes and hatching plots against the Church, take heart from what happened in the days of Joshua. Trust that the Lord is powerful enough to use even the rage of his enemies to fulfil his great purposes for the world. Devote yourself to the Lord, doing everything he commands you, just like Joshua, and you need have no fear. You will live in the good of the promise that Jesus gives you in Matthew 16:18:

I will build my church, and the gates of Hell will not overcome it.

---

[6] We are told in 1 Kings 4:26, 9:22 and 10:26–29 that King Solomon's downfall was partly caused by his disobedience to the Lord's command concerning horses and chariots in Deuteronomy 17:16.

[7] Joshua 11:9, 12, 15. He uses the verb *hāram* in 11:11, 12, 20 and 21.

Go and Get Your Land
(Joshua 11:21–12:24)

So Joshua took the entire land, just as the Lord had directed Moses... Then the land had rest from war.

(Joshua 11:23)

Think of all the promises that God has made to every Christian. Take some time to make a list of them. Let me help you make a start.

How about his promises that he will help us to enjoy deep friendship with him? Jesus says we should expect a deeper experience of friendship with God than was enjoyed by Moses or Joshua or Elijah or John the Baptist: *"Many prophets and kings wanted to see what you see but did not see it, and to hear what you hear but did not hear it."* He assures us that this promise belongs to every single one of us: *"No longer will a man teach his neighbour, or a man his brother, saying, 'Know the Lord,' because they will all know me, from the least of them to the greatest."*[1] You may not be experiencing this yet, but the promise is still yours.

Or how about God's promises that he will forgive us? He doesn't merely overlook our sin and put us on probation. He distinctly remembers forgetting what we have done: *"I will forgive their wickedness and will remember their sins no more."* He doesn't just offset our guilt. He does away entirely with our sense of dirtiness and shame. *"If we confess our sins, he is*

---

[1] Jeremiah 31:34; Luke 10:24; John 17:3; Hebrews 8:11.

faithful and just and will forgive us our sins and purify us from all unrighteousness."[2]

This leads into promises that God will also empower us to break free from our sins. Forgiveness from sin is just the hallway of salvation. Consecration is the corridor that leads us into the full freedom of his palace. That's why it's such good news that *"The grace of God... teaches us to say 'No' to ungodliness and worldly passions, and to live self-controlled, upright and godly lives."* It's why it's so important that we believe him when he says, *"I am the Lord, who makes you holy"* and *"Everyone who sins is a slave to sin... [but] if the Son sets you free, you will be free indeed."*[3] We mustn't settle for anything less than this.

Then there are the promises God makes us about answering our prayers. Seven times in John 14–16 Jesus tells us that *"You may ask me for anything in my name, and I will do it."* This is his constant refrain in the gospels: *"If you believe, you will receive whatever you ask for in prayer."* If your prayer life feels limp and powerless, then it isn't meant to be.[4]

There are many promises that God will make us fruitful: *"some thirty, some sixty, some a hundred times what was sown".* There are promises that we will be filled with the Holy Spirit and trained by him to wield the same authority and power as Jesus. *"Very truly I tell you, whoever believes in me will do the works I have been doing, and they will do even greater things than these, because I am going to the Father."*[5]

Those are a few of the promises that God has given you, just to get your list going. You are going to need it if you want to respond as the first half of the book of Joshua comes to an end. This long list of conquered cities is far more than a soldier's tally of his conquests. They are recorded here to remind us that,

---

[2] Jeremiah 31:34; Hebrews 8:12; 1 John 1:9.

[3] Exodus 31:13; Leviticus 20:8; 22:32; John 8:34–36; Titus 2:11–12.

[4] Matthew 21:22. See also Matthew 7:7–11; 18:19; Mark 11:24; Luke 11:5–13; 18:1–8.

[5] Matthew 28:18–20; Mark 4:20; Luke 24:49; John 14:12; Acts 1:8.

if we trust and act in faith like Joshua, not a single one of the promises that God has given us will ever fail to come to pass in our lives. We are told in 11:23 that *"Joshua took the **entire** land"*, as the detailed list that follows proves. In case we are in any doubt, Joshua spells it out again later to the Israelites in 23:14: *"Not one of all the good promises the Lord your God gave you has failed. Every promise has been fulfilled; not one has failed."*

God's promises towards us are all guaranteed, but that doesn't make them automatic. Joshua tells us in 11:21–22 that he had to fight some pretty fearsome giants to obtain his Promised Land. The Anakites were so large that they made the ten spies that explored the land with Joshua and Caleb conclude in Numbers 13 that they must have misunderstood the promises of God. These were the ancestors of Goliath and the spiritual precursors of whatever makes us feel too scared to lay hold of God's promises. We face up to Anakites whenever we have the courage to share the Gospel with a friend, whenever we pray for someone to be healed, whenever we move house to join a church plant or whenever we deal with a deeply entrenched sin. These verses reassure us that there isn't a giant big enough to stand before us if we believe the promises of God.[6]

Part of our challenge is to study the Bible until those promises take hold of our hearts. It is striking how up-to-speed Joshua is in 12:1–6 on all the contours of the land that Moses conquered on the east side of the River Jordan in Numbers 21. He has taken the time to inform himself about what the Lord has promised to his people. These verses ought to challenge us to study the Bible and to note all the Scripture promises God has given us. When it comes to living in the good of our salvation, ignorance is never bliss. As we will discover in the book of Judges, it always leads to loss and misery.

The apostle Paul appears to see the list of thirty-one

---

[6] Joshua also says in 12:4 that King Og came from the giant race of Rephaites. See Deuteronomy 3:11.

defeated fortress cities in 12:7–24 as a prophetic picture for our own day. He describes the Devil's lies as "strongholds" that prevent us from inheriting our own Promised Land. He teaches us in 2 Corinthians 10:3–5 that *"Though we live in the world, we do not wage war as the world does. The weapons we fight with are not the weapons of the world. On the contrary, they have divine power to demolish strongholds. We demolish arguments and every pretension that sets itself up against the knowledge of God, and we take captive every thought to make it obedient to Christ."* Some of the strongholds listed here are hard to forget – Jericho, Ai and so on – but many of them have gone unmentioned so far in the story. They are like the many promises that God has given us throughout the Bible: easily overlooked but all of them ours for the taking.[7]

So what is your own Promised Land? What has the Lord pledged to give you? What are the strongholds that God wants you to go and conquer today? On a recent holiday, I found a brilliant plaque on the ruins of a German gun emplacement on the D-Day beaches in Normandy. It stated very simply: *"This gun emplacement was the strongest German fortress in Normandy. Nevertheless, it was taken at 8:44am on 6th June 1944."*

Nevertheless – that's a brilliant word. As we come to the end of the first half of the book of Joshua, it's a word that God speaks to you. It's time for you to go and get your land.

---

[7] *Hormah* in 12:14 was where the Israelites had been defeated in Numbers 14:44–45. It doesn't matter if you have tried and failed before. If you trust in the Lord's promises, you will succeed this time.

Joshua 13–24:

God's Gift to Each of Us

Let's Get Personal
(Joshua 13:1–19:51)

The Israelites divided the land, just as the Lord had commanded Moses.

(Joshua 14:5)

The first half of the book of Joshua was national. It described the conquest of the Promised Land by Israel all together. As we begin the second half of Joshua, however, the tone suddenly changes. The focus is no longer on national promises. It gets personal.

Israel has completely conquered the Promised Land. Its central, southern and northern campaigns have now all come to

an end. We are told in 11:23 that *"The land had rest from war."* Fighting continued but it was fundamentally different from here onwards. The Israelites were indisputably the masters of the Promised Land, but there were still pockets of Canaanite survivors to be conquered by each local tribe and clan.

The second half of Joshua begins with the Lord stating the facts plainly. He tells Joshua, *"You are now very old, and there are still very large areas of land to be taken over."* Joshua was aged eighty-four when he crossed the River Jordan, so six years of campaigning from 1406 to 1400 BC brings his age to ninety.[1] The Lord is right: he is too old to lead his nation out to war. He needs to transition in the second half of his book from star player to

---

[1] For a more detailed timeline, see the chapter "Milk and Honey". Some of the key verses for dating Joshua are 14:7, 14:10 and 24:29. Joshua 1–12 takes place between 1406 and 1400 BC, while Joshua 13–24 takes place between 1400 and 1380 BC.

coach, from chief musician to conductor of an orchestra. In 13:2–7, the Lord unveils a second-half strategy to deal with the remaining Canaanites west of the Jordan. *"Be sure to allocate this land to Israel for an inheritance, as I have instructed you, and divide it as an inheritance among the nine tribes and half of the tribe of Manasseh."*

In 13:8–33, Joshua starts by describing the borders of the land that the Lord promised to Reuben, Gad and half the tribe of Manasseh on the east side of the River Jordan. Most people speed-read these verses, but we mustn't. Do you know all the contours of the promises that God has made to you personally? Can you trace their boundaries as confidently as Joshua traces the boundaries here? If not, it may be why there are so many rooms left unexplored in the palace of your salvation. We are warned in 13:13 that God's promises are not automatic. We need to receive them with active faith. *"The Israelites did not drive out the people of Geshur and Maakah, so they continue to live among the Israelites to this day."*[2] So let this chapter inspire you to make a thorough list of God's promises to you personally. Write your own Joshua 13, then go out and get your land.

In 14:1–15:63, Joshua describes the borders of the land that the Lord promised to the tribe of Judah. Judah was by far the largest tribe, and the Lord had ruled in Numbers 26:52–56 that larger tribes ought to be allocated more land than the smaller ones, so the description of the boundaries of Judah is by far the longest. The Lord had also ruled in Numbers 26:52–56 that the tribal allocations ought to be decided by the casting of lots to ensure strict fairness. That's why Joshua gathers all the leaders of the Israelite clans to witness the moment that high

---

[2] Joshua also issues a second warning by mentioning Balaam in 13:22, the prophet who pursued the riches of this world instead of the promises of God, and who lost everything (Numbers 22–24; 31:6–8). We will examine Joshua's two mentions of the tribe of Levi (13:14, 33) in a few chapters' time.

priest Eleazar flips the sacred stones, known as the Urim and Thummim, to determine which tribe ought to settle where.[3]

The description of the land that the Lord promised to Judah is two chapters long, but don't rush it.[4] It includes the city of Jerusalem, still inhabited by the Jebusites. It includes the cities of the Philistines. This is not just a geography lesson. It is a call to stop settling for less than God has given us. It is a call to capture all of our own Promised Land.

In 16:1–17:18, Joshua describes the borders of the land that the Lord promised to Ephraim and to the half-tribe of Manasseh that had resisted the temptation to settle on the east side of the River Jordan.[5] In 18:1–19:48, he describes the borders of the land that the Lord promised to the remaining seven tribes. These chapters stretch our sense of ancient Canaanite geography, since some of these allocations include cities that were given to Judah, Ephraim and Manasseh earlier. Again, this is intentional.[6] It reminds us that God's promises need to be received with active faith. They are never simply automatic. Jerusalem is allocated to both Judah and Benjamin because the Lord will give it to whoever gets there first! Ziklag and Beersheba are allocated to both Judah and Simeon because he is happy to give it to either! Jericho and Bethel are allocated to both Ephraim and Benjamin because, though cleared of Canaanites, those lands have yet to be actively occupied. Endor

---

[3] This is a general piece of leadership wisdom. The greater input people have into decisions, the greater their ownership of them. Christian leaders are to consult and collaborate rather than dictate.

[4] Since Hebrew script reads from right to left, Joshua instinctively describes the southern border of Judah from east to west in 15:2–4. Since our script reads from left to right, we would instinctively do the opposite.

[5] Manasseh was the firstborn son of Joseph (17:1), but Jacob had prophesied that his younger brother Ephraim would be treated as the firstborn when it came to inheritance (Genesis 48:8–20).

[6] We can detect some of his frustration in 18:1–8. He sends scouts out from the Tabernacle to Shiloh to list which places have not yet been conquered, then he gets the high priest to reallocate some of them.

and Jezreel are allocated to both Manasseh and Issachar – I think you get the picture. God makes promises to each one of us, then he waits to see who has the faith to lay hold of them. Let it be you and me. Let's go and get our land![7]

Now comes the grand finale. In 19:49–51, Joshua does something clever to make it clear that these chapters are meant to challenge us personally. Having shifted his focus from the nation of Israel to each of its twelve tribes, he now talks about his own individual inheritance within the tribal land of Ephraim. When asked what share he would like personally in the Promised Land, he is standing before the Lord's high priest in the Tabernacle, so his answer can be taken as a picture of our prayers.[8] Joshua knows exactly what he wants the Lord to give him personally. Ever since he toured the land with Caleb almost half a century earlier, he has had his eye on a beautiful village in the hills named Timnath Serah. Since those hills have already been allocated to Joshua's tribe of Ephraim, it is an obvious place for him to set up his home. It lies on the other side of the hill country to Shiloh, but he sets off to turn the pretty village into a walled town.[9]

So we see that part two of the book of Joshua marks a major change for Israel. In part one we are told about the actions of *"Joshua and all Israel with him"*, but that phrase is never used in part two. From now on, God's people will advance through each tribe and individual laying hold of his specific promises to them. The book of Joshua now gets personal.

[7] We are told in 19:9 that Judah lost some of its allocation because it was clearly *"more than they needed"*. Esther 4:14 agrees: *"If you remain silent at this time, relief and deliverance... will arise from another place."*

[8] Joshua prays and then takes. He doesn't take and then pray. Church leaders need to be squeaky clean in how they handle their finances, leaving no room for any accusation that they have abused their position.

[9] In 18:1, the Tabernacle moves from Gilgal to the town of Shiloh in Ephraim Shiloh means Place of Rest and marks its permanent home from Joshua 18 to 1 Samuel 4.

Perhaps (Joshua 14:6–15)

Perhaps the Lord will be with me, and I will drive
them out as the Lord has spoken.

(Joshua 14:12, New American Standard Bible)

Caleb is the Patrick Swayze of the book of Joshua. As he jumps out of a plane for a risky skydive in the classic 1990s' movie *Point Break*, Patrick Swayze teaches Keanu Reeves his secret: *"Fear causes hesitation, and hesitation will cause your worst fears to come true."*

That's how Caleb acts when Joshua is parcelling out the Promised Land. He was aged forty when Moses sent him and Joshua out as spies from Kadesh Barnea in Numbers 13. That was forty-five years ago, but he can still remember what he saw – the fertile fields, the massive grapes and figs and pomegranates, and the giant-sized Anakites who defended them. *"We should go up and take possession of the land, for we can certainly do it,"* he had urged the Israelites, but he had been outvoted by the ten doubting spies.[1] The moment that Joshua starts talking about individual promises from God, however, he is on his feet. He has been nursing a promise from the Lord for the past forty-five years.[2]

Caleb has many reasons to leave the risk to someone else. For a start, he is too old for battle and he is surrounded by plenty

---

[1] Joshua warns us in 14:8 that we all have a role to play in spurring one another on to great exploits of faith. If our words can *"melt people's hearts"*, they can also make them *"wholehearted"* like Caleb.

[2] Caleb respects the fact that the Lord has chosen Joshua to lead Israel, and not him. He doesn't use God's promise as an excuse to bypass Joshua's authority. He submits to his lead in a very godly way.

of younger warriors. What's more, the promise that the Lord gave him was actually quite vague: *"The land on which your feet have walked will be your inheritance and that of your children forever."* The promise did not name the land and it definitely didn't mention giants.[3] It wasn't even a direct word from the Lord. It came through the mouth of Moses, a man who had failed to enter the Promised Land. Caleb had a pile of excuses why he should hesitate and leave the work to somebody else. That's why he's mentioned here. God wants us to become like Patrick Swayze in *Point Break* too.

Caleb uses a beautiful Hebrew word in verse 12. *'Ūlay* means *perhaps* or *potentially* or *maybe*. It is the same word that the Israelites use in 9:7 to challenge the Gibeonites, *"Perhaps you live near us!"*, and the same word Jonathan uses when he reckons on the Lord being with him in 1 Samuel 14:6: *"Perhaps the Lord will act on our behalf."* Caleb is so determined to lay hold of God's promises that he would literally rather die than wait around for a further sign. He begs Joshua to allocate him the hill country of the Anakites because he has no fear of the giants who live there. He sees them as the men who made his generation of Israelites doubt God's power and die in the desert. He therefore wants to deal with them for the sake of the Lord's reputation. For forty-five years, Caleb has been longing to vindicate the Lord's name or to die trying. He does not hesitate: *"Perhaps the Lord will be with me, and I will drive them out as the Lord has spoken."*

Caleb's words were recorded for us. They remind us that it is impossible to make excuses and history at the same time. It is impossible to wear a crash helmet and a victor's crown. It is impossible to hang on to our safety and on to God's promises as well. That's why Caleb brushes off any suggestion that the task is beyond him. Yes, he was part of the Exodus generation

---

[3] The way that Caleb interprets the promise he received in Numbers 14:24 challenges us to interpret God's promises to us in a manner that requires the most faith, not the least faith. That's how we live out Luke 9:24.

that doubted the Lord, but don't forget that *"I brought him back a report according to my convictions, but my fellow Israelites who went up with me made the hearts of the people sink."* Moses confessed freely that *"You have followed the Lord my God wholeheartedly."*[4] Yes, he is old, but he is not weary. *"I am still as strong today as the day Moses sent me out; I'm just as vigorous to go out to battle now as I was then."*

There are many miracles in the book of Joshua, but I'm not convinced that this was one of them. It is possible that the Lord preserved Caleb's strength, as he did the strength of Moses in Deuteronomy 34:7, but it is just as likely an expression of how Caleb feels on the inside.[5] If he was too weak to defeat these giants without the Lord's help in his forties, Caleb reasons that it will be no harder to fight them in his mid-eighties!

I love Caleb's logic that wherever God's people have failed in the past is the place he most wants to empower them to succeed today. I love the way he sees these giants, not as an obstacle, but as the thing that made the ten spies scared and therefore as unfinished business for the Lord. I also love Caleb's logic that wherever Canaan is most securely defended must be the most important piece of land to capture. What would it mean for you and me to employ that logic in our own situations today?

For me, it has meant going as a missionary to a city that everybody told me was one of the hardest places to reach in Europe. It meant coming back to England and moving into London when most other people at my life stage are moving out into the country. It has meant planting churches into places where people told me that a church could never thrive. It has meant my wife and me giving so much financially to the work

---

[4] The Bible commends Caleb for his *"wholehearted"* faith six times, in Numbers 14:24 and 32:12; Deuteronomy 1:36, and Joshua 14:8, 9 and 14. It led to his promotion as leader of the tribe of Judah in Numbers 34:18–19.

[5] Contrast this with Barzillai, in 2 Samuel 19:31–39, who was younger than Caleb but counted himself out of God's promises and therefore missed out on all that God had for him in his twilight years.

of mission that we often feel nauseous with fear. It has meant repeatedly believing the words of Hudson Taylor, the nineteenth-century missionary to China: *"All God's giants have been weak men who did great things for God because they reckoned on God being with them."*

That's the kind of faith God wants to stir in our hearts through the aged exploits of Caleb. He encourages us that Caleb's *"perhaps"* was all it took for him to capture his share of the Promised Land. Because he refused to get discouraged when his friends died in the desert, because he spent forty-five years nursing God's promises to him, not a bitter sense of disappointment, he was empowered to conquer giants in his old age. Caleb recognized that *"Their cities were large and fortified"*, but he also recognized that his survival into old age was itself all the proof he needed that God was with him.

So away with our excuses. Away with our risk aversion. Away with our demand to receive watertight proof before we step out in obedience to the Lord. Let's not tremble before the giants and the strongholds that lie before us. *"Perhaps the Lord"* is all we need to press forward on to victory.

A Woman's Job
(Joshua 15:13–19 and 17:3–6)

The daughters of the tribe of Manasseh received an inheritance among the sons.

(Joshua 17:6)

Throughout history, churches have generally not been good at helping women to lay hold of all God's promises to them. Sometimes they have even ridiculed the very idea. The eighteenth-century essayist Samuel Johnson argued that *"A woman's preaching is like a dog's walking on its hind legs. It is not done well; but you are surprised to find it done at all"* – and his view was fairly representative of his time.[1] Working to extend the Kingdom of God has often been seen as an essentially male job, which is why we need to spot what Joshua is saying in these two brief interludes within the list of tribal boundaries. He is teaching us that laying hold of the promises of God is as much a woman's job as a man's.

First, let me put my own cards on the table. I am convinced the Bible teaches that churches should be led by teams of elders and that those elders should be godly men who lead their households well. I know that view isn't popular, but I explain in my commentary *Straight to the Heart of 1 Thessalonians to Titus* that it is nevertheless what the apostle Paul teaches us in 1 Timothy 2:8–3:13. I want to state that view up front because I don't want you to think I'm on a modern bandwagon, determined to read something into the book of Joshua that isn't really there.

---

[1] He says this in James Boswell's famous biography *The Life of Samuel Johnson* (1791).

I'm on the conservative end of the spectrum, but I am convinced that Joshua teaches us that godly women have a crucial part to play in helping the Church to inherit all the promises that are given her by God.

Joshua lived in a male-dominated culture. He, the high priest and the twelve tribal leaders of Israel were all men. The first of his two interludes, in 15:13–19, consequently starts as no surprise. Caleb launches his attack on the Anakites, captures their city and renames it after his favourite grandson.[2] If you think that sounds patriarchal, take a read of what happens next. The ageing Caleb decides that it is time to call forth leadership from the young men of Judah so, as leader of the tribe, he offers his daughter's hand in marriage to any warrior who captures the city of Debir.[3] Caleb's nephew Othniel rises to the challenge and emerges as a next-generation leader, the first of the twelve judges who will rule Israel after the death of Joshua.[4] This interlude begins with a man auctioning off his daughter to his nephew on the battlefield. It's about as patriarchal as it comes.

That's why Joshua wants us to read on slowly. In Hebrew society, Caleb's daughter Aksah is expected to know her place. She is to be the blushing bride and not the hero of the story.[5] But we discover she is more passionate to lay hold of God's promises than her new husband. She urges Othniel to ask her father Caleb to allow them to spread out into land that has been allocated to him. When her husband doesn't see the urgency, she takes the

[2] 1 Chronicles 2:42. The name Hebron means *Union*, and Caleb also renamed the city to erase the name of Arba, the father of the Anakites (15:13 and 21:11). Hebron commanded the southern hill country of Judah and would become King David's capital before he captured Jerusalem, 25 miles to the north.

[3] The Canaanite name Kiriath Sepher meant *City of the Scroll*, denoting that it was a centre for pagan learning under the Canaanites. Caleb renames it Debir, meaning *Holy Place*.

[4] Othniel means *Lion of God*. We will read about his leadership in Judges 3:7–11.

[5] The name Aksah means *Ankle Chain*. Caleb expected her to be a pretty little thing, but she is a warrior.

initiative and goes to see her father, asking not just for his land but for some of his waterholes too. Caleb is delighted with his daughter. He recognizes that it's just as much a woman's job to lay hold of all God's promises and to occupy the land.

The second interlude, in 17:3–6, carries a similar theme. A man named Zelophehad has five daughters and no sons, which means that any land he occupies will go outside his family when he dies. The rule was simple in the ancient world: sons inherited land from their fathers, and daughters only got a look-in if they married the right man. Zelophehad had appealed to Moses to make an exception back in Numbers 27:1–11. Moses had brought the case before the Lord and had returned with a landmark ruling: *"If a man dies and leaves no son, give his inheritance to his daughter."* Zelophehad therefore asks Joshua to enforce this decision and he gets more than he bargained for. Joshua doesn't simply declare that his five daughters must share between them the land allotted to the sixth clan of western Manasseh.[6] He decrees that the half-tribe now officially has ten clans! Each of Zelophehad's five daughters is promoted and counted as a clan of her own.[7]

The Lord sees it as so important that we spot what he is saying here about the role of women that he repeats these two interludes elsewhere in the Bible. Aksah's faith is also recorded in Judges 1:12–15. The faith of Zelophehad's daughters is also recorded in Numbers 27:1–11 and 36:1–13. Joshua gives no commentary on these verses other than the fact that his whole book serves as a prophetic pointer to the future victory of Jesus and to our inheritance in him. We need to look to the New Testament for commentary, where Paul explains in Galatians 3:26–29 what is signified by these two striking interludes. He

---

[6] 1 Chronicles 7:15 lists Zelophehad's daughters among the half-tribe that inherited land west of the Jordan.

[7] Don't miss Joshua's startling generosity. Zelophehad was heir to Hepher, one of six clans of Makir (17:2), so Joshua does more than just divide his share among his daughters. He turns the six tracts of land into ten!

says that every believer is *"in Christ"* – whether male or female – it doesn't matter when it comes to sharing in the fruit of what Jesus has done for us. *"You are **all** sons of God through faith in Christ Jesus... There is no male or female; for you are all one in Christ Jesus."*[8]

This doesn't mean that gender roles are to be obliterated in the Church. The New Testament paves a far better path for us by telling us that they are to be redeemed. Husbands and fathers are still to take a leadership role at home and in the church, but they are to champion the complete equality of women in terms of value. They are not to conflate eldership with leadership. Elders are not to monopolize leadership, but to multiply it and direct it. In short, they are to create churches like those planted by the apostle Paul – full of godly women who are released to serve as deacons (Romans 16:1–2), as Bible instructors (Acts 18:26), as church planters (Romans 16:3), as prayer meeting leaders (Acts 12:12), as children's workers (2 Timothy 1:5) and as hard labourers in the Lord (Romans 16:12). The mission that the Lord has given us is so large that it takes the active leadership of every single Christian to capture the whole of our Promised Land.

---

[8] Many English translators take offence at Paul's language and mistranslate his words as *"You are all children of God"*, but the Gospel doesn't obliterate the sexes. It redeems them, teaching that women are in Christ too.

Not a Christian Word
(Joshua 17:12–13)

The Manassites were not able to occupy these towns, for the Canaanites were determined to live in that region.

(Joshua 17:12)

Napoleon Bonaparte was never known for his lack of ambition. When he seized power in 1799, France had been weakened by several years of violent revolution and bankrupted by foreign wars, yet within ten years he had made France the undisputed ruler of Europe. When asked how he did it, his answer was clear. *"Impossible n'est pas français,"* he declared. *"Impossible is not a French word."*[1]

Joshua wants us to understand that impossible is not a Hebrew word either. It isn't a Christian word. It has no place in the vocabulary of those who follow the Almighty.

He is not being unrealistic. As he describes the tribal borders of Israel in these chapters, he confesses very honestly that there were large tracts of the Promised Land that the Israelites failed to subdue. In 15:63, he tells us that the Jebusites quickly rebuilt Jerusalem after Joshua destroyed it as part of his defeat of the southern coalition. The men of Judah not only failed to stop them from rebuilding, but they also failed to capture the city they rebuilt. They were forced to tolerate it as a foreign enclave.[2] Joshua tells us that *"Judah **could not** dislodge*

---

[1] Napoleon wrote this in a letter to General Jean Le Marois on 9th July 1813.

[2] Even when men of Judah finally destroyed Jerusalem, they allowed the Jebusites to rebuild it a second time (Judges 1:8, 21). It would take King David

the Jebusites", but he is simply reeling us in so that he can teach us an important lesson a few verses later.

In 16:10, he confesses that the men of Ephraim had similar difficulties capturing the stronghold city of Gezer. They were able to starve the Canaanites into serving them as forced labourers, but they were unable to dislodge and destroy them.[3]

In 17:12–13, Joshua confesses that the men of Manasseh fared no better with the cities of Beth Shan, Ibleam, Dor, Endor, Taanach and Megiddo. This was even worse than the failure of Judah and Ephraim, not just because it was six towns compared to one, but because none of them was as fortified as Jerusalem or Gezer. The failure of the men of Manasseh to do any more than subject their inhabitants to forced labour was a massive blot on the Lord's reputation as the mighty Conqueror of the false gods of Canaan. Joshua reels us in further when he tells us that *"the Manassites **were not able** to occupy these towns."* He wants to get us nodding about our own struggles as Christians, because a sucker punch is coming.

If you are skim-reading these lists of conquered cities, you will miss it, but Joshua wants us to do a double-take when he tells us that *"The Manassites were not able to occupy these towns, for the Canaanites were determined to live in that region."* They were determined to live in that region? What kind of excuse is that?! Are we supposed to believe that the citizens of Jericho, Ai, Hazor and the other cities that Joshua conquered were therefore **un**determined to hold fast their gates in order to stay alive?! Of course not. Joshua is simply reporting the excuse that the men of Manasseh gave him for their failure to inherit all God's promises. He wants to expose our own lame excuses. He is pointing out that impossible has no place on the lips of a follower of the Almighty.

---

to conquer Jerusalem for good (2 Samuel 5:6–9).

[3] Shamefully for the Israelites and their God, they did not even capture Gezer under King David. They had to rely on Pharaoh to capture it for them and give it as a wedding present to King Solomon (1 Kings 9:16).

The truth was that the men of Manasseh were content with less than God had promised. They were happy to live without capturing those six towns. They turned their attention elsewhere, meaning that the Canaanites were more determined to remain in the land than the men of Manasseh were to expel them. We dare not judge them for this, for we are just as guilty of taking this approach with our calling to make disciples of every nation of the world. We convince ourselves that certain countries are "closed to the Gospel" and that certain sections of our cities are "unreachable". We satisfy ourselves with what we have instead of praying to God to give us the entirety of our Land.

Let's take an example. Niccolò Polo, the father of the famous Marco Polo, was a merchant of Venice who longed to get his hands on the vast wealth of the east. He travelled halfway round the world to become one of the first white men to stand at the court of a Chinese emperor, and he received a stunning invitation. Emperor Kublai Khan had heard about a man called Jesus Christ, who was God, and he wanted a hundred of his followers to come and preach his message to the Chinese. If Niccolò Polo could bring back a hundred missionaries from Europe, the emperor promised that he and his subjects would follow Jesus. Sadly, Europe's Christians had less ambition for their Messiah than Niccolò Polo had for his money. It took them two years to discuss the invitation, and when they did so they could only muster two missionaries who were willing to go. Both of them deserted Niccolò Polo en route back to China due to the hardships of their journey and increasing fear of preaching Christ in pagan lands. China would have to wait six more centuries for the eventual arrival of Hudson Taylor.[4]

Sadly, that tragic story is not unusual. When William Carey pointed out to a gathering of English ministers in 1786 that it

---

[4] Marco Polo and Rustichello da Pisa tell this tragic story in *The Travels of Marco Polo* (c.1300 AD).

was wrong for British businessmen to be so eager to set sail to plunder riches from the Empire and yet for British clergymen to be so eager to stay at home, he was angrily told, *"Young man, sit down, sit down! You're an enthusiast. When God pleases to convert the heathen, He'll do it without consulting you or me."*[5]

Nor is this attitude a thing of the past. In today's Church, ungodly contentment with the status quo can be found everywhere. Every time we write off millions of believers by referring to "the Muslim world", we act like the men of Manasseh. Every time we decide that there is no point sharing the Gospel with one of our work colleagues because they are a Hindu, or a strident atheist or a nominal believer, we show that we are less determined to save their souls than the Devil is to keep hold of them.

Every time we give in to fear and downsize our dreams, we do what the men of Manasseh did when they decided it was easier to leave the towns of Beth Shan, Ibleam, Dor, Endor, Taanach and Megiddo to themselves. Every time we focus on the size of the giants that stand before instead of on the size of the God who sends us, we do what Joshua warns against here. We forget that impossible is not a Christian word.

William Carey ignored his critics and spent the rest of his life as a missionary to India. By the time he died, there were half a million converts in his part of the country alone. He pleads with us not to be like the men of Manasseh: *"Few people know what may be done till they try, and persevere in what they have undertaken."*

---

[5] Both quotes in this chapter come from S. Pearce Carey's excellent biography *William Carey* (1923).

Greener Grass
(Joshua 17:14–18)

Joshua said to the tribes of Joseph – to Ephraim and Manasseh… "Though they are strong, you can drive them out."

(Joshua 17:17–18)

There is a famous story about two men in the same cramped and dark hospital ward. The one whose bed was by the window had lost a lung and was in constant pain. He sat up in his bed all day long and described to his roommate, with laboured breaths, all the things he saw outside. His roommate was recovering from a severe accident and could only lie on his back. Those descriptions from the window were his only access to the outside world. The park, the birds, the children playing – they were all he had to live for.

As time went on, however, he became consumed with jealousy. Why couldn't *he* be the one with the view out of the window instead of receiving a description second-hand? Late one night, the man's remaining lung began to fail. There were no nurses around. His roommate heard him struggling for the buzzer which he could reach from his own bed, but he decided not to. As he heard the final choking of his dying friend, he felt no regrets about the choice he'd made. It was his turn to see out of the window.

Sure enough, the following morning he was promoted. Two of the nurses moved him to the bed next to the window. He asked them to sit him up and then he took his first look out on the world his friend had lovingly described. There was nothing but a brick wall.

The Devil is an expert at provoking jealousy among God's people. He is a master at persuading us that the view from the other bed is better and that the grass is greener on the other side. That's why Joshua, in the middle of his list of tribal boundaries for Israel, warns us strongly against this tactic. He wants us to focus on the green grass of home.

In verse 14, the men of Ephraim and Manasseh come to Joshua and complain, *"Why have you allotted us only one portion of land and one share for an inheritance? We are a numerous people."* Don't miss the irony of their statement, which is meant to show us how foolish we are to envy others. It's not just that the men of Ephraim and Manasseh belonged to two tribes that had been allocated two portions of land by Joshua. It's that half of the men of Manasseh had settled prematurely on the east side of the River Jordan. They were two tribes which had been allocated three portions of land between them! God had been more generous towards them than any other tribe, but that's how discontentment always is. It never stops to thank the Lord for what he has already given us.

Consequently, in verse 15, Joshua rebukes them.[1] He points out that there is plenty of land allocated to them that they have failed to occupy. In addition to Gezer, Beth Shan, Ibleam, Dor, Endor, Taanach and Megiddo, there are plenty of forests for them to convert into farmland. If they are truly as numerous as they claim in their bid to steal land from their brothers, they should have no problem chopping down trees and driving out the Canaanites who claim those forests as their own. Joshua calls their bluff, and so he should, because these are just the kind of excuses that prevent God's people from living in the good of all his promises. We fool ourselves that if only we were

---

[1] Leaders, note Joshua's wisdom in saying no. Although he is an Ephraimite himself, he forces them to take risks and use their own resources because this is the only way a new generation learns the faith of its fathers.

part of a better church, if only we lived in an easier community to reach with the Gospel and if only we were less busy then we would be more fruitful, but Joshua insists firmly that our real problem is internal. We need to stop fantasizing about other places and to start fighting where we are. It's like the proverb says: *"Those who work their land will have abundant food, but those who chase fantasies will have their fill of poverty."*[2]

In verse 16, the men of Ephraim and Manasseh continue to make excuses. They complain to Joshua that *"The Canaanites who live in the plain have chariots fitted with iron."* Stop for a moment and consider how irrelevant that excuse is to Joshua's command for them to clear the forest areas of the land the Lord has allocated them. Chariots cannot be used to fight a battle in a forest. The place that Joshua was ordering them to conquer was in fact the one place where they were safe from their biggest fear! But that's how it is with the Devil's deceptions. They rarely make sense. When Christians convince themselves that they are ministering in a spiritually difficult area, they never stop to reflect on whether they have ever lived in an area that is spiritually easy or whether this is just what people say to bat away the scary promises of God.

James Fraser, the great missionary to the Lisu people of China found that this was often his own greatest obstacle to fruitful ministry. He wrote in his diary that

> *The temptation I have often had to contend with is persistent under many forms: "If only I were in such and such a position" for example, "shouldn't I be able to do a great work! Yes, I am only studying engineering at present, but when I am in training for missionary work things will be different and more helpful." Or "I am just in preparation at present, taking Bible courses and so on, but when I get out to China my work will begin." "Yes,*

---

[2] Proverbs 12:11; 28:19.

I have left home now, but I am only on the voyage, you know; when I am really in China, I shall have a splendid chance of service." Or, "Well, here in the Training Home, all my time must be given to language study – how can I do missionary work? But when I am settled down in my station and able to speak freely, opportunities will be unlimited!" etc. etc. It is all IF and WHEN. I believe the devil is fond of those conjunctions... The plain truth is that the Scriptures never teach us to wait for opportunities of service, but to serve in just the things that lie next to our hands... The Lord bids us work, watch and pray; but Satan suggests, wait until a good opportunity for working, watching, and praying presents itself – and needless to say, this opportunity is always in the future.[3]

James Fraser stopped fantasizing about tomorrow and started fighting hard today. His efforts triggered a revival among the Lisu that many historians believe led directly to the remarkable Christian transformation of China at the end of the twentieth century. So, in verses 17–18, Joshua urges the men of Ephraim and Manasseh to stop making excuses and to start making inroads against the enemy. Their brothers succeeded in verse 1 because they *"were great soldiers"* – in other words, because they stopped tut-tutting and started training. When we fail to live in the good of all God's promises to us, the issue is rarely with the enemy. It is almost always with our own hearts. Joshua tells the men of Ephraim and Manasseh forcefully that *"Though the Canaanites have chariots fitted with iron and though they are strong, **you can drive them out**."*[4]

So away with excuses. Away with fantasies of what we

---

[3] Quoted by Eileen Crossman in her biography entitled *Mountain Rain* (1982).

[4] In Judges 4, the Lord demonstrates that he is capable of turning the iron-axled chariots of the enemy into a liability. A sudden rainstorm swamps Sisera's heavy chariots so that his army is destroyed.

might do for God if we were somewhere else, sometime else or someone else. Away with comparison altogether, and with the foolish notion that the grass is somehow greener on the other side. Focus instead on the green grass of your own allocation of the Promised Land. Don't let the Devil rob you of what the God who keeps on giving has promised to give you today.

The Accursed
(Joshua 20:1–21:42)

The towns of the Levites in the territory held by the Israelites were forty-eight in all, together with their pasture-lands.

(Joshua 21:41)

God just keeps on giving, even when his people let him down. If we want proof of this, we need look no further than the way he singled out the tribe of Levi.

In Genesis 34, the Lord had singled out Levi in a bad way. Hearing that his sister Dinah had been raped by a Canaanite, Levi had teamed up with his brother Simeon to deceive, trick and murder the rapist and his friends. He and his brother pretended to help the Canaanites to find forgiveness from the Lord. Tricking them into being circumcised, they took advantage of their weakness to murder them and ransack their city. In response, in Genesis 49:5–7, the Lord had placed a curse on Simeon and Levi. He decreed that their two tribes would be scattered throughout the land of Canaan for their crimes:

Simeon and Levi are brothers – their swords are weapons of violence... Cursed be their anger, so fierce, and their fury, so cruel! I will scatter them in Jacob and disperse them in Israel.

You must have noticed that the tribe of Levi has already been singled out several times in the book of Joshua, so this is why. Levi was one of the two accursed tribes of Israel.[1]

But the God who keeps on giving wasn't willing to leave it there. Joshua explains to us in 20:1–9 that, while killing people is always wrong, it isn't always equally wrong. What matters is the motive of a person's heart. We recognize this fact ourselves by sending murderers to prison yet honouring soldiers as heroes when they return home from war. The Lord makes a similar distinction here. He creates six *"cities of refuge"* throughout the Promised Land so that anyone who kills a person accidentally and without evil motive has a place to run to find legal protection until their case can be brought to a fair trial.[2]

The Lord is excited. He has found a way to keep on giving to the tribe of Levi. He has singled them out, not as rogues, but as the perfect custodians of these six cities of refuge, since they have proven by their actions that their ancestor was driven by a very different motive to his brother Simeon when he killed the Canaanite rapist and his friends.[3] Simeon had pretended to act out of a passion for the Lord's name. He had appealed to the sanctity of sex within marriage and to the importance of not intermarrying with the Canaanites – but this was hard to believe when he later took a Canaanite concubine and had sex with her.[4] As a result, we are told in 19:9 that *"the Simeonites received their*

---

[1] It was singled out in 13:14, 33; 14:4 and 18:7 as a tribe that would inherit no land of its own.

[2] Moses had already designated three cities of refuge on the east side of the Jordan, commanding that three more be designated on the west side once the land had been conquered (Numbers 35:6–34; Deuteronomy 4:41–43). The Lord's commitment to fairness and to giving everyone an opportunity to prove their motive is also emphasized by his insistence in 20:9 that these cities were to be a refuge for non-Israelites too.

[3] Numbers 35:6 stipulated that these six refuge cities should be given to the Levites. All six are listed in 21:1–42.

[4] Genesis 46:10; Exodus 6:15. Simeon's descendants took a lead in Israel's sexual sin (Numbers 25:14).

inheritance within the territory of Judah." They would quickly be absorbed by their larger neighbour and largely disappear from the map of Israel, affirming the words of King David: *"The Lord searches every heart and understands every motive behind the thoughts. If you seek him, he will be found by you; but if you forsake him, he will reject you for ever."* [5]

Levi had lied and murdered alongside Simeon, but his motive was different. He never took a Canaanite concubine, and the actions of his children showed that his intentions had been pure. When the Levites strapped on swords to kill their relatives for worshipping the golden calf in Exodus 32:25–29, Moses commended their unusual passion for God's name: *"You have been set apart to the Lord today, for you were against your own sons and brothers."* When they did it again, in Numbers 25:7–13, in response to seeing their relatives worshipping foreign gods by having sex with foreign women, the Lord rejoiced that it proved that their tribal leader *"was as zealous for my honour among them as I am"*. The Lord had found a perfect way to keep on giving to the Levites. He would make them custodians of his holy Word, his holy Tabernacle and his holy promises to Israel.

That's why Joshua has already told us four times that the Levites were not allocated any of the land of Canaan. The Lord had cursed them with being scattered throughout Israel, and so scattered they would be. The Lord would simply turn the curse of scattering into a blessing. He would allocate them the forty-eight towns that are listed in 21:1–42, scattered across the lands of all twelve tribes of Israel, so that they could act as spiritual guardians for their nation as a whole. The three clans of Levi – the Kohathites, Gershonites and Merarites – would receive some of the best towns in the land, including the highly desirable cities of Hebron, Gibeon, Shechem and Kedesh.[6] They

---

[5] 1 Chronicles 28:9. Unintentional killing was merely punished by exile to the city until the high priest died.

[6] Kedesh means *Set Apart As Holy*, so the Hebrew text of 20:7 tells us that the Israelites *kedeshed Kedesh*. This scattering gave them space and authority,

must have been left gaping with astonishment at God's generous mercy towards them, because the principle of Jeremiah 17:10 is truly amazing: *"I the Lord search the heart and examine the mind, to reward each person according to their conduct, according to what their deeds deserve."*

So don't be put off by this long list of forty-eight cities. They are recorded here for you. If you have sinned, these verses call you to run to the Lord for forgiveness with the same speed as a person running to one of these six cities of refuge. In Jesus Christ, you have a far better high priest than was ever born to the tribe of Levi.[7] He is your true Redeemer.[8]

If you know your sin has been intentional, these verses encourage you to repent in a way that Simeon failed to do. The Lord wants them to stir you to listen to the apostle Paul when he warns you in 1 Corinthians 4:5 to *"Judge nothing before the appointed time; wait until the Lord comes. He will bring to light what is hidden in darkness and will expose the motives of the heart."* Let the contrasting fates of the two accursed tribes of Israel spur you on to repent of your sins while there is still time

for you to receive mercy. The God who keeps on giving will turn the curse of your sin into the blessing of his salvation.

---

but not sole occupancy of these cities. The 12 tribes did not so much lose these cities as gain some Levites within them who had authority to keep calling them back to God.

[7] Jesus is revealed as the true and better Aaron in Hebrews 3–10. Aaron's family, which served as priests in the Tabernacle and Temple, is helpfully allocated the towns nearest to Jerusalem in 21:10–19. The priests get 13 towns, their fellow Kohathites get 10 towns, the Gershonites get 13 towns and the Merarites 12 towns.

[8] The Hebrew word *gō'ēl*, which means *avenger of blood* in 20:3, 5 and 9 also means *guardian-redeemer* throughout the book of Ruth. Jesus is both the true Avenger on sin and the true Redeemer of sinners.

Long-Distance Relationship
(Joshua 21:43–22:34)

Then Joshua blessed them and sent them away, and they went to their homes.

(Joshua 22:6)

I once attempted a relationship with a girl who lived in the Czech Republic. I was living in England, and it didn't work well at all. It doesn't matter how many messages you send, how many phone calls you make and how many great memories you have shared, there is simply no substitute for actually being in the same room together! When Joshua finally disbands the army of Israel and sends the twelve tribes back home, they quickly discover that long-distance relationships don't work well for the people of God either.

In 21:43–45, the future still looks bright for Israel. They have taken possession of the land of Canaan and settled right across the map. Yes, there are still pockets of Canaanites left, but none of those beleaguered groups any longer dares trouble them. *"The Lord gave them rest on every side, just as he had sworn to their ancestors."* Yes, there are still Canaanite strongholds left to capture, but whenever they shook off their contentment with less than what God had promised them and marched out onto the battlefield, *"not one of their enemies withstood them; the Lord gave all their enemies into their hands. Not one of all the Lord's good promises to Israel failed; every one was fulfilled."*

This is what normally happens when the Church is united and every believer plays their part in laying hold of the promises of God. It is important that we recognize that the current Christian landscape is not normal. The same God who told Israel, *"I am the Lord your God, who brought you out of Egypt to give you the land of Canaan"* now also says to us, *"Ask me, and I will make the nations your inheritance, the ends of the earth your possession"* and *"Go into all the world and preach the gospel to all creation."*[1] We have not properly understood the message of the book of Joshua unless we grasp the commentary in Hebrews 3–4, which explains that Jesus is a better Conqueror who has defeated a more wicked enemy and now sends us into all the world with better promises about his Kingdom. The weak Church that we see today does not reflect the weakness of Jesus, but the weakness of his followers – their apathy, fear, unbelief and tragic disunity.

In 22:1–12, we begin to see this principle played out in the final days of Joshua. The two and a half tribes of Israel that settled on the east side of the River Jordan had already disobeyed the Lord. Joshua had graciously overlooked the fact that fewer than half of their fighting men made good on their promise to cross the River Jordan with him in 4:12–13.[2] He continues to be gracious towards them now as he sends them back across the Jordan, commending them for having followed him as they did Moses before him.[3] There is an important leadership principle here, to be as generous in our praise of people as the Lord is towards us. We should imitate the way the New Testament speaks so highly of stubborn old sinners such as Abraham, Sarah, Lot, Jacob and David. But we must not be naïve. These two and half tribes instantly do something very foolish.

Moses had warned them in Numbers 32:23 that if they harboured compromise in their hearts then *"You may be sure that your sin will find you out."* Sure enough, before they cross

---

[1] Leviticus 25:38; Psalm 2:8; Mark 16:15.

[2] They didn't need over half their men to stay behind to guard their lands while they were away. Besides, they had *all* pledged to cross the River Jordan in Numbers 32:25–27.

[3] Joshua's summary of the Law in 22:5 is similar to that of Jesus in Matthew 22:35–40.

the River Jordan to return home, they start to worry that the strain of a long-distance relationship with the other tribes of Israel will end with their exclusion from the people of God. They therefore ignore the stipulation in the Law of Moses that no altar was to be built as a rival to the one at the Tabernacle.[4] In clear defiance of the Law, they build another altar closer to their new home.[5] Compromise has become such a way of life for them that they fail to realize the gravity of what they are doing. When the nine and a half western tribes hear what they have done, they gather together to destroy them. Sin has turned Israel's victory into civil war.

In 22:13–20, Joshua demonstrates how to preserve unity among God's people. In any long-distance relationship, it is very tempting to distrust one another – whether it's the twelve tribes of Israel, the different churches in a denomination or the different denominations that make up the Church as a whole. It is very easy to take the moral high ground and to set out on the warpath against one another.

The nine and a half western tribes would have been well within their rights to do so. They even had a Bible verse for it. The Lord had commanded in Deuteronomy 13:12–18 that any Israelite city that turned away from him was to be *hērem*, subject to destructive judgment like the Canaanites. But instead of marching out to war immediately, they seek first to understand their brothers properly. There is a major spiritual lesson here: never judge long-distance brothers and sisters before giving them a chance to be heard.[6]

The western tribes send a delegation, led by Phinehas, the

---

[4] Leviticus 17:8–9. This wasn't just to provide unity for the people of Israel. It was also because the altar at the Tabernacle burned with fire from heaven. Any other altar spoke about manmade schemes for salvation instead of faith in the divine Saviour who would one day come from heaven (Leviticus 9:23–10:2).

[5] Joshua emphasizes in 22:19 and 28 that this was a replica altar, a sinful alternative to the one at Shiloh.

[6] A representative from each of the 9½ western tribes sets out to give them a hearing in 22:14.

next in line to become high priest. He had led the slaughter of the sinful Israelites in Numbers 25, so nobody could ever accuse him of being soft on sin. He reminds the eastern tribes that God was with him when he led the slaughter at Baal Peor, but then he takes a more conciliatory tone. He emphasizes unity, reminding them that Achan's sin affected Israel as a whole and offering to reallocate some of the land west of the Jordan to their tribes if it helps them return wholeheartedly to the Lord.[7]

To their credit, the eastern tribes respond to Phinehas with great humility in 22:21–34.[8] They insist that their altar was never meant to serve as an alternative to the one at Shiloh, but as a spiritual marker that proved their commitment to the Lord. Personally, I don't believe them, and I'm not convinced that Phinehas believed them either. But he decides to give them the benefit of the doubt – whatever they intended when they built the altar, there is nothing sinful about their reinterpretation of its meaning now – so war is averted. Peace returns to the people of Israel, although this episode serves as a warning that the book of Judges is likely to be turbulent. The Israelites are going to need plenty of spiritual markers. They name the altar: *A Witness Between Us – that the Lord is God.*

Long-distance relationships are difficult within a local church, let alone across a denomination and across the global Church. Let's therefore learn from Phinehas and his friends how to respond when we disagree with one another. Let's seek to understand before we judge. Let's bend over backwards to preserve Christian unity. Let's be tough on sin but gentle with one another. Let's be quick to believe the best of one another. Let's fight to win our long-distance brothers and sisters back to the Lord.

---

[7] It is not enough for Christians to tell people not to live together before marriage, not to have abortions, and so on. They must also offer to help bear the cost of choosing the path of holiness instead.

[8] The Hebrew phrase *"God of gods, the Lord; God of gods, the Lord"* is only used in 22:22 and in Psalm 50:1. The eastern tribes use this intense description of God's uniqueness to pledge their absolute loyalty to him.

Final Warning
(Joshua 23:1–16)

> *"If you violate the covenant of the Lord your God, which he commanded you, and go and serve other gods and bow down to them, the Lord's anger will burn against you."*
>
> (Joshua 23:16)

Leadership is a lot about timing. Joshua was very good at it. He knew when the moment had come to cross the River Jordan. He knew when it was time to attack Jericho.[1] He knew when it was time to transition from fighting as one national army under his lead into fighting as tribal armies under local leaders. Now he spots that the time has come for Israel to make a third transition. Knowing that he is elderly and about to exit the stage, he gathers the Israelites to issue them a final warning.[2]

Don't underestimate the brilliance of Joshua's leadership timing. We will see in the next chapter that he made mistakes, but he didn't do so here. Leaders who share his sense of timing are sadly few and far between. It is rare to find somebody like Tim Keller, who told the congregation of Redeemer Presbyterian Church in Manhattan in the 1990s that *"to grow we need to become mobile and avoid having buildings"*, then just a few years later changed tack: *"In order to grow we now need to buy buildings."* Tim Keller is also unusual for his willingness to stand

---

[1] Note the references to this in 1:11; 2:22; 3:2 and 6:14–15: *"three days... three days... three days... sixth day... seventh day."*

[2] We will see in the chapter "Milk and Honey" that the events of this chapter took place in *c.*1380 BC.

down as Senior Pastor while still in his mid-sixties and to divide his megachurch into three new churches because he believed the time had come for a new *"vision of not being a megachurch"*. It is far more common to see what the missionary Oswald Sanders lamented: *"Advance is held up for years by well-meaning but aging men who refuse to vacate office and insist on holding the reins in their failing hands."* [3]

Joshua sees that the moment has come for a handover. He can see storm clouds on the horizon for the Israelites, so he gathers them to issue a final reminder that they need to hold firm to the promises of God if they want to continue enjoying the Promised Land. Perhaps Joshua was as sceptical as I am about the earnest protestations of the eastern tribesmen that their motives for building a replica altar were good, or perhaps he can simply see that Israel's passion for the things of God is already starting to wane. Whatever the reason, he preaches a farewell sermon to Israel that serves as a conclusion to his entire book of prophecy. We need to read it carefully and respond.

In verses 3–5, Joshua reminds the twelve tribes of Israel that it was the Lord who empowered them to conquer the Promised Land. They must never forget this and become proud and complacent, as if able to bring blessing on themselves: *"It was the Lord your God who fought for you."* Joshua also reminds them that he has allocated more land to them than they have yet occupied. They must not become satisfied with less than God has promised them. They must fight hard to live in the good of every square inch of their salvation. Remember that this book is listed among the "Former Prophets" in the Hebrew Old Testament. Joshua's words are relevant to us too. We must never forget that God wants to lead us into an ever-deeper experience of our salvation.

In verses 6–11, Joshua points out to the Israelites how much they are currently living in the blessing of the Lord. In

---

[3] Oswald Sanders in his book *Spiritual Leadership* (1967).

happy times for God's people it is easy to forget how much difference it makes when we obey the Scriptures (verse 6),[4] separate ourselves from sin (verse 7) and devote our lives to the Lord (verse 8).[5] Joshua therefore points out that these things have made an immeasurable difference to their experience of their salvation. Their parents thought that entering the Promised Land was impossible, yet *"to this day no one has been able to withstand you."* Their parents struggled to believe the Lord's promise in Leviticus 26:8 that five Israelites would rout a hundred enemy soldiers and that a hundred would rout 10,000, yet Joshua points out that the Lord has done ten times more than this for them: *"One of you routs a thousand, because the Lord your God fights for you."* Whenever God's people love and trust him, nothing can stop them.[6]

In verses 12–16, Joshua warns the Israelites what will happen to them if they cease to obey the Scriptures by separating themselves from sin and devoting their lives to the Lord. They need only remember the blessings and curses that they read out to one another from the tops of Mount Gerizim and Mount Ebal in 8:30–35.[7] Since the Lord has been true to all his promises to bless his obedient people, they can be sure he will be equally true to all his curses if they turn their backs on him. It would be nice if we could convince ourselves that the stark choice that Joshua sets out for the Israelites is no longer relevant under the

---

[4] Joshua's charge to Israel in 23:6 strongly echoes the Lord's charge to him in 1:7. See 2 Corinthians 1:3–4.

[5] Note the progression in 23:7. Partnership with unbelievers leads to thinking and talking like unbelievers, which in turn leads to acting like unbelievers.

[6] Joshua doesn't tell the Israelites to *obey* the Lord in 23:11, but to *love* him. If we love the Lord, we will naturally obey him (John 14:15). Joshua is telling preachers to aim at this root if they want fruit.

[7] Joshua says literally in 23:14 that he is going to die *today*. If this means that Joshua 23–24 are two halves of the same speech, then Joshua had already moved the Tabernacle from its normal home at Shiloh to the city of Shechem (24:1), which was very poignant, since Shechem lay in the valley between Gerizim and Ebal.

New Covenant, but that simply isn't true. The New Testament echoes these verses with many similar warnings. Joshua speaks these words for our sake too.[8]

He is warning *leaders* to be as aware as he is of key moments when they need to transition the manner in which they lead. He is flagging the same danger that William Shakespeare observed: *"There is a tide in the affairs of men, which, taken at the flood, leads on to fortune. Omitted, all the voyage of their life is bound in shallows and in miseries. On such a full sea are we now afloat; and we must take the current when it serves, or lose our ventures."*[9]

But Joshua is primarily warning *all believers*. He is asking us to reflect on whether the Church in our own generation is experiencing the non-stop blessing that the Lord promises to those who love him wholeheartedly, or the defeat and fruitlessness that he promises to the half-hearted, the complacent and the disobedient.

Be in no doubt about it: this is the most important question for every generation of believers. As we will see in the book of Judges, each new generation either reoccupies or loses the Promised Land, and many generations of God's people fail. So how will you respond to Joshua's final warning? He assures the twelve tribes of Israel that

> *Not one of all the good promises the Lord your God gave you has failed. Every promise has been fulfilled; not one has failed. But just as all the good things the Lord your God has promised you have come to you, so he will bring on you all the evil things he has threatened... if you violate the covenant of the Lord your God.*

---

[8] Note the echo of 23:13 in 2 Corinthians 12:7. See also Galatians 6:7–8 and 2 Timothy 2:26.

[9] Brutus says this in *Julius Caesar* (Act IV, Scene III). Church leaders take note: had Joshua not transitioned his leadership style at the start of chapter 13, the land would never have been occupied.

Success and Succession
(Joshua 24:1–33)

"As for me and my household, we will serve the Lord."

(Joshua 24:15)

Success without a successor spells failure. Joshua knew that full well. He had been trained by the very best, and he could trace most of his achievements back to the constant investment that Moses made in him as an emerging leader.

Moses had taught Joshua how to know the Lord as his friend. He not only modelled for him the importance of prayer when he interceded on the mountaintop at Rephidim so that Joshua could win a battle in the valley. He also took him up Mount Sinai, brought him into the Tabernacle and laid hands on him to receive the Holy Spirit. Rather than feeling threatened by the growing intimacy that his protégé was developing with the Lord, Moses was delighted that Israel's knowledge of the Lord would not diminish after he was gone.[1] When older leaders become competitive with the younger generation that God has called them to disciple, they make Church history like the opening of a Russian doll. The successes get smaller and smaller with each successive generation.

Moses had taught Joshua how to serve the Lord. He had asked him to act as his dogsbody for almost forty years, offering no guarantee that he was on a career ladder towards eventual leadership of Israel. He never appealed to Joshua's selfish

---

[1] Exodus 17:8–16; 24:13; 33:7–11; Numbers 11:14, 27–29; 12:3; Deuteronomy 34:9.

ambition by stringing him along with promises of position. He simply asked him to act as his gofer to express his love for the Lord. By the time that Joshua was officially recognized as successor to Moses, only a few weeks before the older man's death, Joshua had already been dead for many years. He had died to his own pride and ambition as a sweaty servant to Moses in the desert. He had been made ready to lead Israel for the Lord.

Moses had taught Joshua to obey the Lord in everything. Fifty times in Exodus, Leviticus, Numbers and Deuteronomy we are told that Moses and the Israelites did *"everything just as the Lord commanded"*. It is no coincidence, therefore, that the book of Joshua says something similar about the younger leader at least twenty-five times too.[2] Joshua believed that God was the deciding factor in any situation. He had been trained by Moses to expect the realities of heaven to trump earthly realities every time.

But there isn't a new next-generation leader for Israel in the final chapter of Joshua. Eleazar the high priest has trained up his son Phinehas to take over from him at the Tabernacle, but Joshua has not trained up anyone to lead the nation as a whole. Aaron handed over to his son Eleazar, who handed over to his son Phinehas, yet Moses handed over to Joshua, who handed over to nobody. That's the great tragedy of the final chapter of the book of Joshua. Sadly, we can see the book of Judges coming.

Joshua can see it coming too, but he has left it too late to do anything about it. All he can do is shift the Tabernacle from its permanent home at Shiloh to the city of Shechem, in the valley between Mount Gerizim and Mount Ebal, summoning the twelve tribes of Israel to hear the second half of his final warning.[3] He proclaims the Word of God to them in verses 2–13, reminding them that by faith Abraham turned his back on the

---

[2] Joshua 1:12–18; 4:1–8, 10, 16–18; 5:15; 8:8, 18–26, 27, 30–35; 10:40; 11:9, 12, 15, 20; 14:2, 5; 15:13; 17:4; 19:50; 21:1–3, 8; 22:2, 5, 9; 23:16.

[3] Joshua says literally in 23:14 that he is going to die *today*, so it appears he gave the speech in Joshua 23 on the same day at Shechem too. These two final chapters form two halves of a single final warning.

idols of Mesopotamia, that by faith Moses led their fathers out of Egypt and across the Red Sea, and that by faith they have now conquered the sinful nations on both sides of the River Jordan. These are the verses that inspired the writer of Hebrews to liken the Promised Land to God's salvation promises to us. The Lord describes the land as his "Sabbath-rest" because the Israelites are now farming fields they did not clear, living in cities they did not build and eating from trees they did not plant. They are living in the good of following the God who keeps on giving.

In verses 14–16, Joshua clearly suspects that the Israelites are not going to remain faithful to the Lord. He knows that some of them have already taken the idols of the Canaanites they defeated into their homes, so he pleads with them to recognize that they are simply the gods of Mesopotamia dressed up in different clothes.[4] To become idolaters would be to reject their nation's history with the Lord and to tell him that they want no further share in his promises to Abraham. Knowing that he has but a few breaths left to take on earth, Joshua uses them to lay a choice before the Israelites who outlive him. They can either choose to serve the gods that failed to protect the Canaanites against them, or they can choose to serve the God of Abraham, but they can't choose both. It's decision time.

Joshua looks around. He has been a successful leader in his own lifetime but what of the long term? Nowhere in the sea of faces is a successor like him. Othniel has settled down to farming. The other army officers have largely hung up their spears. Joshua blurts out the only thing he thinks that he can guarantee: *"As for me and my household, we will serve the Lord."* But that's the tragedy of this final chapter. We never hear another word about his sons and daughters. They are part of the problem in the book of Judges, never part of the solution. When Christians fail to think big and to raise up great leaders for the future, they

---

[4] Ur of the Chaldees worshipped the moon-god Nanna, just as Jericho worshipped the moon-god Yarikh.

sabotage their own families too. John Donne reminds us, *"No man is an island, entire of itself."*[5] Success without a successor is failure.

In verses 16–28, the book of Joshua therefore descends into an argument. The Israelites insist that they will serve the Lord wholeheartedly, even without an obvious leader, while Joshua insists they do not have it in them. He records their protestations in the book he has been writing – verse 26 appears to describe his final entry in the book of Joshua – but then he is forced to erect a pile of stones as a spiritual marker in lieu of a leader.[6] His final words to Israel sound far more like a curse than a blessing: *"See! This stone will be a witness against us. It has heard all the words the Lord has said to us. It will be a witness against you if you are untrue to your God."* It's a tragic end to Joshua's ministry.

In verses 29–33, one of Joshua's friends takes over to record the death of Joshua and Eleazar. He also records that Joseph's mummified bones, which had been carried up from Egypt, were buried in Shechem too.[7] But that is all. The book ends with dry rocks and dead bones, not with a flesh-and-blood leader. There is no new Joshua for Israel.

The writer therefore ends with an ominous premonition: *"Israel served the Lord throughout the lifetime of Joshua and of the elders who outlived him and who had experienced everything the Lord had done for Israel"* – the implication being that afterwards they did not. What a tragedy. What an end to a mighty ministry. Joshua's death leaves Israel leaderless.

---

[5] John Donne says this in his "Meditation 17" (1624).

[6] Joshua 24:22–26 parallels Deuteronomy 31:24–26, just as Joshua 24:29–33 parallels Deuteronomy 34:5–12.

[7] Jacob had bought the land of Shechem and cleared it of Amorite squatters. The New Testament commends Joseph for wanting his bones to be buried there, since it proved he believed his children would one day inherit the Promised Land (Genesis 33:19; 48:22; 50:24–25; Exodus 13:19; Hebrews 11:22). Conveniently, Shechem had been allotted to the tribe of Manasseh, one of Joseph's two sons.

A Dying Man to Dying Men
(Joshua 24:1–33)

"Choose for yourselves this day whom you will serve."

(Joshua 24:15)

We can't end the book of Joshua with that final chapter, full of failure and foreboding. We can't finish more aware of his mistakes than of his miracles. It's very natural for the person who stepped in to write the book's five final verses to want to end in a way that dovetails nicely into the book of Judges, but we have a far better sequel to Joshua. We have the New Testament, which proclaims that Joshua *did* have a successor! His ministry, though flawed in places, was a prophetic pointer-perfect ministry of the true and better Conqueror, Jesus Christ, so let's not end the book with thoughts of failure.[1]

Let's end it instead by appreciating Joshua as the consummate preacher and prophet to his nation. If we were still in any doubt that his book deserves its place among the "Former Prophets", the last traces of doubt evaporate now.[2] The great Puritan preacher Richard Baxter claimed that he preached *"as a dying man to dying men"*, but for Joshua that is far more than a metaphor. It is what he truly does in his final chapter.

---

[1] We have already noted that the angel told Mary and Joseph to name their son after Joshua for a reason. This is masked in English purely because *Joshua* follows the Hebrew spelling and *Jesus* the Greek spelling.

[2] In Joshua 1:1, Moses was called *"the servant of the Lord"* and Joshua was merely *"Moses' assistant"*. Ironically, it is only as he dies that he is finally hailed in 24:29 as *"the servant of the Lord"* too.

Joshua's sermon teaches us that preachers *are called to speak for God*. He doesn't start his message to the Israelites with an anecdote or an apology. He leaves them in no doubt from the very start that *"This is what the Lord, the God of Israel, says."* There should always be a prophetic edge to Christian preaching, a sense that we are speaking words inspired by the Holy Spirit and not simply the words of a well-crafted essay. The apostle Paul commends people in 1 Thessalonians 2:13 for receiving his preaching, *"not as the word of men, but as it actually is, the word of God"*. That's how we ought to proclaim the news about an even better Conqueror whenever we have opportunity today.

Joshua's sermon also teaches us that preachers *are called to speak from Scripture*. We are reminded in verse 26 that the sixth book of the Bible is still being written as he speaks, so he only has the first five books of the Old Testament to preach from. Nevertheless, note how Bible-based he makes his sermon to the Israelites. He talks about Abraham, Isaac, Jacob and Esau from the book of Genesis. He talks about Moses and Aaron's exploits in the book of Exodus and about their battlefield victories in the book of Numbers. He refers to events described in Deuteronomy and in the early chapters of his own book. In case we miss how much he points to the Scriptures, he deliberately uses two curious metaphors from the Torah.[3] John Piper encourages us to follow Joshua's example here:

> *Where the Bible is esteemed as the inspired and inerrant Word of God, preaching can flourish. But where the Bible is treated merely as a record of valuable religious insight, preaching dies.*[4]

---

[3] Compare 24:12 with Exodus 23:28 and Deuteronomy 7:20. Compare 24:13 with Deuteronomy 6:10–12.

[4] Both of the John Piper quotes in this chapter come from *The Supremacy of God in Preaching* (1990).

Joshua's sermon teaches us that preachers *are to awaken people to the promises of God*. He does not merely wave theological statements under the noses of his hearers. He paints a vivid picture of Israel's history to awaken them from their drowsy complacency. Eugene Peterson argues that a preacher *"deals with the difficulty everyone has in staying alert to the magnificence of salvation"*.[5] That's what Joshua models for us here. He paints the history of Israel in shocking colours, even adding detail in verse 14 that is mentioned nowhere else in the Bible – that the Hebrews had actually started worshipping the false gods of Egypt before the Lord delivered them through Moses! He tells such a compelling narrative that, by the time he reaches his appeal, all of his listeners want to get on board.

Joshua's sermon also teaches us that preachers *are to call for an active response.* We need to hear this, because it is tempting to react against the manipulative altar calls of the white-suited evangelist by not calling for any immediate response at all. Joshua has no time for this overreaction. If the Lord himself makes an appeal at the end of the Law of Moses, in Deuteronomy 30:15–20, Joshua is not ashamed to follow his lead. It is a biblical principle that people only act differently if they set their heart towards a different course of action. Our words and actions reflect the overflow of our hearts, so Christian preaching always ought to challenge people to reorientate their hearts more fully towards the promises of God.[6] John Piper calls it *"a tragedy to see pastors state the facts and sit down. Good preaching pleads with people to respond to the Word of God"*. Joshua begs the Israelites to turn from their pagan idols to the true God. As preachers for the true and better Joshua, we dare not challenge people to do anything less.

Joshua's sermon teaches us that preachers *are to be passionate about what they say*. There is a way of telling someone

---

[5] Eugene Peterson in *Five Smooth Stones for Pastoral Work* (1980).

[6] 2 Chronicles 12:14; Daniel 1:8; Luke 6:45. The Lord makes another passionate appeal in Haggai 2:18–19.

their house is on fire that convinces them that it isn't. There is a way of preaching about the holiness of God, the seriousness of sin and the reality of judgment that reassures people that the Gospel is not as urgent as many people say. Richard Baxter warns that *"As long as men have eyes as well as ears, they will think they see your meaning as well as hear it; and they are apter to believe their sight than their hearing, as being the more perfect sense of the two."*[7] Joshua knows this, so he nails his colours to the mast, declaring that, even if every Israelite rejects the Lord, he and his family will gladly worship him on their own. Is it any wonder that the Israelites protest their own allegiance to the Lord, when they see such intense passion in the eyes of Joshua? We need a little less laughter and whole lot more tears if we want to move people to do the same.

Joshua's sermon teaches us that preachers *are to focus their hearers' attention on the Lord*. He is acutely aware that he is dying without a successor. He knows that setting up a pile of rocks as a spiritual marker for Israel is no substitute for a flesh-and-blood leader. He therefore focuses on the true and better Leader that he knows will outlast him. His entire sermon is about the Lord: *"He is a holy God; he is a jealous God."*[8] Joshua preaches as a dying man to dying men, but he preaches about the God who will outlive him. As he dies, he focuses the eyes of Israel on the far better Leader they have in heaven.

Joshua ends the sermon of a lifetime. He dies and is buried in the Promised Land. The curtain falls on the book of Joshua and rises on the book of Judges, but his words still echo across the stage. The God who keeps on giving has not died with Joshua. He invites a new generation of Israelites to follow him and occupy the Promised Land.

---

[7] Richard Baxter in *The Reformed Pastor* (1656).

[8] Joshua's words echo those of Moses in Exodus 34:14 and Leviticus 11:44. They warn the next generation of Israelites not to trifle with the Lord. He will step into the empty shoes of a successor to Joshua.

Judges:

God's Gift to Sinners

Backwards
(Judges 1:1–2:5)

"You have disobeyed me. Why have you done this?"

(Judges 2:2)

Life is like a treadmill at the gym. If you're not moving forwards, you're moving backwards and you are heading for a fall.

The final chapter of Joshua hinted that this would happen to the Israelites after the generation that conquered the Promised Land died. Sure enough, things begin to go wrong from the very start. Even the repetition of several stories from the book of Joshua is meant to communicate that the Israelites are moving backwards, not forwards.

In 1:1–8, the Israelites are still living in the good of Joshua's ministry.[1] They instinctively go to the Tabernacle to receive their military strategy from the Lord, presumably by asking the high priest to flip his sacred stones, the Urim and Thummim, and they receive a happy answer: *"Judah shall go up; I have given the land into their hands."* Our first hint that the faith of Israel is beginning to unravel is that the men of Judah are too afraid to fight the Canaanites unless the Simeonites help them. This intermingling of the armies of Simeon and Judah triggers our memory that the Lord cursed the smaller tribe with being scattered and swallowed up by its larger neighbour. It serves as a reminder that God calls his people to choose a blessing or a curse. Israel is about to choose badly.

The first campaign against the Canaanites in the book of

---

[1] Joshua 24:31 told us that *"Israel served the Lord throughout the lifetime of Joshua and of the elders who outlived him."* Even after Joshua died, there was a short period in which Israel continued to obey the Lord.

Judges is a huge success. Adoni-Bezek means *Lord of Lightning*, and he is king of Jerusalem. Like his predecessor Adoni-Zedek, in Joshua 10, we are meant to see him as an imposter, a demonic parody of the true Messiah who would one day die on a cross outside the walls of his city. He has a savage reputation for mutilating his prisoners of war by chopping off their thumbs and big toes to stop them from fighting in the future, humiliating seventy defeated kings by keeping them alive and treating them like dogs around his table.[2] When he is defeated by the men of Judah and loses his own thumbs and big toes, he recognizes it as an act of divine retribution. His bleeding hands and feet proclaim that one day a far better King of Jerusalem would gladly surrender his hands and feet to Roman nails for the sins of the world. For a moment, it looks as though things might not turn out too badly for this new generation of Israelites.

In 1:9–18, there are further positive developments. The writer of Judges repeats the account of Caleb, Othniel and Aksah from Joshua 15:13–19, then he carries on the story further. The descendants of Jethro, the father-in-law of Moses who served as priest to the Lord in the land of Midian, decide to stop living as nomads in the ruins of Jericho and to join forces with the tribe of Judah. This rejection of *Moon City* seems to signify a renewal of their ancient allegiance to the Lord.[3] The men of Judah capture one of the Canaanite cities that has been holding out against them, renaming it Hormah, which comes from the Hebrew word *hāram* and means *Judged By Destruction*, suggesting their continued devotion to the Lord. They even capture Gaza,

---

[2] Such barbaric treatment of prisoners was not uncommon in the ancient world (16:21). It brings some perspective to the slaughter in Joshua. We can't judge Bronze Age people by the standards of today.

[3] Moses married the daughter of Jethro (also known as Reuel) and invited his son Hobab to help him lead Israel through the desert. The Kenites were Hobab's descendants (Judges 4:11; Numbers 10:29). The *City of Palms* was another name for Jericho (Deuteronomy 34:3; 2 Chronicles 28:15).

Ashkelon and Ekron, three of the stubborn hold-out cities of the Philistines. The tribe of Judah seems to be going forwards.

Except it isn't doing so under the surface. Whenever a nation turns away from the Lord, it tends to maintain a veneer of faith for a few years. That veneer starts to crack in 1:19–21, where we are told that the men of Judah *"were unable to drive the people from the plains, because they had chariots fitted with iron"*. That's a bad sign, because iron chariots had proved no problem for Joshua in his campaign against the northern coalition. Something sinister is clearly taking place in the hearts of Judah. They have forgotten that they have a determined enemy. They have become satisfied with less than God has promised them, forgetting that it's not enough to take spiritual ground; we also need to keep the ground we have taken. After allowing the sinful Jebusites to rebuild Jerusalem, they leave it to Benjamin to recapture the city. When the tribe of Benjamin fails, the tribe of Judah simply learns to live without it. They have lost their former desire to move forward in partnership with the Lord, and very quickly they find themselves hurtling backwards.

The focus shifts towards the other tribes in 1:22–36. Things start well for them when they find a male equivalent of Rahab, who sides with the God of Israel to help them capture and destroy the Canaanite city of Bethel.[4] However, the writer of Judges repeats some of the failures we were told about in Joshua 17:12–18. The tribe of Manasseh fails to capture several Canaanite towns because the pagans are more determined to survive than the Manassites are to inflict God's judgment on them. The tribes of Ephraim, Zebulun, Asher and Naphtali fare no better, contenting themselves with turning the Canaanites into forced labourers instead of driving them out of their land.

---

[4] Both Bethel and Hebron had already been captured but the Canaanites had been allowed to rebuild (Joshua 10:36–37; 12:10, 16). Holding on to ground taken is just as essential as capturing it. Note another ominous sign here too. The man does not convert to Israel's God; he goes to join the pagan Hittites.

The tribe of Dan fares even worse, giving up on capturing the fertile lowlands because *"the Amorites were determined also to hold out."* By the end of the first chapter of Judges, Israel's passion is clearly waning to lay hold of all the land that the Lord has promised to give them.

In 2:1–5, the Lord confronts their growing apathy. The Angel of the Lord, who appeared in Joshua 5:13–6:5, now appears again to reinforce the message of their dead leader. He rebukes the Israelites for making peace treaties with the Canaanites and declares that the God who keeps on giving is about to shower them with all the curses that their fathers spoke from the top of Mount Ebal. Don't miss the significance of the Angel leaving Gilgal, the place where God rolled away the previous generation's shame at having been redeemed from Egypt but left landless, and his going to Bokim, which means *People Weeping.* Since the Israelites no longer want to pursue friendship with the Lord, they are about to form a close friendship with misery instead. Since they have lost interest in God's promises to their nation, they are about to forfeit the Promised Land.

This is all pretty sobering. It informs us that whenever a generation of believers stops powering forward in faith, it soon starts sliding backwards. There is no standing still in the face of our determined enemy, the Devil. The book of Judges warns us that each new generation of believers needs to hold on to what it has inherited from its parents and to reach out in faith for the Lord to take them further forwards into his salvation.

In his anger against Israel the Lord gave them into the hands of raiders who plundered them.

(Judges 2:14)

It can't have escaped your notice that the Church in the Western world isn't doing very well. The full scale of its collapse has been masked by mass immigration from more Christian parts of the world, but here's an analysis by *The Spectator* magazine:

It's often said that Britain's church congregations are shrinking, but that doesn't come close to expressing the scale of the disaster now facing Christianity in this country. Every ten years the census spells out the situation in detail: between 2001 and 2011 the number of Christians in Britain fell by 5.3 million – about 10,000 a week. If that rate of decline continues, the mission of St Augustine to the English, together with that of the Irish saints to the Scots, will come to an end in 2067. That is the year in which the Christians who have inherited the faith of their British ancestors will become statistically invisible... [They are] one generation away from extinction.

If you don't know *The Spectator*, you might assume that it's a Christian magazine. It isn't. Even nonbelievers are astonished at the speed of the Church's decline. Their verdict on church leaders in Britain, Europe and America is pretty damning: *"They're led by middle-managers who are frightened of their own shadows. They run up the white flag long before the enemy comes down from the hills... It can't be stressed too often that the secularisation that happens inside churches is as important as the sort that happens outside them."[1]*

There are plenty of explanations for the Church's sudden shift into terminal decline. A lot of them sound like the men of Judah in 1:19 ("we lack resources"), like the men of Manasseh in 1:27 ("it is pretty tough territory here") and like the men of Joseph in 1:35 ("don't worry, we still hold all the positions of power"). Some of the excuses even sound like the ones that the Angel rebukes sharply in 2:2 ("we'll never get a hearing for the Gospel unless we compromise on certain issues"). It's hardly surprising that many Western believers, born into such a spiritual landscape, doubt the victory promises of God altogether. They have never seen the Church advancing in obedience to the Lord.

That's why we need the commentary that the book of Judges gives us here. Before it launches into the actions of the twelve judges of Israel, it gives a big-picture perspective of events as viewed from the director's chair.[2] Whenever the fortunes of God's people take a nosedive, it does not indicate that he has grown tired of keeping his promises.[3] The writer tells us in 2:14–15 (quite shockingly, given how often Joshua says the Lord is fighting for the Israelites) that *"In his anger against Israel the Lord gave them into the hands of raiders who plundered them. He sold them into the hands of their enemies all around, whom they were no longer able to resist. Whenever Israel went out to fight, the hand of the Lord was against them to defeat*

---

[1] These quotes come from an article entitled "2067: The End of British Christianity" (13th June 2015).

[2] The English word "judge" conjures up images of a courtroom, but in a Hebrew context it really meant *rulers*. Elders ran each tribe or city's internal affairs, while the judge presided over all those eldership teams. Technically, there were 14 judges of Israel, but the actions of Eli and Samuel are recorded in 1 Samuel.

[3] Many people in the days of the judges must have incorrectly assumed that the age of miracles was over.

them, just as he had sworn to them."[4] The disasters that befall Israel in the book of Judges are therefore not a sign that God has given up on his promises. Quite the opposite. Even when his people suffer setbacks, he is still in the director's chair.[5]

In 2:6–10, we are given a first explanation. God uses Church decline to drive his people back to their Bibles and back onto their knees. These sentences sound so similar to Joshua 24:29–31 that it is highly likely that the writer who finished off the book of Joshua also wrote the book of Judges. He says that ignorance about God's actions in the past, about his commands in the present and about his promises for the future always fosters apathy towards him.[6] The Israelites had not read enough Scripture to feel a proper sense of frustration that the conquest of Canaan had descended into cat-and-mouse games with the enemy and a decision to live and let live. Their view of the world was based on their puny experience of God, instead of on the panorama of his promises. The Lord let them feel the heavy burden of defeat in order to drive them to their knees.[7]

In 2:10–15, we are given a second explanation. The Israelites who failed to capture the cities of the Canaanites in chapter 1 had begun themselves to worship the idols of the Canaanites.[8] They were sacrificing to the storm-god Baal and embracing all the sexual perversions associated with the fertility-goddess

---

[4] This talk of God handing us over to our enemies is echoed in Joshua 23:15; Romans 1:24–28 and James 4:6.

[5] Revelation 2:5 says that only Jesus can close down churches, not the Devil. The Lord loves his people too much to leave church communities unchecked in their rebellion against him.

[6] This ought to encourage churches to invest more heavily in their children's ministries. The Church is only ever one generation away from extinction or revival, depending on how well it teaches its children.

[7] The Hebrew words for *groaning* and *oppressing* in 2:18 are the same words used in Exodus 2:24 and 3:9 to describe Israel's suffering in Egypt. God's judgment retaught his people the lessons of the past.

[8] The Canaanites were slaughtered to eradicate their grotesque immorality and child sacrifice from the land. The ease with which their sins spread to the Israelites explains why Joshua was so intolerant towards them.

Ashtoreth.[9] When the Lord sees so-called believers mingling his commands with those of idols – whether idols in the form of metal and stone, like those of the Canaanites, or idols in the form of strident ideas that set themselves up against the Word of Christ, like those of our own day – he decimates their faith communities until their distress forces them back to repentance.[10]

In 2:16–3:6, we are given a third explanation. The writer introduces us to the salvation cycle of the book of Judges. **Sin** leads to a period of **oppression**, which leads to **repentance**, which leads to the provision of a judge who works **deliverance** and provides a period of **peace** for God's people. Through this salvation cycle, the Lord rekindles the faith and devotion of the Israelites towards him, but when each judge dies they soon go back to their sinful ways.[11] The Lord therefore uses the Canaanite survivors to reveal the true state of the hearts of Israel towards him. He uses these nations to train the Israelites for war, in the same way that he uses the demonic forces that attack the Church to prepare believers for an eternity of ruling with him over his new creation when Jesus returns.[12] On that day, we will look back on the ups and downs of Church history and worship him for his wisdom, seeing them in true perspective from the director's chair.

So before we dive into the detail of what happened to each of the twelve judges of Israel, let's take a deep breath and remember the big picture behind the story. We need this perspective in our own days of Church decline and disappointment. The God who keeps on giving wants to use these verses to encourage us. None of his promises have failed.

---

[9] Baal means *Lord* and he was said to be in charge of rain and harvests. His worship often involved child sacrifice (Jeremiah 19:5). Ashtoreth, also known as Astarte, was a goddess of love, fertility and war.

[10] Ezekiel 14:3 speaks about *idols in our hearts*. See Ephesians 5:5 and 2 Corinthians 10:1–6.

[11] 2:19 says each time they backslid, they became even more sinful. This cycle was in fact a downward spiral.

[12] This is why Acts 14:22; Romans 5:3–4; 1 Peter 1:7 and James 1:2–4 tell us to rejoice in our earthly trials.

Secret Weapon
(Judges 3:7–11)

The Spirit of the Lord came on him, so that he became Israel's judge and went to war.

(Judges 3:10)

Israel had a secret weapon in the book of Judges. It wasn't chariots with axles made of iron. It was the presence of the Lord, and it delivered them victory every single time.

In the days of Moses and Joshua, the presence of the Lord had been hidden from the people in the inner sanctuary of the Tabernacle, but in the book of Judges it goes mobile and takes to the battlefield. We are told repeatedly that God's Spirit descended on the judges to empower them to overcome the enormous odds stacked against them. The Holy Spirit was the secret weapon that enabled them to recapture the Promised Land.

Othniel is a great example. These verses about him are full of stock phrases that are used to describe the problems facing the other eleven judges of Israel. The people *"did evil in the eyes of the Lord"* and *"served the Baals and the Asherahs"*.[1] As a result, *"the anger of the Lord burned against Israel so that he sold them into the hands"* of their enemies. These verses are also full of stock phrases that are used to describe the ministry of the other judges. *"When they cried out to the Lord, he raised up for them a deliverer"*, and the most important stock phrase of them all:

---

[1] Most scholars believe that Asherah and Ashtoreth were two different fertility goddesses. *Ashtoreths* in 2:13 and *Asherahs* in 3:7 are therefore probably collective nouns for the two goddesses together.

"The Spirit of the Lord came on him." Othniel relied on Israel's secret weapon. The book of Judges is as much about the Holy Spirit as the book of Acts.

It is important that we grasp that none of the twelve judges was anything special. The book of Judges is not a hero story, unless that hero is the Holy Spirit. Othniel's name means *Lion of God*, and for a brief moment he lived up to his name when he captured the city of Debir to win the hand of his cousin Aksah in marriage from her father Caleb. Once he settled down to married life, however, we have already seen that his new wife had more passion to possess the Promised Land than he did. When Joshua looked around for a successor, he evidently did not think him a promising enough candidate. Nor is there any record of his attempting to capture Jerusalem or to help his fellow tribesmen of Judah to drive the stubborn Canaanites from their lands. On the contrary, we are told in verse 8 that he allowed the Arameans to occupy Israel for eight years before he eventually challenged them. Since they came from the north and he lived in the south, he preferred to turn a blind eye to their presence in the land.[2] Like many Christians today, Othniel had become an expert in rationalizing away his failure.[3]

It is only when the Lord unleashes his secret weapon upon Israel that Othniel is suddenly transformed into the lion-hearted warrior his parents hoped that he would be. *"The Spirit of the Lord came on him, so that he became Israel's judge and went to war."*[4] Don't believe it when people tell you that the first sign of being filled with the Holy Spirit is speaking in tongues or prophesying. Throughout the book of Judges, the first sign is

---

[2] Aram was in modern Syria, beyond the northern border of the Promised Land. It included the former homes of Abraham, Rebekah, Leah and Rachel. Cushan-Rishathaim means *Cushan the Doubly Wicked*.

[3] Joshua died in *c.*1380 BC yet Othniel only became judge of Israel in *c.*1367 BC. See the timeline in the chapter "Milk and Honey".

[4] The Hebrew text uses verbs to say literally that these 12 individuals *judged* Israel, not nouns to say that they were *judges* of Israel. It saves the noun for 11:27 to stress that the Lord alone was the true Judge of Israel.

always a sense of supernatural courage. The peace-loving farmer Othniel became a courageous soldier for the same reason that the shepherd-boy David became *"a brave man and a warrior"*. We must not forget that the apostle Paul contrasts the Spirit of God with *"a spirit of timidity"*, or that the early Christians were contagious in their faith because *"they were all filled with the Holy Spirit and spoke the word of God boldly."*[5] When the Lord anointed Othniel with Israel's secret weapon, he burst out of his sleepy retirement, defeated the Arameans and brought peace to the land of Israel for forty years.[6]

The rule of Othniel as the first judge of Israel therefore marked more than just a military turning point. It also marked the start of a spiritual revolution. Before the death of Joshua, the Holy Spirit came infrequently on a handful of Israel's leaders (Numbers 11:25; 27:18), but after Othniel such anointing becomes mainstream for the judges. It was the only reason why such flawed and faltering people achieved victory for Israel. Gideon is a coward, but the Spirit of the Lord anoints him in 6:34 to give him courage to defeat the Midianites. Jephthah is an outlaw, but the Spirit of the Lord anoints him in 11:29 to drive the Ammonites out of the Promised Land. Samson is a weakling when it comes to fighting sin, but the Spirit of the Lord anoints him in 14:6 to kill a lion with his bare hands, in 14:19 to single-handedly butcher thirty Philistines and in 15:14 to break the ropes around his wrists and kill 1,000 Philistines with a piece of jawbone. A lot of religious art misses the point. We are told in 16:20 that Samson was not particularly muscular. It was the Holy Spirit who gave him his supernatural strength.

That's why it helps to remember that Joshua and Judges are listed in the Hebrew Old Testament among the "Former Prophets". The life of Joshua serves as a prophetic pointer to Jesus and the twelve judges serve as prophetic pointers to

[5] 1 Samuel 16:18; Acts 4:13, 31; 2 Timothy 1:7.

[6] This is another stock phrase throughout the book of Judges: *"So the land had peace for X years, until Y died."*

the twelve apostles who followed him. The death of Joshua unleashes an explosion of the Holy Spirit's activity throughout Israel to prefigure what happened after the death, resurrection and ascension of Jesus the Messiah.[7] This is superb news for beleaguered churches in our own day. The Lord wants to anoint us with his Holy Spirit to lead us into victory.

He wants to empower us to push back the forces of evil, like Othniel in 3:10, to rout the demonic hordes that stand against us, like Gideon in 7:21, to demolish the Devil's strongholds in our land, like Jephthah in 11:33, and to break spiritual chains that hold people captive to Satan, like Samson in 15:14. We are not to treat the book of Judges as a collection of quirky stories to keep the children entertained at church on a Sunday. We are to see it as a prophetic picture of what the risen Lord Jesus wants to do through his followers today. They remind us of the New Testament promises about the Holy Spirit:

> *If you then, though you are evil, know how to give good gifts to your children, how much more will your Father in heaven give the Holy Spirit to those who ask him!... You will receive power when the Holy Spirit comes on you; and you will be my witnesses... The promise is for you and your children and for all who are far off – for all whom the Lord our God will call.*[8]

So let's move out of the cosy farmlands of timid Christianity and onto the battlefield with Othniel. Let's ask the Lord to fill us with his Holy Spirit and to empower us to overcome the work of Satan. Judges is not just a history book. It is calling you to war.

---

[7] Acts 2:33. In Luke 1–2, the Holy Spirit falls on everyone associated with the birth of Jesus – on Zechariah, on Elizabeth, on John the Baptist, on Mary and on Simeon. See also Luke 3:22; 4:1, 14 and 16–21.

[8] Luke 11:13; Acts 1:8; 2:39.

The Impossible
(Judges 3:12–31)

*After Ehud came Shamgar son of Anath, who struck
down six hundred Philistines with an ox-goad.*

(Judges 3:31)

Most people rush over the accounts of the second and third
judges of Israel. Many Christians haven't even heard of Ehud
and Shamgar. But let's slow down and dwell on the strangeness
of these verses. They teach us to how to accomplish the
impossible.

Let's start with Shamgar in verse 31 and work backwards,
because judges don't get any stranger than him. We are not
told what tribe he comes from. Some scholars even think his
foreign name betrays he was an outsider to Israel. Whatever his
ethnicity, he clearly came from a family of idolaters, since his
mother was named after the Canaanite war-goddess Anath.[1]
How did a man from such a dubious family manage to kill 600
Philistines, armed only with an ox-goad, which is essentially a
big stick for controlling cattle? How did he score other victories
like it, since 5:6 tells us that there were many other *"days of
Shamgar"* too? How did he manage to accomplish so much with
so little? We have to look elsewhere for an explanation of how
he achieved the impossible.

We get our first clue in the account of Ehud, the second
judge of Israel, in verses 12–30. Ehud also achieved the

---

[1] Like most Hebrew historians, the writer of Judges gives us the name of
people's fathers, not their mothers (see 13:2–24). Since Anath was a girl's
name, he must name Shamgar's mother here for a reason.

impossible, since the Moabites had taken advantage of the power vacuum created by Othniel's death to cross the River Jordan and to dominate the Promised Land. Setting up camp amid the ruins of Jericho,[2] they were helped by the Ammonites and Amalekites to oppress Israel for eighteen years.[3] By the end of that time their rule looked permanent. King Eglon of Moab had built himself a two-storeyed palace and set up Moabite idols at Gilgal, in the very place where Joshua had once led the Israelites to consecrate themselves to the Lord.[4] The writer uses the word *hāzaq* in verse 12, the same word that described the Lord *hardening* the hearts of the Canaanites in Joshua 11:20, to emphasize that the Lord had made Moabites *hard* enough to resist any Israelite attempt to overthrow their rule and to recapture the Promised Land.

Ehud achieves the impossible because he is a weak man. Like many of the other men of Benjamin, he is left-handed (somewhat ironic, given that Benjamin is Hebrew for *the Son of My Right Hand*), and the writer uses this to express his gaucheness.[5] The Hebrew text says literally that he was "a man impeded in his right hand" – in other words, through either defect or disease or disuse, he had become a man incapable of

---

[2] Jericho was also known as the *City of Palms*, particularly between its destruction by Joshua and its rebuilding under King Ahab. See Judges 1:16; Deuteronomy 34:3 and 2 Chronicles 28:15.

[3] The Moabites and Ammonites were descended from Lot's drunken incest with his daughters, and the Amalekites from Esau (Genesis 19:30–38; 36:12). The sins of the patriarchs come back to haunt Israel.

[4] The idols at Gilgal are mentioned twice, in 3:19 and 26, to contrast strongly with Joshua 5. Ehud may have been so scared that he left King Eglon's palace without acting and only retraced his steps two miles from Gilgal back to Jericho when he was angered afresh into action by the sight of these pagan idols.

[5] For other left-handed men of Benjamin, see Judges 20:16 and 1 Chronicles 12:2.

battle.[6] He was the runt of Benjamin.[7] God loves to use weak people to achieve the impossible.

The Moabite camp amidst the ruins of Jericho lay within the tribal boundaries of Benjamin. Ehud is therefore tasked with taking Israel's tribute to the king. Too weak to say no to his countrymen and too weak to raise any fear among the Moabites, he is the perfect undercover agent to carry out God's plan. That's how we achieve the impossible. <u>We stop relying on our own strength and we trust in the Lord.</u>

It was precisely because Ehud was on the bottom rung of the social ladder that he became messenger to King Eglon. It was because he was impeded in his right hand that a sword strapped to his "wrong" leg went undetected by the security guards on the door. It was because even his left hand was weak that his weapon was small enough to hide under his clothes (at only fifty centimetres long, it was more of a dagger than a sword).[8] It was precisely because he looked so inoffensive that the king of Moab saw no threat when Ehud asked if he could share some secret news with him alone. The fact that Ehud wasn't judge material was what made him perfect as a judge! The guards think it more likely that King Eglon is taking a long trip to the bathroom than that a man like Ehud could become an assassin, giving him time to escape and call the Israelites to

.

---

[6] The Greek Septuagint translation misses the point, telling us that Ehud *"used both right and left hand alike"*. No – the Hebrew text conveys that his right hand was so weak that he was unfit for war.

[7] We will discover in Judges 20:27–28 that Benjamin was slaughtered down to only 600 men *before* Ehud became judge. In other words, he was the runt of the runt of a very sinful tribe!

[8] This may be why he failed to pull the sword out of King Eglon's belly, despite potentially needing it to evade the guards. God empowered him to stick the sword in, but he lacked the power to pull it out.

fight.⁹ It's a great example of God turning human weakness into strength to achieve the impossible.¹⁰

Ehud's weakness is turned to strength through his faith in the God of Joshua. He escapes to the hill country of Ephraim and blows a *shōphar*, a ram's-horn trumpet like the ones the priests blew to bring down the walls of Jericho. We saw in Joshua 6 that this acted as a prophetic pointer to God giving his people victory through the blood of Jesus. The same is true here. For eighteen years the Israelites have been too scared to overthrow the Moabites, but the death of one fat man emboldens an entire nation, not just to throw off their rule, but to conquer the land of Moab and to rule over it for the next eighty years!

Ehud's weakness is also turned to strength by the power of the Holy Spirit. The writer is not explicit here, but he explains further on a similar occasion in 6:34: *"The Spirit of the Lord came on Gideon, and he blew a shōphar."*¹¹ Rallied by Israel's secret weapon, the entire nation rises up in arms to defend every crossing point over the River Jordan so tightly that 10,000 Moabite soldiers are slaughtered. No one makes it home alive.¹²

Ehud means *United*, but the sudden unity he brought to Israel was impossible. Shamgar means *Sword*, which emphasizes that his slaughter of 600 Philistines with a big stick was impossible too. These verses are meant to show us that all we need to accomplish the impossible in God is faith in the blood of his Son and in the power of his Spirit. He is the one who loves

---

⁹ Eglon means *Little Cow* and he was evidently an overeater, prone to long trips to the bathroom. His extreme fatness is meant to convey how repulsive it is when we love earthly pleasures more than the Lord.

¹⁰ Hebrews 11:32–34 says that this is one of the greatest themes of the entire book of Judges. See also 2 Corinthians 12:7–10; Philippians 4:13; Ephesians 6:10 and John 3:34.

¹¹ In the same way, Judges 15:14–15 explains how Shamgar managed to kill 600 Philistines with a stick.

¹² Ehud blows a trumpet in the hills of Ephraim, not of Benjamin, trusting God's Spirit to rally the entire nation.

to turn our impediments into opportunities. He is the one who loves to turn our weaknesses to strength. He is the God who keeps on giving.

So whatever challenges face you today, these verses are for you. Cry out to the Lord, admit your weakness and believe this is a message from God for you. The God who empowered Ehud and Shamgar to accomplish the impossible now wants to work in you.

The Stomach of a Judge (Judges 4:1–24)

THE STOMACH OF A JUDGE (JUDGES 4:1-24)

*"Because of the course you are taking, the honour
will not be yours, for the Lord will deliver Sisera into
the hands of a woman."*

(Judges 4:9)

Queen Elizabeth I of England knew that her culture looked down
on women. Waving off her troops from Tilbury docks to fight the
Spanish Armada in 1588, she felt the need to reassure them: *"I
know I have the body of a weak and feeble woman; but I have the
heart and stomach of a king, and of a king of England too."*[1]

Unlike sixteenth-century England, the Bible never looks
down on women. We have already seen how Joshua commends
Aksah and the daughters of Zelophehad for their passion to
possess the Promised Land. Now the book of Judges commends
two more mighty women for their faith in the face of a fresh
crisis for Israel. Their names were Deborah and Jael.

To understand this chapter, we need to grasp how much
the Lord detests male passivity. It was Eve who ate forbidden
fruit in the Garden of Eden, but since Adam was with her and did
nothing to stop her, he is the one who takes the blame. The Lord
comes looking for Adam, not for Eve, and the New Testament
traces our sin back to Adam's lack of leadership, not to Eve's
act of eating.[2] This is important, because when God saves us he

---

[1] John Knox had recently published his outrageously titled *First Blast of the
Trumpet Against the Monstrous Regiment* [that is, *Rule*] *of Women* (1558). It
was directed at Mary Queen of Scots but upset Elizabeth too.
[2] Genesis 3:6, 9; Romans 5:12–19; 1 Corinthians 15:22.

begins to shape us back into the men and women he created us to be. He teaches male bullies not to use their strength to oppress women, but to cherish and promote them. He teaches passive men not to abdicate the task of leadership, but to lead their families well.

Deborah is aware of this. She knows that women are often tempted to give up on men by seizing authority for themselves, so that's what she steadfastly refuses to do as the fourth judge of Israel. She is introduced as *"Deborah the wife of Lappidoth"* – in other words, as a woman who recognizes the authority of her husband. She is described as *"a prophet"* – in other words, as a Spirit-filled leader who recognizes that her task is to unite the elders of the twelve tribes by helping them to listen to the true Judge of Israel.[3]

Deborah can see that none of the male leaders in her nation have the stomach of a judge. The twelve tribal leaders have allowed King Jabin of Canaan to oppress Israel for twenty years from the rebuilt northern fortress city of Hazor.[4] They are so afraid of his 900 iron chariots, the superweapon of their day, that they have forgotten Israel has a superweapon too.[5] Rather than despise those male leaders, she encourages one of them to fight, in the same way that a mother might persuade her son to captain the school rugby team. Barak leads the tribe of Naphtali, which is home to the city of Hazor. His tribe had allowed the Canaanites to rebuild it after Joshua destroyed it, so his tribe needs to take a lead in dealing with the problem now. Deborah prophesies that the Lord will use Barak to defeat the Canaanite army with only

[3] This was in fact the calling of all 12 judges of Israel. The Hebrew text uses the verb *judging* to describe their ministry, and the noun *Judge* to describe the Lord in 11:27. Deborah simply grasped this the most clearly.

[4] Hazor means *Fortress*. It was in land belonging to the tribe of Naphtali (Joshua 19:32–39). The Israelites had destroyed it but then allowed it to be rebuilt (Joshua 11:1–14). This reminds us that compromise with the Devil is always foolish. He only uses it to bide his time to launch a fresh attack later.

[5] Iron axles and joints made chariots stronger and far harder to destroy. See Joshua 17:16 and Judges 1:19.

10,000 men. Don't miss how much she affirms his leadership instead of seeking to supplant it. This is what she means when she reflects in 5:7 that the men of Israel *"would not fight; they held back until I, Deborah, arose, until I arose, a mother in Israel"*. It is what she means in 5:9 when she insists that *"My heart is with Israel's princes."* Deborah is a very humble enabler of others.

Barak, on the other hand, is the archetypal passive male. He refuses to obey the Lord unless Deborah agrees to hold his hand. *"If you go with me, I will go; but if you don't go with me, I won't go."* Deborah agrees, but she tells him that there is a price to pay.[6] The honour of slaughtering the Canaanite general Sisera will not be his. It will go to a woman with more stomach for a fight than him, as a lesson to all the men of Israel.[7]

The name of Deborah's husband Lappidoth means *Torches*, but he sheds no light on Israel's problems. Barak means *Flash of Lightning*, but he is slow to obey. The men of Israel are more consumed with the size of their enemies than with the size of their God, so Deborah keeps on prophesying. When Barak hesitates in fear to lead the 10,000 men he has mustered into battle, Deborah encourages him, *"Go! This is the day!"*[8] When he baulks at marching out at the head of the army, she continues: *"Has not the Lord gone ahead of you?"* Deborah mothers Barak onto the battlefield, where the Lord steps in to help him. God transforms the iron chariots of the Canaanites from superweapon into liability by sending such a heavy rainstorm that a flash flood fills the valley. That's more than just a poke in the eye for their so-called storm-god Baal. It also mires their heavy iron chariots in the mud. Their charioteers are unable to move, and their infantry are too boxed in to flee.[9]

---

[6] Deborah warns him literally in 4:9 that *"the road you are taking will not lead to your glory."* By God's grace, his shame is redeemed in Hebrews 11:32, which commends him for the little faith Deborah drew out of him.

[7] The fact our culture sees no shame in 4:9 and 9:54 shows how much the godly Deborah has to teach us.

[8] Kedesh in Naphtali was even further north of Galilee than Hazor. Zebulun was another northern tribe.

[9] We only discover this detail about how Barak won the battle in 5:20–21.

None of them survives. Sisera abandons his chariot and his dying men to take refuge in the tent of a Kenite, one of the descendants of the father-in-law of Moses, who are meant to be his allies.[10] Like Deborah, however, Jael continues to fly the flag of faith in Israel's God long after the men of her nation have done a dirty deal with the Devil. While Sisera sleeps in safety, she hammers a tent peg through his skull.[11]

All of this is pretty gruesome, but this chapter tells us that it isn't as gruesome as the spectacle of men who fail to take a lead. If you are a man, don't make excuses like Barak, who initially did nothing to stop Sisera and his men from raping Israelite women (5:30). Grasp that the Devil is raping the Church across the Western world. Rise up and lead!

If you are a woman, be encouraged to play your own leadership role too. Recognize that Deborah led differently from the eleven male judges of Israel, but don't miss the fact that she led better than any of them. The writer doesn't have a single bad word to say about her.[12] Don't be afraid to say what Queen Elizabeth said back at the docks in Tilbury:

> *The enemy perhaps may challenge my sex because I am a woman; but I likewise charge them for being nothing more than men... If God is with us, who can be against us?!*[13]

---

[10] Exodus 3:1; Numbers 10:29; 24:21–22; Judges 1:16.

[11] Sisera is not a Canaanite name and *Harosheth Haggoyim* means *Woodland of the Foreigners*, so it is likely that he was a foreign general executed by a foreign woman. Jabin means *Intelligent* but he was outwitted by Jael.

[12] By telling us she was a *prophet* (4:4), he emphasizes that the Lord is just as willing to fill women with his Spirit as he is men. See Exodus 15:20; 2 Kings 22:14; Luke 2:36; Acts 2:18 and 21:9. Note also that women were last at the cross of Jesus, first to the tomb of Jesus and first to believe in the resurrection of Jesus.

[13] This comes from William Leigh's account of her speech in his sermon *Queen Elizabeth Paralleled* (1612).

We Fall Apart
(Judges 5:1–31)

"When the princes in Israel take the lead, when the people willingly offer themselves – praise the Lord!"

(Judges 5:2)

Tourists to the Egyptian city of Luxor are invited to marvel at how Barak managed to defeat the Canaanites in 1257 BC.[1] Engraved on a high wall in the Temple of Amun-Ra at Karnak is the ancient historian Tjaneni's account of the victory of Pharaoh Thutmose III over the Canaanites exactly 200 years before. The Battle of Megiddo, in 1457 BC, was the largest battle ever fought by the pharaoh, and Tjaneni says he captured 924 chariots on the battlefield. That alerts us to the scale of Barak's victory. Without a single chariot of his own, he managed to defeat an army large enough to defy a pharaoh.

Throughout Joshua and Judges, iron chariots are touted as the greatest weapon the enemy has in his armoury. In our own day, this might represent financial challenges. It might be Christian apathy, unbelief and contentment with the status quo. It might represent bitter persecution from the government or media. Whatever it means for you, the iron chariots felt like an insurmountable problem to the men of Israel. Deborah therefore sings a song to explain how those superweapons were defeated. With typical humility, she agrees to sing it as a duet with Barak. Listen carefully to their words.

The big theme of Deborah's song is: *We stand together, or*

---

[1] We will look at how to date the book of Judges in the next chapter, "Milk and Honey".

we fall apart. She works very hard on her song lyrics to ensure that we don't miss it: our victory depends on our unity. The song begins by celebrating that, for once, the tribal leaders of Israel led as one man and all their tribesmen did as they were told. This is one of the biggest themes in the book of Judges. The final verse of the book laments that *"In those days Israel had no king; everyone did as they saw fit."* Deborah warns that disunity among God's people always leads to defeat and disgrace, while unity among God's people always leads to victory. The opening line of the song can even be translated, *"Bless the Lord that the leaders in Israel [finally] took the lead and that the people [finally] volunteered willingly!"*

This was the secret of Deborah's success. She used the fact she was a woman to her advantage. Instead of attempting to monopolize leadership, like some sort of king, she mothered the male tribal leaders and city elders of Israel. She didn't try to force them into unity. That never works. She showed them that she cared for them and that her aim was to empower each one of them to be the very best leader they could be.[2]

Some of the names in the song are a bit obscure for modern readers, so we need to read it slowly to see what Deborah wants to teach us. We were told in 4:10 that Barak summoned 10,000 soldiers from the tribes of Zebulun and Naphtali, but Deborah adds that she also won over the leaders of four more tribes. When they saw that she wanted to bring the best out of them, like a mother, they became bigger men. The leaders of Ephraim became as courageous as their fathers had been when they drove the Amalekites out of their land.[3] The leaders of Benjamin marched north to join them. The captains of Makir, the largest clan within the tribe of Manasseh, also threw in their lot with

---

[2] Like a mother, she also wrote songs for minstrels to play at the waterholes to remind Israel of its history with God (5:11). Church leaders need to be storytellers to foster similar unity in their own day (Psalm 110:3).

[3] Judges 12:15 refers to part of Ephraim as *"the hill country of the Amalekites"*.

Zebulun and Naphtali. Issachar is the sixth tribe mentioned, and Deborah is particularly pleased that her empowering style of leadership attracted people of all classes to fight. She celebrates in verse 10 that Barak's final army included both the rich *("you who ride on white donkeys")* and the poor *("you who walk along the road").*[4]

Deborah's excitement isn't simply that this meant a lot more soldiers to fight the battle. Her song teaches us the same principle as the Psalms: *"Behold, how good and pleasant it is when brothers dwell in unity!... For there the Lord has commanded the blessing."* When the nation of Israel banded together under Barak, even iron chariots could not stand in their way, not just because they were physically stronger, but because unity among God's people always attracts his blessing. Similarly, the rapid advance of the early Church was due to the way in which the Holy Spirit changed their attitudes so that *"All the believers were one in heart and mind."*[5] God's Spirit fosters unity as a precursor to his blessing.

Deborah sings that the unity of God's people under Barak resulted in miracles. The Lord did not defeat the Canaanite chariots through weight of numbers – verse 8 says that many of the Israelite soldiers were unarmed![6] – but by sending such heavy rain that the earth seemed to shake (verses 4–5) and the River Kishon burst its banks near the city of Megiddo and flooded the Valley of Jezreel, where Sisera's chariots were waiting for Barak's army to come down from Mount Tabor (verses 19–21).[7] In an instant, their famous iron chariots became a liability,

---

[4] Deborah also celebrates in 5:2, 9 and 13 that both *"the princes"* and *"the people"* played their role.

[5] Psalm 133:1–3 (English Standard Version); Acts 4:32.

[6] The Philistines pursue a similar policy of forcibly disarming the subject Israelites in 1 Samuel 13:19–22.

[7] Mount Tabor and Megiddo were on opposite sides of the Valley of Jezreel. Sisera waited in the valley because chariots cannot operate on rugged mountain terrain (1:19). The Hebrew for *Mount Megiddo* becomes *Armageddon* in the Greek text of Revelation 16:16, which uses this battle with Sisera as a

sinking into the mud and mire.[8] Unity ushered God's favour towards Israel. As in the days of Joshua, he fought alongside his people.

No wonder the Devil loves to create division within churches, denominations and the body of Christ as a whole. He knows that we stand together or that we fall apart, so he works very hard to create disunity and strife among God's people.[9] Thankfully, Deborah's song informs us that God is willing to work with whatever unity he finds. It didn't matter that the men of Reuben spent so long debating that they missed the battle (verses 15–16). It didn't matter that the men of Gad and Manasseh, on the east side of the River Jordan, and the men of Dan and Asher on the Mediterranean coast saw the Canaanites as someone else's problem (verse 17).[10] It didn't even matter that Meroz, one of the towns of Naphtali, was too afraid to fight alongside its brothers (verse 23).[11] The song says that the Lord focuses more on our unity than on our disunity. He will work with whatever we give him. Even a little unity among God's people goes a long way.

So let's learn from Deborah to lead as loving parents, not as dictators, so that we become a joy to follow.[12] Let's join forces with other leaders, without any sense of competition, believing

---

prophetic picture of God's final showdown with his enemies. *Taanach* in 5:19 was a village near Megiddo.

[8] This is a great illustration of Psalm 20:7. When we rely on idols, they always turn on us and let us down.

[9] Luke 9:46 treats disunity among believers as demonic – literally, *"a disagreement entered in among them."*

[10] *Gilead* was shared between the tribes of Manasseh and Gad (Joshua 13:24–25, 29–31). Tribes which saw the Jordan as their moat or the Mediterranean Sea as their getaway route forfeited any share in the victory.

[11] It didn't matter to Israel's victory, but it certainly mattered to God. We can sense how strongly he feels about Christian disunity from how fiercely he curses Meroz in 5:23. See also Jeremiah 48:10.

[12] Deborah calls herself a mother (5:7), emphasizes the role played by Barak and Jael (5:1, 12, 15, 24–27) and shares the credit for victory with Israel's leaders (5:2, 8, 9, 13–15). She must have been a joy to follow.

that we are more together than we can ever be apart. Let's follow the leaders that the Lord has placed over us. Disunity in the book of Judges always leads to defeat, while unity always results in great blessing. We stand together, or we fall apart.

Milk and Honey
(Judges 5:24–31)

"Most blessed of women be Jael... He asked for
water, and she gave him milk."

(Judges 5:24–25)

The Lord had a peculiar way of describing the land of Canaan to the Hebrews. He promised to lead them into *"a good and spacious land, a land flowing with milk and honey"*. That phrase is used so often to describe the Promised Land in the first six books of the Bible that the Devil even uses it when trying to diddle the Hebrews out of it.[1]

During the time of the judges, the Devil often succeeded. Milk and honey meant for the Israelites flowed into the mouths of foreigners. That's why we mustn't miss the significance of the Hebrew names of the two godly women who rescued them and granted them forty years of unity, peace and victory. Jael means *Mountain Goat* and Deborah means *Bee*. A goat and a bee restored to Israel its land of milk and honey.

That's why Deborah sings in verse 25 that Jael offered a drink of milk to Sisera as he hid from Barak's army.[2] It's why she emphasizes that Jael's husband was named Heber, meaning Team. She is using Jael as a prophetic pointer to the victory

[1] Canaan is described this way in Exodus 3:8, 17; 13:5; 33:3; Leviticus 20:24; Numbers 13:27; 14:8; 16:14; Deuteronomy 6:3; 11:9; 26:9, 15; 27:3; 31:20; and Joshua 5:6. The Devil uses the same phrase to describe his counterfeit promised land in Numbers 16:13 and 2 Kings 18:31–32.

[2] Here we see Deborah's understanding of a woman's world. She knows that no one but a husband, son or brother would ever dare to enter the tent of a married woman, making it a safe place for Sisera to hide.

that comes through the unity of God's people. It doesn't matter that Jael's actions were brutal.[3] It doesn't matter that she was a foreigner. She united herself with God's people in the same way that the Israelites cursed at Meroz chose to become tacit allies of the Canaanites. Deborah stirs our determination by contrasting Jael with Sisera's mother, longing for her son to come back with plunder from the Promised Land.[4] Because Jael treated Israel as her true nation, she helped them to enjoy afresh their *"land flowing with milk and honey"*.[5]

Deborah ends her song by celebrating that a new day has dawned for Israel. The Israelites have become like *"the sun when it rises in its strength"*.[6] We are told in 5:31 that this revival of Israel's fortunes lasted for forty years. We are also told in 4:23–24 this was a period of slowly taking back all that the Canaanites had taken. Victory at the Battle of Mount Tabor broke the power of King Jabin, but God's people had to keep on pressing forward for the next forty years to recapture the whole of the Promised Land.[7]

This is a vital lesson. Regaining lost ground takes time. Nations can be transformed *through* a day, but they are rarely transformed *in* a day. Crisis moments of victory are crucial, but we must not forget that most of the Church's advance takes place quite unspectacularly – as we read the Bible, pray, love one another, share the Gospel and help those who are in need. It

---

[3] Don't judge Jael by twenty-first-century standards. We are told in 5:30 that Sisera was a serial rapist.

[4] Again we see Deborah's understanding of how a woman thinks. Her description of a soldier's mother is very poignant, dreaming about what gift her son will bring home for her, little knowing he will never return.

[5] Don't be fazed by the fact that Judges 4 says Jael killed Sisera while he slept and Judges 5 implies more of a struggle. It appears that Sisera woke as she attacked him, but too late to escape.

[6] This same picture is also used in 2 Samuel 23:4; Psalm 37:6; Proverbs 4:18; Daniel 12:3 and Matthew 13:43.

[7] There is a play on words in 4:23 when the Hebrew text says that Israel subdued *(kāna')* Canaan *(kenā'an)*.

may not sound as glamorous as the battlefield, but it's genuine warfare. The timeline of Joshua and Judges is as much about small advances as big ones.

1406 BC	Crossing the River Jordan and capturing Jericho[8]
1406 BC	Campaign against the Southern Coalition
1405–1400 BC	Campaign against the Northern Coalition
1400–1380 BC	Twenty years of peace and gradual growth
1380–1375 BC	Death of Joshua and five more years of peace
1375–1367 BC	Eight years of Aramean oppression
1367–1327 BC	Othniel's victory leads to forty years of peace
1327–1309 BC	Eighteen years of Moabite oppression
1309–1229 BC	Ehud's victory leads to eighty years of peace in the south, aided by Shamgar
1277–1257 BC	Twenty years of Canaanite oppression in the north[9]
1257–1217 BC	Deborah's victory leads to forty years of peace
1217–1210 BC	Seven years of Midianite oppression in the south
1210–1170 BC	Gideon's victory leads to forty years of peace
1170–1167 BC	Abimelek rules as a self-appointed king in Shechem
1170–1125 BC	Forty-five years of peace elsewhere under Tola and Jair
1125–1107 BC	Eighteen years of Ammonite oppression in the east
1107–1101 BC	Jephthah's victory leads to six years of peace in the east[10] Ibzan, Elon and Abdon are also active at some point during this period
1140–1120 BC	Samson fights the Philistines for twenty years in the west
1120 BC	Eli succeeds Samson as judge at the start of 1 Samuel

---

[8] Scholars debate these dates constantly. This initial date comes from 1 Kings 6:1, which tells us that 966 BC was the 480th year after the Exodus. The dates thereafter come from the text of Joshua and Judges, allowing for some overlap between the dates of some judges who served in different parts of Israel.

[9] There is overlap here because Judges 5:6 says that in *"the days of Shamgar"* people lived in fear. Although he brought relief from the Philistines in the south-west, he did not challenge the Canaanites in the north.

[10] The book of Judges is scant on historical markers, but Judges 11:26 clearly marks the date as c.1107 BC. This helpfully clarifies that Jephthah actually ruled in the east *after* Samson ruled in the west.

Some of these precise dates are still the subject of debate among Bible scholars, but what is undisputed is that most of Israel saw peace for most of these 300 years. So don't despise the little spiritual advances of your day-to-day life. Crisis moments are few and far between, but spiritual warfare takes place every day. The unity fostered by Deborah, the fourth judge of Israel, didn't just have to be produced. It also needed to be preserved. The defeat of King Jabin and the Canaanites was not just about coming together, but about staying together. Christian unity is never an event, always a lifestyle.

The history of the city of Constantinople bears tragic testimony to this. Now the Muslim city of Istanbul, its founders hoped it would advance the Christian cause across the globe, and initially their prayers were granted. From the fifth to thirteenth century it was the largest and wealthiest city in Europe, sending missionaries to countless nations. Shaped like a triangle, two of its sides were protected by the sea and the third side by walls so tall and thick that even Attila the Hun took one look at them and decided to try elsewhere. Nevertheless, when the Church split in 1054 into a Catholic west and an Orthodox east, the city was terribly weakened. It was Catholic Crusaders who sacked the city in 1204, leaving it wounded and very vulnerable to the Turks outside its walls. When they besieged and captured the city in 1453, they were assisted in the task by Catholic sailors and artillerymen. One of the greatest Christian missionary-sending cities in history fell because the Church was disunited. The Devil loves to divide and conquer.

So learn this lesson from the days of Deborah. Seek unity within your local church. Seek unity between the churches in your denomination. Seek unity across the Church at large. Where there are differences, call out major issues, but never major on minors. If we want to inherit all the promises that God has given us, then we must not act as rivals. Let's march shoulder to shoulder, as brothers and sisters. We stand together but we fall apart.

Ignorance Is Not Bliss
(Judges 6:1–13)

"I am the Lord your God... but you have not listened to me."

(Judges 6:10)

The life of Deborah warns us not to miss out on the promises of God through disunity. What happened after she died warns us not to miss out on them through stupidity.

This was the case with Constantinople. It didn't just fall through Christian disunity. It also fell because one of its defenders forgot to shut a door in its walls. The Walls of Theodosius were five metres thick and twelve metres high. They were so solid that they still survive today (I walked along them earlier this year with my family). But all of that counted for nothing when a foolish soldier, rushing back from a raid on the Ottoman camp, forgot to close the Wooden Circus Gate behind him. Within minutes, Ottoman soldiers had crept inside, captured the gatehouse and flown the Muslim crescent from the walls. Through a moment of stupidity, Constantinople became Istanbul.

The Israelites were every bit as neglectful as the Christian defenders of Constantinople. The Lord had instructed Joshua to *"Keep this Book of the Law always on your lips; meditate on it day and night, so that you may be careful to do everything written in it. Then you will be prosperous and successful."* Joshua had passed this instruction on to God's people, chiselling the Law on great tablets and urging them to *"Be very careful to keep the commandment and the law that Moses the servant of the Lord gave you... Be careful to obey all that is written in the Book of the Law of Moses, without turning aside to the right or to the left."*[1] Israel's enjoyment of God's blessings was linked to their obedience to his Word.

After the death of Joshua, Israel quickly forgot this. The writer of Judges tells us that the fundamental problem throughout this period was that *"Another generation grew up who knew neither the Lord nor what he had done for Israel. Then the Israelites did evil in the eyes of the Lord."* Ignorance is never bliss when it comes to the promises of God. When we neglect his Word, our faith soon begins to shrivel and die. Created to worship something, we very quickly start to worship idols whenever we lose sight of the Lord. It is shocking but entirely unsurprising that when the Israelites neglected the Scriptures, *"they forgot the Lord their God and served the Baals and the Asherahs."*[2] That's what happens whenever God's people neglect studying his Word. These terrible verses were written for us today.

Deborah died in around 1217 BC. Very quickly the Israelites forgot the songs sung by the minstrels at their waterholes about the way she led them to receive great victories from the Lord (5:11). As a result of their ignorance, they fall back into idolatry and Deborah's forty years of peace give way to seven years of harsh oppression by the Midianites.[3] Now here's the deepest tragedy: because they have neglected the Scriptures, they begin to tolerate this situation as something normal. They exchange Joshua's theology of conquest and promise for a watered-down theology of caves and poverty. Unaware that the Midianites are descended from the son that Abraham sent away so that Isaac's children could inherit the Promised Land, they find ways to accommodate themselves to being oppressed by the

---

[1] Joshua 1:7–8; 8:30–35; 22:5; 23:6.

[2] Judges 2:10–15; 3:7–8.

[3] When offended by the slaughter in Joshua and Judges, it helps to remember that these seven years of misery were caused by Israel's failure to destroy the Midianites as commanded (Numbers 25:16–18; 31:1–54).

Midianites.[4] Unaware that the Amalekites are descended from Esau, who lost the Promised Land to Jacob, they try to persuade themselves that their nations can get along.[5] Forgetting that the Lord parted the Red Sea and the River Jordan, they start assuming warriors who fight on camels are unbeatable.

Pitiful though it sounds, this is also what happens to Christians who neglect the Bible. It doesn't take long for churches to start accepting the status quo that the Devil has inflicted on their land. They find their own equivalent of mountain clefts, caves and strongholds in which to hide. So long as they are left to practise their religion in peace, they soon learn to accept the loss of any influence over the rest of the land. Even when the Devil robs them of the Gospel harvest that the Bible promises them, they learn to live without it. They develop a theology of caves and poverty and camels, convincing themselves that modern people are too busy, too affluent or too distracted to give the message of Jesus the time of day. Soon they view the Church's failure as quite normal.

That's why the opening verses of Judges 6 are encouraging. The writer assures us that the Israelites forfeited the Promised Land, not because the Lord is weak, but because he is strong! We are told in Revelation 2:5 that only one person has the power to close down churches, and it is not the Devil. It is Jesus, who is fiercely committed to judging any Christian community that does *"evil in the eyes of the Lord"*. Whenever the Church looks like Israel after the death of Deborah, these verses teach us to assume that the Lord must be impoverishing his people to make them cry out to him for mercy. If they repent, he promises not to ignore them. If they submit to his discipline and return to his Word, he pledges to revive them and to reverse the decline

---

[4] We find out one of Gideon's work-around tactics in 6:11. Abraham should not have taken a rival wife to Sarah in Genesis 25:1–6. Now his sins come back to bite the descendants of Isaac.

[5] Genesis 25:19–34; 36:1–12. The *"other eastern peoples"* in 6:3 are probably the Moabites and Ammonites.

in their fortunes. *Seven years* in these verses describe a literal period in the history of Israel but, as in the book of Revelation, the number seven also speaks of God's perfection. It assures us that the Lord disciplines his people for a short time to bring them back to a place of blessing. The Church's cave-and-camel moments are a gift from the God who keeps on giving.[6]

As we are about to see in the life of Gideon, the Lord revives his repentant people by raising up those individuals who have not neglected the Scriptures. We do not know the name of the prophet who provokes a revival in verses 7–10 through a vivid retelling of the story of Israel. All we know is that the prophet has clearly studied the first six books of the Bible and that he has the courage to share what he has found.[7] As for Gideon in the verses that follow, he has very little going for him except for the fact that he has clearly meditated on God's Word. He instinctively asks, *"If the Lord is with us, why has all this happened to us? Where are all his wonders that our ancestors told us about?"* Ignorance is not bliss. It is through reading about the parting of the Red Sea and of the River Jordan that Gideon is made ready for his dramatic showdown with the Midianite army.

So well done for reading this commentary. Well done for poring over the books of Joshua, Judges and Ruth. The Lord will use your study to make you part of his solution for your generation. Ignorance is not bliss. It always leads to loss and misery and pain. But when God's people start to study the Scriptures, revival is never far away.

---

[6] In God's perfect plan, a short period of testing can do us good. Israel's prosperity brought on apathy, but Israel's adversity brought on repentance and revival.

[7] When the prophet uses the word *Amorite* as shorthand for the seven nations of the Promised Land in 6:10, he is following the lead of Genesis 15:16. See also Joshua 10:5 and 15:63.

How the Light Gets In
(Judges 6:11–40)

"The Lord is with you, mighty warrior... Go in the strength you have and save Israel."

(Judges 6:12, 14)

You don't have to be a fan of Leonard Cohen to love the chorus of his classic song "Anthem". It goes like this:

Ring the bells that still can ring.
Forget your perfect offering.
There is a crack, a crack in everything.
That's how the light gets in.
That's how the light gets in.

153

Gideon can truly say he has a crack in everything. Like Ehud and the other judges, his greatest strength is his weakness, his greatest qualification that he has no qualifications at all. We can see at least four reasons in these verses why the Lord ought to have rejected him as the fifth judge of Israel. They ought to encourage us that God can work through us today. Forget your perfect offering. God has one of those already. When you see cracks in your own life, don't try to paper them over. That's how the light gets in.

First, Gideon is terrified of the Midianites. Threshing wheat requires space. Lots of it. Nobody in their right mind, wanting to beat corn until the edible grain has been separated from the inedible chaff that surrounds it, would choose to do so in the cramped confines of a winepress. Gideon is so scared that Midianite raiders might arrive at any moment that he has thrown all sense out of the window. Later, he betrays his crippling fear again when the Lord commands him to destroy his father's altar to Baal. He obeys at night to avoid being seen by his family and neighbours.[1] Despite this tendency towards cowardice, the Lord decides that Gideon should be the next judge of Israel. He sees his character flaws as opportunities to display his power through him. The Angel of the Lord appears to him and tells him he is precisely the kind of person God loves to use: *"The Lord is with you, mighty warrior."*[2] Yes, there are a whole lot of cracks in his courage, but that's how the light of God is going to get in.

Second, Gideon comes from a very feeble family. His tribe is Manasseh, one of the three tribes that settled on the east side of the River Jordan instead of pressing on into the Promised Land. His clan belongs to the half of Manasseh that settled west of the Jordan, but it is still the weakest in the entire tribe. If that's not bad enough, Gideon confesses that he is the least of his father's sons within the clan.[3] He protests to the Angel of the Lord that he isn't judge material. The Angel of the Lord smiles back: *"Go in the strength you have and save Israel out of Midian's hand. Am I not sending you?"* What matters isn't the strength of the messenger, but the strength of the Master whose authority is wielded.

Third, Gideon's own father is an idolater. He offers sacrifices on an altar to the storm-god Baal and he dances round an image of the fertility-goddess Asherah. Gideon's own family are therefore part of Israel's problem rather than of its solution.

---

[1] Revival always has to start at home (Exodus 4:24–26). Gideon had a right to be afraid – his neighbours try to lynch him in the morning! – but it would take a lot more courage than that to fight the Midianites. The Lord will lead Gideon through incremental steps of faith until he is ready for the big one (1 Samuel 17:36–37).

[2] The Lord also speaks prophetic titles over people and then helps them to grow into those shoes in Matthew 16:17–18 and John 1:47.

[3] See Joshua 17:2. Gideon's response is part humility and part truth.

Again the Angel of the Lord smiles. Even amidst a tangled web of weakness, the Lord knows how to find something he can use. Gideon's father has given him a Hebrew name that means *Chopper*, so the Angel of the Lord treats this as an unwitting prophecy. He commands Gideon to take an axe to his father's false gods. Sure enough, it turns out that Gideon's father possesses more faith in the Lord than he lets on. He stands up to the lynch mob that gathers to murder his son for chopping down the objects in his shrine, acquiring his son the new nickname Jerub-Baal, in the context meaning *Let Baal Fight His Own Battles*.[4] Against all expectation, Gideon's father suddenly sides with the Lord against Baal.

I personally find this very challenging. How many of the reasons that I give why God can't use me are as unfounded as those given by Gideon? How much of my desire to bring the Lord a perfect offering is, in fact, a sinful forgetfulness that he has already got one? My fruitfulness depends on the sacrifice of Jesus, not on my own exertions for him.

Gideon is readier to become the fifth judge of Israel than he knows. Unlike the rest of his generation, he has clearly studied the Law of Moses. He knows not to mix yeast in the grain offering that he sacrifices on a rock before the Lord.[5] He also knows enough to suspect his supernatural visitor is a theophany, like the ones experienced by Abraham, Jacob, Moses and Joshua, since he cries out, *"Sovereign Lord! I have seen the angel of the Lord face to face!"*[6] He even knows to build an altar

---

[4] Gideon is famous for laying down fleeces, but here he becomes a living fleece himself. His father effectively tells his neighbours that if nothing bad happens to Gideon then Baal is a fraud. The neighbours take this fleece seriously, since the nickname clearly stuck. It is used 13 times in Judges.

[5] The Hebrew word *minehāh* in 6:19 is the technical word used throughout Leviticus for the grain offerings sacrificed to the Lord at the Tabernacle. The detail about not using yeast is meant to echo Leviticus 2:11. The Angel of the Lord brings fire out of the rock to echo the fire that came out of the Tabernacle in Leviticus 9:24.

[6] Gideon appears to be aware of the Lord's warning in Exodus 33:20.

like those erected by Abraham and to name it *Yahweh Shālōm*, meaning *The Lord is Peace*. Where the altar of Baal once stood, there is now an altar to the Lord. Gideon hasn't got much going for him, but he might just have faith enough for the Lord to work through him to deliver Israel.

Gideon still has a fourth flaw, however. He still struggles to believe what he has read in the Word of God.[7] He requests a sign to prove that the Lord is truly with him, and is given one when the Angel of the Lord suddenly disappears. Rather than scold him when he asks for a third sign (for the fleece to be dry and the floor wet instead), the Lord celebrates the baby steps of faith that he is taking. In order to check these last two signs, Gideon at least plucks up the courage to step out of the winepress and onto his proper threshing-floor![8] Through each of these signs, Gideon develops faith the size of a mustard seed that will eventually move the mountain of the Midianites.[9]

It's just as the great theologian Leonard Cohen told us: *"Ring the bells that still can ring. / Forget your perfect offering. / There is a crack, a crack in everything. / That's how the light gets in. / That's how the light gets in."* These twelve Spirit-filled judges come after the death of Joshua to remind us that we only start our own work after Jesus has finished his. God already has a perfect offering, so we don't have to offer one ourselves. Our cracks and weaknesses don't prevent us from partnering with the Holy Spirit. That's how the light gets in.

---

[7] Many Christians today still talk about "laying down fleeces" to receive guidance from the Lord, so don't miss the fact that the writer does not present this as a good thing! He wants us to believe his Word outright, for we have far more proof than Gideon.

[8] In fairness to Gideon, he uses a Hebrew perfect tense in 6:37 to state that the fleece is not for revelation, but for final confirmation – to be sure that *"I have known"*. We are allowed to lay down similar "fleeces" ourselves, but we already have more proof than Gideon. Better simply to believe the Lord (Exodus 17:7; John 20:29).

[9] Matthew 17:20. Gideon will require yet another sign in 7:9–15.

Coming on Too Strong
(Judges 6:33–7:8)

"You have too many men. I cannot deliver Midian into their hands, or Israel would boast against me, 'My own strength has saved me.'"

(Judges 7:2)

We've all seen what happens when a guy comes on too strong with a girl. It's pretty embarrassing for everyone concerned. She feels uncomfortable, he feels hurt and we feel sorry for both of them. We've seen it all before. Coming on strong may be well-meaning, but is always self-defeating. Christians need to understand that they can do the same thing with God. Gideon came on too strong and it almost cost him victory.

157

In the previous chapter, we examined Gideon's weakness. He didn't have a hope in hell, which is why he was able to access the power of heaven. The Angel of the Lord encouraged him to *"Go in the strength you have"* because our challenge is never our weakness, only ever our delusion that we are strong. Gideon obeys and sets out in faith, despite not yet having experienced the Holy Spirit in the same way as Othniel and the other judges of Israel.[1] When he hears in 6:33 that the Midianites and their allies have forded the River Jordan to strengthen their control of the Promised Land, he suddenly feels weaker than ever. That's why the Lord chooses this moment to invest him with divine power. We are told literally in 6:34 that *"Then the Spirit of the Lord clothed Gideon."*

---

[1] As we saw in the chapter "Believing Is Seeing", we often need to set out in faith *before* God empowers us.

Clothed is an unusual way of describing a person suddenly receiving the Holy Spirit. We tend to talk more today about being "filled" or "baptized" or "soaked" in the third Person of the Trinity, but this phrase is also used throughout the Bible. We are told in 1 Chronicles 12:18 that Amasai was clothed with the Holy Spirit when he pledged his loyalty to the outlaw David. We are told in 2 Chronicles 24:20 that Zechariah was clothed with the Holy Spirit when he preached the Word of God to people who didn't want to hear. Jesus says in Luke 24:49 that we are to expect the same thing, since we too can be *"clothed with power from on high"*. The apostle Paul encourages us that this is part of our own Promised Land. He urges you to *"clothe yourselves with the Lord Jesus Christ"*.[2]

Recently I dressed up in a tiger suit to preach the Gospel to a bunch of children. I was clothed head, body, hand and foot so that not an inch of my skin was visible. When the children looked at me, they didn't see me. All they saw was tiger. That's what the writer of Judges wants us to sense here. God's Spirit descended so powerfully on Gideon that onlookers could hardly recognize him. All they saw was God's power enveloping him.[3]

Gideon is barely recognizable as the timid farmer who hid from the Midianite raiders in a winepress a few verses earlier. He blows a *shōphar* – a ram's-horn trumpet – to express the same faith as Joshua before the walls of Jericho and as Ehud when he blew a ram's-horn trumpet in 3:27. Like the *"oil and wine"* that the Good Samaritan uses to heal the man's wounds in the parable, this faith in the blood of God's Son and in the power of God's Spirit proves an explosive combination. The

---

[2] Christians have been clothed with Christ (Galatians 3:27) so they need to clothe themselves daily with Christ (Romans 13:14). Heavenly reality needs to be drawn upon daily as an earthly reality.

[3] The prophet Samuel emphasizes this in 1 Samuel 10:6 when he promises Saul that *"The Spirit of the Lord will come powerfully upon you… and you will be changed into a different person."*

Lord rallies the five northern tribes of Israel behind Gideon.[4] The farmer now heads up an army of 32,000 men!

Now Gideon has a new problem. People look at him and think he may be strong to fight invaders *"thick as locusts"* in the Valley of Jezreel, whose camels *"could no more be counted than the sand on the seashore"*. The Lord therefore surprises us at the start of chapter 7, not by telling Gideon he can't lead him to victory because his army is too small, but by telling him he can't because his army is too large![5] He says, *"You have too many men. I cannot deliver Midian into their hands, or Israel would boast against me, 'My own strength has saved me.'"* The problem isn't that Gideon is too weak to fight the Midianites, but that people might now think he stands a remote chance of victory! The Lord has resolved to work only through weak people so that the glory always goes to him and him alone. He explains in Isaiah 42:8, *"I am the Lord; that is my name! I will not yield my glory to another."*

That's why the Lord sends home 20,000 soldiers who lack confidence that he is the Deliverer of Israel.[6] Gideon is horrified, but the Lord hasn't finished yet. *"There are still too many men."* Next, he sends home 9,700 soldiers who are confident in their own strength. Sending home the first group of frightened soldiers was one thing, but this was quite another. Their only crime was kneeling to drink water from a fountain instead scooping water with their hands and remaining standing in case the enemy suddenly attacked them. Nevertheless, the Lord insists that it is equally vital. <u>He will neither work through those who have no faith in him nor through those whose faith is in themselves</u>. Gideon is left with only the 300 soldiers who trust

---

[4] The Midianites were camped in the *Valley of Jezreel*, in the tribal land of Issachar, just east of where Barak had defeated the Canaanites (7:1). Issachar's northern neighbours therefore help them. Unknown to Gideon, at around this time the Midianites murdered Gideon's brothers on Mount Tabor (8:18).

[5] We are given an estimated number of 135,000 men in 8:10. That's 450 times the size of Gideon's final army.

[6] *The Fountain of Harod*, in 7:1, means literally *the Fountain of Trembling* – presumably named after the 20,000.

in God and God alone, but God says this at last means he is ready for victory. He uses a Hebrew perfect tense to reassure Gideon literally in 7:7 that *"I **have given** Midian into your hand."*[7]

The Lord has taught this lesson to every man and woman who has spearheaded the advance of his Kingdom throughout the centuries of Church history. He taught it to the twelve disciples in Matthew 9:12–13.[8] He taught it to the apostle Paul in 2 Corinthians 12:1–10: *"My power is made perfect in weakness... That is why, for Christ's sake, I delight in weaknesses... for when I am weak, then I am strong."* He teaches it to any individual that he wants to empower. The one thing he cannot abide in us is when we come on too strong.

The Lord taught this same lesson to Martin Luther in the sixteenth century, when he decided to work through him to launch the greatest revival Europe has ever seen. When the whole world stood against him, he discovered that the God of Gideon helped him. Reflecting on the words of Isaiah 40:29–31, he wrote later in his *Commentary on Isaiah*:

> *It is as if God were saying: "You must be weary and emptied, so that there is no way out for you. Then I will give you strength. First you must become nothing, then consolation and strength will come." This happened to me, Martin Luther, who against my will came up against the whole world, and then God helped me.*

---

[7] The Lord also uses a Hebrew perfect tense to promise literally in 7:9, *"I have given the camp into your hands."*

[8] Matthew wrote his gospel for Jewish readers, so he particularly emphasizes the link between the 12 disciples, the 12 tribes and the 12 judges. Matthew 19:28 talks about their *"judging the twelve tribes of Israel"*.

One Day (Judges 7:9–22)

When the three hundred trumpets sounded, the Lord
caused the men throughout the camp to turn on each
other with their swords. The army fled.

(Judges 7:22)

Many Christians don't believe in revival. They think that it's
naïve to expect the Lord to transform the spiritual landscape of
a nation in a day. On one level, they are right, as we will see in
the next chapter. But on another level, they are entirely wrong.
What the Lord did through Gideon should fill us with faith for
what he can do in a single day with us.

The God who spoke "cannot" over Gideon's army in verse
2 now reveals himself unmistakably as the God Who Can.
Forget the movie *300*. What Leonidas and his famous group of
Spartans achieved at the Battle of Thermopylae was nothing
compared to what the Lord now does through the 300 weak
men that followed Gideon. Ancient occupying armies disarmed
the people they conquered, which explains the battle cry of the
300: *"A sword for the Lord and for Gideon!"* The soldiers appear
to be confessing their utter weakness – Gideon is the only one
among us who has a sword, but a sword in the hand of the Lord
more than makes up for the fact that each of us is armed only
with a trumpet and a torch! People who doubt that God can
change their nation in a day focus too much on the earthly odds
that are stacked against them, and not enough on the heavenly
power that is unleashed when we confess our weakness.

Gideon places his confidence in God the Father. It is easy
to despise him for wanting yet another sign from the Lord by

infiltrating the Midianite camp with his servant to do a final piece of reconnaissance.[1] Don't miss his faith, however. When he hears that one of the Midianites has had a dream that suggests the Lord will grant him a great victory, he bows down and worships before the battle in verse 15. He uses a Hebrew perfect tense to state with certainty to his men, *"The Lord **has given** the Midianite camp into your hands."*[2]

Gideon also places his confidence in Jesus, the Son of God. He knew far less about him than we do, but he prophesies about him when he tells his men to expect victory through sounding ram's-horn trumpets. The Hebrew word *shōphar* is used eight times in this chapter. Over 1,000 years before the Lamb of God shed his blood on the cross at Calvary, Gideon obtains victory through faith in the Messiah who is to come.[3]

Gideon also places his confidence in the Holy Spirit.[4] What happens next can only be explained with reference to the anointing he received in 6:34. Hearing the sound of 300 trumpets and seeing 300 torches flickering in the darkness around their camp, the Midianites assume that they must represent a massive army. Panicking, nobody thinks to try and rush the soldiers that surround them. Confused in the darkness, they turn instead and slaughter one another. The sword of the Lord and the sword of his servant Gideon have transformed the spiritual landscape of Israel in a single day.

---

[1] This was the fourth sign demanded by Gideon, after 6:17–22, 36–38 and 39–40. Note that this time the Lord volunteers to grant a further sign in order to settle Gideon's pre-match nerves.

[2] Romans 4:17 encourages us that we imitate God whenever we accept his Word above what we can see.

[3] Gideon needed to trust in the prophetic picture he was given, without adding extra innovations of his own. Timing mattered, since at the changing of the guard the Midianite soldiers were either tired or unready. Unity mattered too, since victory only came through all 300 soldiers playing their own part in the darkness.

[4] Paul appears to be thinking back to this passage in 2 Corinthians 4:6–7 when he likens our feeble bodies to the *clay jars* that kept the torches concealed until the moment of attack. God's Spirit is the light within us.

These verses are included among the writings of the "Former Prophets" to encourage us. They are meant to stir us to expect sudden revival in our own day too.[5] They encouraged a twenty-six-year-old Welsh miner named Evan Roberts to believe in God when the spiritual state of his nation was at such a low ebb that one Welsh clergyman reflected,

> *The ministry has lost its power and its convicting edge... Preaching is scholarly, interesting and educational but there is little anointing and convicting in it. Consciences are not pricked as in days gone by, and old phrases of long ago – such as conviction, conversion, repentance, adoption, dying to sin, self-loathing, etc – have become alien and meaningless... Family worship is quickly disappearing... Congregations in many places are lessening... The prayer meeting is nearly extinct... The authority of the Bible and the foundational truths of Christianity are being judged in the court of reason... The desire for pleasure has totally captivated the age. If this were my last message to my fellow countrymen throughout the length and breadth of Wales before I am taken to the judgment, take note – it would remain thus: The greatest need of my dear nation and country at this time is spiritual revival through a specific outpouring of the Holy Spirit.*[6]

It was the clergyman's last message. He died only one month later, but his words inspired Evan Roberts to pray. Though an uneducated miner, he believed the book of Judges that God makes weak people strong when they cry out to him. He reflected later,

---

[5] Gideon is speaking to us when he says in 7:17, *"Watch me. Follow my lead... Do exactly as I do."*

[6] Dean Howell of St David's wrote this in the December 1902 edition of the magazine *Y Cyfaill Eglwysig*.

For a long, long time I was much troubled in my soul and my heart by thinking over the failure of Christianity. Oh! It seemed such a failure – and I prayed and prayed, but nothing seemed to give me relief. But one night, after I had been in great distress praying about this... I found myself with unspeakable joy and awe in the presence of the Almighty God... I saw things in a different light, and I knew that God was going to work in the land, and not in this land only, but in all the world.[7]

That one day of personal breakthrough for Evan Roberts resulted in a year of revival during which 100,000 Welsh people were converted. Among them was the great preacher Martyn Lloyd-Jones, but most were rough-and-ready manual labourers like Evan Roberts. Together, they saw over a million converts across the rest of the United Kingdom and brought to birth the Pentecostal movement in the United States.[8]

So let's be encouraged by the dream that Gideon heard about in the Midianite camp.[9] It proclaimed that the God who keeps on giving can take a simple barley loaf – the cheapest, lowest-quality bread on sale in ancient Israel – and use it to perform a mighty miracle. Let's also be encouraged by the New Testament counterpart to the dream, in John 6:9, where Jesus uses five small barley loaves to feed 5,000 hungry mouths. Both Gideon in the Old Testament and Jesus in the New encourage us to believe that the Lord transforms nations in a day by clothing ordinary people with his Holy Spirit.

Let's also remember the title that the Nicene Creed gives to the third Person of the Trinity. *"I believe in the Holy Spirit, the*

[7] Evan Roberts in an interview with W. T. Stead in *The Bruce Herald* (28th March 1905).

[8] For more on this, see Kevin Adams in *A Diary of Revival* (2004).

[9] Going to spy on the vast and sprawling camp ought to have made Gideon's heart sink. It was hearing that God had given a dream of a mighty barley loaf to a Midianite that gave him the courage to fight and win.

Lord and **Giver of Life,** who proceeds from the Father and the Son, who with the Father and the Son together is worshipped and glorified." The Holy Spirit is the *Giver of Life* and the granter of revival. That's great news for frightened Hebrew farmers and for frustrated Welsh miners. It is also great news for you and me.

The Plod
(Judges 7:23–8:21)

Gideon and his three hundred men, exhausted yet keeping up the pursuit, came to the Jordan and crossed it.

(Judges 8:4)

In the last chapter, we saw how the Lord can transform a nation in a day. In this chapter, we're going to see how the Lord doesn't. One day of breakthrough in the life of Evan Roberts brought about the Welsh Revival, but he had to chase it hard for two years before he finally collapsed on the battlefield. Gideon secured victory over the Midianites in a moment, but it was how he behaved in the hours after his victory that turned a moment of triumph into a lasting deliverance for Israel.

In 7:22–25, Gideon shows us how to turn the breakthroughs the Lord gives us into lasting victory. He is not satisfied by seeing many of the Midianites turning on each other. He is not even satisfied with the knowledge that the five northern tribes of Israel will slaughter many of those who flee.[1] He calls for fresh troops from the tribe of Ephraim to the south to prevent any of the Midianites from making it home across the River Jordan. He will not rest until their power has been broken beyond all possible recovery. Seizing all the major crossing points along the river, he ensures that none of the Midianites or their allies escapes the slaughter. As a result, two of the greatest Midianite

---

[1] *"Israelites from Naphtali, Asher and all Manasseh"* in 7:23 describes a re-enlistment of the 31,700 soldiers he dismissed before the battle (6:35). Now that the victory is clearly the Lord's, they get to share in its plunder.

generals are captured and decapitated. Oreb means *Raven* and Zeeb means *Wolf*, reminding us that these were men who preyed on Israel. The scene is gory, but God wants to use it to teach us to be equally ruthless with sin and with the evil spirits that seek to ravage our own nations to destroy a great multitude of souls.[2]

In 8:1–3, Gideon shows us how to keep our eyes fixed on the prize. The Ephraimites had failed to rally to Gideon when he blew the ram's-horn trumpet in 6:34. Since their land bordered that of Manasseh, this was clearly a deliberate choice. If soldiers from the far north of Israel could hear the call to battle, the soldiers of Ephraim cannot have missed it. They were simply too scared to risk fighting with him. Having already let some of the fleeing Midianites escape over the River Jordan, they now have the temerity to complain that Gideon started the battle without them. We can tell how furious this must have made him from the way he treats the town of Sukkoth a few verses later, but for now he suppresses his anger and keeps his focus on the pursuit.[3] The Devil loves to distract Christians from ramming home the victory of Jesus. In a famous sermon on Nehemiah 6:3 – *"I am doing a great work, so that I cannot come down. Why should the work cease, whilst I leave it and come down to you?"* – the great revivalist Charles Finney claims that lack of focus is what brings many a revival to a halt.

> *Revival will cease whenever Christians get the idea that the work will go on without their aid. The church are co-workers with God in promoting a revival, and the work can be carried on just as far as the church will carry it on,*

---

[2] Although the bloodbath here feels quite offensive, don't miss this lesson for today. The Lord had already decreed judgment on the many sins of the Midianites and ordered their execution in Numbers 31:1–3.

[3] Joseph's second-born son Ephraim was treated as his firstborn ahead of Manasseh (Genesis 48:8–20; Jeremiah 31:9), so the fact that Gideon hailed from Manasseh reopened old wounds. Gideon models the wisdom of Proverbs 15:1 by deflecting anger with a gentle reply. Jephthah will be less patient in 12:1–6.

> and no farther... Let them keep about their work, and not
> talk about the opposition... Nothing is more detrimental
> to revivals of religion, and so it has always been found,
> than for the promoters of it to listen to the opposition,
> and begin to reply.[4]

Gideon replies humbly to the Ephraimites and keeps on pursuing the enemy. Despite his hunger and intense fatigue, we are told in 8:4 that *"Gideon and his three hundred men, exhausted yet keeping up the pursuit, came to the Jordan and crossed it."*

In 8:5-9, Gideon shows how seriously God regards the laziness of many Christians.[5] The towns of Sukkoth and Peniel, both in the territory of Gad on the east side of the Jordan, represent anyone who claims to be a believer in Christ yet tries to hedge their bets by compromising with the world.[6] The citizens of both towns are too frightened to nail their colours to the mast as part of God's people by feeding Gideon's hungry soldiers in case it provokes reprisals from the Midianites.[7] The writer of Judges has already warned us in 5:23 that the Lord curses lazy believers, but now he uses the humiliation of the elders of Sukkoth and the destruction of Peniel to warn us the Final Day of Judgment will be as great a day of loss for the lazy as a day of rejoicing for those believers who persevere.[8]

In 8:10-21, Gideon shows us why such relentless follow-

---

[4] This sermon forms the fifteenth of the lectures in his famous *Lectures on Revival* (1835).

[5] Don't be surprised by this. Proverbs 18:9 says that *"One who is slack in his work is brother to one who destroys."*

[6] Joshua 13:24-28. The unbelief of these two cities was a betrayal of their history in God (Genesis 32:30-31; 33:17). They did the opposite of Rahab, as Israelites who threw in their lot with the enemies of God.

[7] *"Do you already have the hands of Zebah and Zalmunna in your possession?"* is the opposite of faith. Where there is no willingness to risk everything by nailing our colours to the mast for Jesus, there is no faith at all.

[8] The fact that only the elders of Sukkoth are punished, while all the men of Peniel are executed, reassures us that God knows the motives of our hearts. Nobody will be punished who does not deserve it on that Day.

up must always follow victory. Many a breakthrough has been thrown away by people moving too speedily from victory into rest, instead of pursuing a long-lasting breakthrough. Compare Gideon's laser-sharp focus with the half-heartedness of Joab on the battlefield in 2 Samuel 2:25–3:1 and 10:13–16,[9] or the way in which the Israelites allowed the Canaanites to rebuild many of the cities destroyed by Joshua.[10] It was only because Gideon refused to stop fighting that 8:28 tells us, *"Midian was subdued before the Israelites and did not raise its head again."*[11]

William Carey, the pioneer missionary to India, referred to this principle as "the plod". Having sailed from England to Calcutta in 1793, he failed to see a single convert for his first seven years. During that time, his young son died of dysentery and his wife had a mental breakdown from which she never recovered. He pressed on in faith, determined to see the victory God had promised him. Finally, he saw his first Indian convert in 1800, which seemed to break open the floodgates for many more. William Carey worked tirelessly for the next thirty-four years, translating the Bible into twenty-four Indian languages, founding sixty mission stations and seeing half a million Indians come to faith in Christ before he died. When I visited the museum in his home, I found the following statement among his papers: *"If anyone should think it worth his while to write my life, if he give me credit for being a plodder he will describe me justly. I can plod. I can persevere in any definite pursuit. To this I owe everything... Few people know what may be done till they try, and persevere in what they have undertaken."*

In 8:20–21, Gideon shows us that each new generation of believers has to learn this. The name of his eldest son Jether means *Remnant* or *Best Part*, but he lacks the commitment of his

---

[9] We also see this principle in Judges 4:23–24; 1 Samuel 7:13, 14:29–30; and Psalm 18:37.

[10] Joshua 11:1–11; Judges 4:2; Joshua 12:10; 15:63; Judges 1:8, 21.

[11] The 135,000 mentioned in 8:10 were slaughtered in Gideon's pursuit, not by each other in the battle (7:12).

father.[12] The Lord has passed judgment on two Midianite kings named Zebah and Zalmunna, meaning *Sacrifice* and *Devoid of Protection*, but he lacks the stomach to carry it through. One of them taunts him as he dies – *"As is the man, so is his strength"* – and his words serve as a warning to us too. Don't stop plodding. Don't give up asserting the victory of Jesus until the Devil's forces are completely driven from your land.

---

[12] The slaughter of Gideon's brothers at Mount Tabor, only mentioned in 8:18, presumably took place in 6:33.

The King of Israel
(Judges 8:22–9:57)

"I will not rule over you, nor will my son rule over you. The Lord will rule over you."

(Judges 8:23)

THE KING OF ISRAEL (JUDGES 8:22–9:57)

The Canaanites had more kings than a history book of England. Thirty-three of them are listed among the dead in Joshua 12. Every Canaanite city had one.

This made the Israelites feel like the odd nation out. They often hankered after having a king of their own. After all, they had been conquered so far by an Aramean king, a Moabite king, a Canaanite king and two Midianite kings. Surely they needed a strong king to reinstate the unity that had briefly existed during the days of Deborah? When Gideon finally returns from his pursuit of the Midianites, the tribal leaders therefore go to meet him and offer to make him their king and his sons their new royal dynasty.

We know from 6:15 and 8:19 that Gideon was the youngest of several brothers. So he must have been tempted to act like Prince Hans in the Disney movie *Frozen*, willing to sink to any depths in order to leapfrog his way to becoming king. To his credit, he responds instead with a Bible study on the theme of kingship. He points out that Israel already has a King and that his name is the Lord. That's why Moses sang in Exodus 15:18 that *"The Lord rules as King forever and ever."* It's why Numbers 23:21 declared that *"The Lord their God is with them; the shout of the King is among them."* Yes, the Lord had promised in the Law of Moses to anoint a human king to reign over Israel, but he had also prophesied that this Messiah would come from the tribe of Judah, not from the tribe of Manasseh.[1] Gideon therefore declines the offer of the tribal leaders: *"I will not rule over you, nor will my son rule over you. The Lord will rule over you."*

We do not know who wrote the book of Judges, but a strong tradition in the Jewish Talmud says it was written by the prophet Samuel. If this is true, it explains why so many verses are devoted to Israel's brief first experiment with monarchy, since Samuel was rejected as the fourteenth and final judge of Israel in favour of the new King Saul. It was Samuel to whom the Lord said, *"They have rejected me as their King"*, and who was sent to anoint David as a better messiah for Israel.[2] If Samuel wrote this book, it also explains its positive view of kingship in 17:6 and 21:25 but, whoever the author, these warn that God's people have a toxic tendency to turn God's anointed leaders into little gods themselves. For *king* in these verses, we can read *pastor* or *priest* or *pope*, because this sin has a thousand faces.

Gideon resists the temptation to usurp a position that belongs only to God. He insists that he is simply called to judge Israel for a season on behalf of its true Judge and King.[3] But temptation is subtle. Gideon has imbibed more of Canaanite culture than he knows. The trouble starts when he plunders some of the crescent-shaped necklaces that the Midianites wore to worship their moon god.[4] It worsens when he asks the Israelites for twenty kilograms of gold so that he can make himself a set of clothing worthy of a king. Such clothing was known as an *ephod* and it was only ever worn by a priest or a

[1] Genesis 17:6, 16; 35:11; 49:10; Deuteronomy 17:14–20.

[2] 1 Samuel 8:7. The book of Judges records the lives of 12 judges in order to prefigure the 12 Spirit-filled disciples of Jesus (Matthew 19:28). The final two judges, Eli and Samuel, therefore appear in 1 Samuel.

[3] Jephthah is even more explicit in 11:27 that the Lord is the true Judge of Israel.

[4] The Hebrew word *saharōn* in 8:21 and 26 means literally *moon-shaped* and is the same word used in Isaiah 3:18. *Ishmaelites* in 8:24 is a generic term for any desert dweller. Compare Genesis 37:25–28 and 36.

king, so when he puts it on display in his hometown of Ophrah, people start to worship it, despite it being as ridiculous as worshipping the Crown Jewels at the Tower of London. Gideon has already taken many wives, like a king, but his decision to commission this set of royal clothes for himself takes this mistake to a whole new level.[5]

Gideon betrays a growing sense of pride in his leadership position by naming a son born to one of his concubines Abimelek. The name means *My Father is the King* and it speaks volumes.[6] By the time he dies, his seventy sons are ruling Israel like princes and the Israelites are ready to move off the gateway drug of Gideon's ephod into worshipping Baal-Berith, a demonic parody of Yahweh whose name means *Lord of the Covenant*.[7]

The sins of Gideon come home to roost on his family and nation in chapter 9. Abimelek's mother came from Shechem, a city which polluted the people of God in Genesis 34 but which was now home to the memorial stone that marked the renewal of God's covenant with Israel in Joshua 24. Abimelek persuades the city of Shechem to crown him king and to allow him to raid the treasury of the temple of Baal-Berith in order to expand his rule.[8] He proceeds to murder all but one of Gideon's seventy sons, including Jether, who pays a heavy price for his failure to follow through on his father's victory.[9] Only Jotham escapes to

---

[5] Many readers view this *ephod* and the one in Judges 17–18 as an idol, but the Hebrew word is used almost 50 times in the rest of the Old Testament to refer to the high priest's magnificent robe.

[6] The Lord had forbidden the king of Israel from taking multiple wives in Deuteronomy 17:17. In addition to his many wives (8:30), Gideon took concubine slaves (9:18) – effectively a royal harem.

[7] The Hebrew word *māshal* that is used twice in 9:2, meaning *to rule*, is also used three times in 8:23.

[8] When believers worship false gods, the Lord still uses those false gods to judge them. When Europeans first began to worship science, they were destroyed by their own gadgetry in World War One.

[9] Jotham means *The Lord Is Perfect*, and he mercifully survives to ensure that Gideon's name is not wiped out from Israel. However, he plays no further part in the story. There will be no comeback for this royal family.

climb Mount Gerizim (ironically, the mountain of blessing in Joshua 8:30–35) to call down a curse that his killers kill one another.[10] He declares that Gideon's dead sons were all like fruitful olive trees, vines and fig-trees, whereas Abimelek is as useless as a thorn-bush. He and Shechem are welcome to each other.

Only the Lord can be the true King of Israel. That makes Abimelek an antichrist, a false messiah. Although he manages to establish himself as king of Israel for three years, the nation quickly descends into civil war.[11] When Shechem toys with the idea of appointing a different king, Abimelek destroys the city, murders its people and burns the temple of its false god Baal-Berith.[12] Turning his attention to the neighbouring city of Thebez, he tries to do the same to their allies. We are meant to recall the shame of Sisera when Abimelek is killed by a brave woman dropping a millstone on his head from on top of the citadel walls.[13] Israel's first experiment with monarchy has ended in disaster. It always does when human leaders forget that they are called to govern for God and start acting like trumped-up little gods themselves.

Israel's problem was never that the nations around them had kings while they had none. It was always that they refused to submit to the Lord, the only true King of Israel.

---

[10] Even now, Jotham still invites Israel back to the Lord: *"Listen to me... so that God may listen to you."*

[11] The Hebrew text of 9:23 says literally that *"God sent an evil spirit between Abimelek and the men of Shechem."* He is sovereign even over the Devil's attempts to defeat his people. Satan always overstretches himself.

[12] Gaal is a Canaanite survivor, whose name means *Loathing*. He is meant to express the Lord's contempt for manmade messiahs like Abimelek – or ourselves. Zebul and the other supporters of Abimelek in Shechem are destroyed too, because the Devil shows no loyalty to those foolish enough to serve his purposes. El-Berith in 9:46 means *God of the Covenant* and is the same idol as Baal-Berith, *the Lord of the Covenant*.

[13] The shame of Abimelek's death would still be remembered in 2 Samuel 11:21.

The Dirty Dozen
(Judges 10:1–11:29)

*Jephthah said to them, "Didn't you hate me and drive
me from my father's house? Why do you come to me
now, when you're in trouble?"*

(Judges 11:7)

It can't have escaped your notice that the people Jesus chose to
be his twelve disciples weren't the type of people most rabbis
wanted. There was Peter, the fisherman who wasn't very good
at catching fish. There was Thomas the doubter, Nathanael the
cynic and Matthew the collaborator with Rome. There were
James and John, the quick-tempered brothers who tried to
buttonhole Jesus into granting them greatness even as he talked
about laying down his life for the world. The other six disciples
were also-rans. There wasn't one among them that showed the
least glimmer of potential.

We can tell that the twelve judges of Israel were meant
to prefigure those dirty dozen disciples from what the book of
Judges says and doesn't say about them. Tola was the sixth judge,
but his name means *Maggot* and the twenty-three years of his
rule are summarized in two short verses in 10:1–2.[1] Jair was
the seventh judge, ruling through his thirty sons who rode on
thirty donkeys between thirty towns east of the Jordan, known
somewhat uncreatively as *The Settlements of Jair*. Jair's name
means *He Will Enlighten*, but he is even less impressive than

---

[1] Tola came from Issachar in the north, but he ruled from the hill country of
Ephraim because it was more central to the nation as a whole. It also gave him
easier access to the Tabernacle at Shiloh.

Tola. Three short verses summarize the twenty-two years of his rule in 10:3–5. We are told that Tola *"saved Israel"* (although it's not quite clear what from), but we are never told that Jair saved Israel from anyone.

After the deaths of these two unimpressive judges, Israel plunges even deeper into sin. While it's true that the book of Judges is cyclical (**sin** leads to **oppression**, which leads to **repentance**, which leads **deliverance** and **peace**, which leads to a fresh descent into **sin**) we must not exaggerate this. The sequence of events is less a repeated cycle and more of a downward spiral.[2] Gideon is a worse judge than Deborah and leaves Israel in a worse state than ever. In addition to worshipping the gods of Canaan (Baal, Asherah and Ashtoreth[3]) the Israelites now start worshipping the gods of Aram, Sidon, Moab, Ammon and Philistia too.[4] No longer are they simply led astray by the idolatrous survivors of Joshua's campaigns. They have now become eager importers of idols from foreign lands.

The Lord therefore brings Israel to a place of desperation so that they will finally come to their senses and run back into his arms. For eighteen years, he allows the Philistines to ravage their lands to the west and the Ammonites their lands to the east.[5] The two and a half tribes on the far side of the River Jordan bear the brunt of it (their land is tellingly described in 10:8 as *"the land of the Amorites"*) but the Ammonites also ford the river to launch raids on the southern tribes. The Lord's initial response to their panicked cries for help isn't promising: *"You*

---

[2] We were warned of this in 2:19. If we stop moving forwards with the Lord, we quickly move backwards.

[3] Asherah and Ashtoreth were two distinct fertility goddesses, but they were often worshipped together as *the Ashtoreths* (2:13 and 10:6) and as *the Asherahs* (3:7).

[4] The main Ammonite god was Molek, who demanded child sacrifice (Leviticus 18:21; 2 Kings 23:10).

[5] This was fitting, since they were worshipping the gods of Ammon and Philistia. Jephthah delivers Israel from the Ammonites in Judges 10–11. Samson will need to follow up with the Philistines in Judges 13–16.

*have forsaken me and served other gods, so I will no longer save
you. Go and cry out to the gods you have chosen. Let them save
you!"* [6] But he is simply testing them to see if they are genuinely
repentant. [7] As soon as they throw away their foreign idols, they
discover the truth: *"He could bear Israel's misery no longer."* [8]

The stage is now set for the eighth judge of Israel, who is
even less impressive than Tola and Jair. For a start, he belongs
to one of the tribes east of the Jordan, those compromisers
who had settled for something less than the Promised Land. [9]
Worse, his father conceived him while paying a sinful visit to
a prostitute (perhaps even to a foreign prostitute at a pagan
shrine), so his own clan treats him as an outsider to Israel. [10]
We find him living as an outlaw in a foreign land as the leader
of a band of *"worthless men"* – the same phrase used in 9:4 for
the band of mercenaries Abimelek hired. [11] As an illegitimate,
part-foreign, exiled mercenary leader, Jephthah is perhaps the
dirtiest of the dirty dozen judges of Israel.

But Jephthah had two big things going for him. They were

---

[6] The *Maonites* in 10:12 came from the city of Maon in the hill country of
Judah (Joshua 15:55; 1 Samuel 23:24–25; 25:2). The fact that Judges makes
no other mention of their oppression confused the Greek translators of the
Septuagint such that they mistranslated it as *Midianites*. They were either
Canaanite allies of Hazor in Judges 4 or they teach us that the book of Judges
only records a selection of Israel's troubles.

[7] Turning *to* the Lord is only half of repentance. We also need to turn *from* our
sins (1 Thessalonians 1:9). *"Do with us whatever you think best"* also reminds
us that true repentance comes without conditions (10:15).

[8] Even when disciplining Israel, the Lord remained the God Who Keeps On
Giving. He loved Israel enough to bring them back to a place where they could
receive all the blessings he longed to shower on them.

[9] The land of Gilead was split by the River Jabbok between the tribes of
Manasseh and Gad, and 12:4 tells us that Jephthah came from Manasseh.
Jacob had built the altar at Mizpah in Genesis 31:44–54.

[10] I love this. It means that the Lord was just as sovereign over the unplanned
conception of Jephthah as the much-prayed-for conception of Samuel. Even if
your parents didn't plan your life, God did!

[11] Although clearly a foreign land in 2 Samuel 10:6–8, Tob is Hebrew for *Good*
and the Lord blessed him there.

the same two things that helped the dirty dozen disciples too, so we need to pay careful attention.

First, *he studies the Scriptures*. The name Jephthah means *He Opens*, and it is clear from these verses that he opens God's Word far more often than do the leaders of Israel. He corrects the elders of Gilead for placing their faith in his skill as a fighter, reminding them in 11:9 that the Lord alone grants victories to Israel. When the elders nod in agreement that *"the Lord is our witness"*, he leads them to the altar at Mizpah and insists that any deal between them must be struck in the presence of the Lord. He instinctively quotes the Law of Moses to correct the warped account of Israel's history peddled by the Ammonite king. Most impressive of all, Jephthah is the only one of the dirty dozen judges to proclaim explicitly that the Lord is the true Judge of Israel. In stark contrast to Abimelek, he refuses in 11:27 to usurp any title that belongs only to God alone.[12]

Second, *he is familiar with the Holy Spirit*. While the rest of the Israelites worship idols, Jephthah opens himself up to the Lord in prayer. There is not a trace of manipulation in his sudden promotion. He does not go looking for the elders of Gilead. They come looking for him.[13] They see he is *"a mighty warrior"* who still has courage to conduct raids on their enemies at a time when most Israelites have simply accepted their new masters.[14]

That's it. That's just about all that Jephthah has going for him. He is a man of God's Word and of God's Spirit. But those are the two things the Lord uses to turn natural zeroes into

---

[12] In the same way, Christian leaders ought to beware stealing credit from the Lord by too eagerly adopting the title *father* (Matthew 23:9) or *senior pastor* (Hebrews 13:20; 1 Peter 5:4).

[13] Those who rely on the flesh have to chase hard after promotion. Those who partner with the Holy Spirit can be promoted in a moment (Genesis 41:1–46; Esther 6:1–8:2).

[14] Note how much 10:18 echoes 1:12. Jephthah is emboldened by the same Holy Spirit as Othniel.

supernatural heroes. The great crescendo of these verses comes in 11:29: *"Then the Spirit of the Lord came on Jephthah."*

So don't write yourself off from playing a major role in God's purposes for your nation. Your past and your present need not define your future. Devote yourself to the Word of God and to the Spirit of God, because the Master who recruited a dirty dozen judges and a dirty dozen disciples is still recruiting very unlikely men and women today.

Selective Reading
(Judges 11:12–40)

*The king of Ammon, however, paid no attention to
the message Jephthah sent him.*

(Judges 11:28)

Leaders are guardians of the story of their people. Think of
Abraham Lincoln after the Battle of Gettysburg: *"Four score and
seven years ago, our fathers brought forth on this continent a new
nation, conceived in liberty... Here we highly resolve that these
dead shall not have died in vain – that this nation, under God,
shall have a new birth of freedom."*[1]

Or think of Winston Churchill during World War Two:
*"Bearing ourselves humbly before God, but conscious that we
serve an unfolding purpose... we are fighting by ourselves alone;
but we are not fighting for ourselves alone."*[2] Think of Barack
Obama: *"We've been warned against offering the people of this
nation false hope. But in the unlikely story that is America, there
has never been anything false about hope."*[3] Leaders have to
know their people's story.

Jephthah understood this. He was a master storyteller. He
shows us what a difference it makes when we catch people up
into the Bible's big story. His name means *He Opens* and much

---

[1] Lincoln delivered this Gettysburg Address over the graves of his soldiers on
19th November 1863.

[2] Churchill said this in a speech in the House of Commons on 14th July
1940.

[3] Obama stated this defiantly after losing the New Hampshire Democratic
primary on 8th January 2008.

of his strength as a leader came from how he opened up the Scriptures to a nation that had forgotten its story. When *"another generation grew up who knew neither the Lord nor what he had done for Israel"* (2:10) the Israelites became easy pickings for the Devil. They didn't know how to answer the king of the Ammonites when he stole their land, claiming here in verse 13 that *"When Israel came up out of Egypt, they took away my land from the Arnon to the Jabbok, all the way to the Jordan. Now give it back peaceably."*

The king's argument sounded convincing. That's the power of storytelling. But Jephthah knew the Word of God better than to be deceived. In reply to the king, he opens up the Law of Moses. He points out that the king of the Ammonites is guilty of selective reading. It simply isn't true that the Israelites stole the land east of the River Jordan from the Ammonites (Deuteronomy 2:19; 3:16). They captured it from the *Amorites* – similar spelling but an entirely different people group – and they did so as an act of self-defence when the Amorites responded to their friendly messages with war (Numbers 21:21–31). Note how methodical Jephthah is in his overview of the past few hundred years to prove that the king's selective reading of history is in fact a barefaced lie.[4]

Jephthah hasn't finished. He also adds some commentary to the story. He points out that *"the Lord, the God of Israel"* delivered the land of the Amorites into Israel's hands. *"The Lord, the God of Israel, has driven the Amorites out before his people Israel."* Jephthah presents the present-day struggle as something much more significant than a squabble between two nations over a stretch of land. It is a clash between the true God and an imposter. *"Will you not take what your god Chemosh gives you? Likewise, whatever the Lord our God has given us, we*

---

[4] Jephthah does not point it out, but their actions actually prove this. If they were simply out to reconquer their historic lands, they would not have crossed the Jordan to raid Judah, Benjamin and Ephraim in 10:9.

will possess."[5] The same God who empowered the Israelites to defeat the Moabites under Moses and Joshua in 1407 BC will help them hold on to the Promised Land now.[6] Jephthah throws down the gauntlet and gets ready to fight. *"Let the Lord, the Judge, decide the dispute this day between the Israelites and the Ammonites."*[7]

The king of the Ammonites refuses to listen. He prefers his own false take on the story. The Lord therefore anoints Jephthah with the Holy Spirit and empowers him to assert the truth in the face of a revisionist lie. The eighth judge of Israel defeats the Ammonites and destroys the twenty major cities of their kingdom, dealing with their made-up story once and for all. It is time for peace and celebration, but the chapter ends with needless tragedy. It turns out that Jephthah has been doing some selective reading of his own.

Jephthah was a fighter who loved the battle stories in the Law of Moses. He could quote every detail about the early battles in the Bible and every contour of the land of Canaan, but he hadn't been as diligent in studying the character of the Lord. He had skim-read many of the verses that describe the Lord as the God who keeps on giving, so he imagined him to be a better version of the pagan idols. Since those gods demanded gifts from their worshippers, Jephthah assumed that the God of Israel wanted such gifts too. If Chemosh and Molek wanted child sacrifice, then surely the Lord would want it too.

---

[5] Chemosh was the main god of the Moabites (1 Kings 11:33) but, as descendants of the two daughters of Lot, the Ammonites and Moabites often acted like one nation (Genesis 19:36–38). This lay at the heart of the king's claim, since the Amorites had driven out the Moabites before the time of Moses (Numbers 21:26–29).

[6] 11:26 acts as an important marker for dating the book of Judges. Moses defeated the Amorites in 1407 BC, so Jephthah defeated the Ammonites in *c.*1107 BC.

[7] Only in 2:16–19 does the writer use a Hebrew noun to describe these 12 leaders as *judges*. Normally he uses a Hebrew verb to say instead they *judged*, and here he explains why: The Lord was the true Judge of Israel.

Jephthah must have known that the most likely thing to come bounding out of his door to greet him on his return from the battlefield was his daughter. It wasn't likely to be a pet cat or a stray squirrel. He was about to pay a hefty price for his selective reading. If only he had read Genesis 22:8 – *"God himself will provide the lamb for the burnt offering"* – he would have known that God loves giving to us, not demanding gifts from us.[8] If only he had read Deuteronomy 12:31 and 18:1–12 – *"You must not worship the Lord your God in their way, because in worshipping their gods, they do all kinds of detestable things the Lord hates. They even burn their sons and daughters in the fire as sacrifices to their gods... Let no one be found among you who sacrifices their son or daughter in the fire... Anyone who does these things is detestable to the Lord"* – he would have known that God detests the idea of child sacrifice. Tragically, Jephthah had not read the detailed stipulations of the Law of Moses. He therefore assumed that Yahweh was simply a better version of Chemosh and Molek.

Jephthah has only one daughter and, sure enough, she rushes out to greet him on his return from the battlefield. To her credit, she courageously insists that her father follow through on his foolish vow. She doesn't know the Scriptures either.[9] She spends two months in the hills with the friends who would have been her bridesmaids, weeping over the fact that she will die a virgin before they see her wedding day.[10] The tragedy is that, even now, Jephthah could have spared them all such misery by simply opening up God's Word. Leviticus 27:1–8 would have informed him that any son or daughter dedicated to the Lord

---

[8] The same Hebrew word 'ōlāh is used to refer to the *burnt offering* in Genesis 22:8 as in Judges 11:31.

[9] We are not told why God chose not to intervene and stop them, as he did with Abraham and Isaac. We are simply warned that he sometimes lets people reap the consequences of their selective reading of the Bible.

[10] The Hebrew word for *friends* in 11:37–38 is feminine. These two months were all about mourning her virginity, not about losing it before she died.

could be redeemed for a few shekels of silver. Jephthah had saved Israel from the Ammonites because he studied sections of Scripture carefully. Tragically, he failed to save his daughter because he skim-read other sections of Scripture.

Let's not be selective in our reading of the Bible. Paul pleads with us in 2 Timothy 3:15–17: *"The Holy Scriptures... are able to make you wise for salvation through faith in Christ Jesus. All Scripture is God-breathed and is useful for teaching, rebuking, correcting and training in righteousness, so that the servant of God may be thoroughly equipped for every good work."*

Louder Than Words
(Judges 12:1–15)

"I saw that you wouldn't help... Now why have you come up today to fight me?"

(Judges 12:3)

On 30th September 1938, the British prime minister Neville Chamberlain arrived back in London from several days of discussion with Adolf Hitler. Brandishing a piece of paper above his head on the airport runway, he announced excitedly that it bore the Führer's signature and promise for *"our two peoples never to go to war with one another again"*. Later that day, he made the same declaration outside 10 Downing Street: *"I believe it is peace for our time. We thank you from the bottom of our hearts. Go home and get a nice quiet sleep."* The crowds that cheered him loudly would fall silent less than a year later when World War Two began. They were to learn the hard way that actions speak louder than words.

We learn the same lesson from this point onwards in the book of Judges. We are halfway through, and it is all downhill from here. There will be no more godly Deborahs or courageous Gideons, just a solemn warning about what happens when people promise to serve the Lord and then continue living for themselves. These chapters can be a bit depressing, especially when we realize that they are a prophetic picture of the Church in our own day, but I hope to show you that they are full of hope. They point towards the arrival of a better Judge, whose actions completely marry up with his words.

Judges 12 prepares us for the downwards trajectory of

the second half of Judges. In verses 1-6, the men of Ephraim march out to confront Jephthah for fighting the Ammonites without them. They cross over the River Jordan and meet him at the town of Zaphon, in the territory of Gad, as he is returning in high spirits from his triumph. They bring him back down to earth with a bump. *"We're going to burn down your house over your head."*[1]

If you feel like you are experiencing déjà vu here, it is because you are. The Ephraimites reacted the same way to Gideon's victory over the Midianites in 8:1-3. They loved the fact that their tribal name meant *Doubly Fruitful*. They loved the fact that Jacob had given the blessings of the firstborn to their ancestor Ephraim instead of to his elder brother, Manasseh. They loved the fact that theirs was the tribe of Joshua, the tribe that hosted the Tabernacle and the tribe that lay at the geographical heart of Israel. They loved their reputation as the leading tribe of Israel, but their actions spoke louder than their words. Jephthah points out that he called for their help to fight the Ammonites but that they refused until they saw that victory was won. They were afraid to take a lead in the battle in case their foreign masters won the day and launched reprisals. Jephthah insists that leadership is not about talk, but about courage. They have no right to be offended.

Sadly, Jephthah's own actions speak louder than words too. He was a man of God's Word who knew the story of God's people, but once again his selective reading spells disaster for Israel. In his anger with the men of Ephraim, he forgets that they are brothers. Instead of responding peacefully like Gideon, he responds harshly: I acted, you dithered; the Lord helped me, he didn't help you. Proverbs 15:1 teaches us that *"A gentle answer turns away wrath, but a harsh word stirs up anger"*, and so it proves. When the Ephraimites accuse Jephthah and his east-

---

[1] This threat epitomizes the lawlessness of the second half of Judges. See also 14:15 and 15:6.

bank family of being less Israelite than they are – *"You Gileadites are renegades from Ephraim and Manasseh"* – it is like a red rag to a bull. Having been rejected by his brothers, he simply cannot bear further rejection in his moment of triumph. Seizing all the crossing points along the River Jordan and taking advantage of their distinctive accent, he comes close to destroying the tribe of Ephraim.[2] The man God called to serve as Israel's saviour becomes Israel's slaughterer instead.

So, in verse 7, we discover that Jephthah's time as judge ended in disaster. Othniel oversaw forty years of peace, Ehud eighty years, Deborah forty years and Gideon forty years. Jephthah, on the other hand, only ruled Israel for six short years. Starting well in leadership is important, but it's how well we finish that determines our legacy. Gideon allowed his sinful ambition to plunge Israel into idolatry. Jephthah allowed his bitterness over having been rejected as a child to plunge Israel into slaughter. Jephthah knew how to tell his nation's story from the Word of God. He talked a great game for Israel. Tragically, his final years remind us that our actions speak louder than our words.

In verses 8–10, we are told about the ninth judge of Israel. Ibzan comes from Bethlehem in Judah, the birthplace of King David and of Jesus, but he is nothing like either of them.[3] Although we must assume that the Lord anointed him with the Holy Spirit, like his fellow judges, the writer makes it clear that he relied mainly on earthly power, by marrying his sixty children into each of the key clans of Israel. There is no record that he delivered Israel from anyone, because human scheming

---

[2] There were 32,500 Ephraimite fighting men when they were counted 300 years earlier in Numbers 26:35–37. Despite their population growth since then, this still decimated their tribe. See Proverbs 16:18.

[3] Some readers put Joshua 19:10–16 and Judges 12:11–12 together to argue that Ibzan actually came from the tribe of Zebulun. However, the context of 17:6 and 21:25 points more strongly towards the town in Judah.

cannot replace the Holy Spirit. His marriage certificates were as valueless as Neville Chamberlain's piece of paper.

In verses 11–12, we are told about the tenth judge of Israel. Elon means *Great Tree* or *Mighty Leader*, but his actions speak louder than his words. We are not told that he delivered Israel from anyone. We are not told anything about him except that he came from the tribe of Zebulun, ruled for ten years, died and was buried near his home.

Abdon means *Service* and his father's name means *Praise* but, once again, actions speak louder than words. He was a proud Ephraimite who relied on human strength, leading Israel by sending his seventy sons and grandsons around the country on donkeys.[4] Note how much his nepotistic style of government is based on that of Jair, in 10:3–5. It is meant to serve as a picture of what happens to believers whenever they place their hope in the donkey work of human effort instead of in their partnership with the Holy Spirit. We are not told that Abdon delivered Israel from anyone. His rule was as brief as that of Jephthah, Ibzan and Elon. He was a judge in name, but actions speak louder than words.

So let's use these verses to reflect soberly on how much we rely on the Holy Spirit ourselves. How much do we allow our past to dictate our present, like Jephthah, and miss out on the future God wants to give us? How much do we shy away from taking risks, like the Ephraimites, preferring the badge of leadership to actually leading?[5] How much do we rely on human strength instead of on the Holy Spirit, like Ibzan, Elon and Abdon? Our own actions speak far louder than our words.

---

[4] There is plenty to discourage us in Judges 12, but the fact God uses a proud Ephraimite in spite of all they said and did in 12:1–6 gives us hope. Praise God that his grace is always far greater than our sin.

[5] Following the paperback strategies of Christian leaders who have taken risks before us can never offset our own risk aversion, because their faith-filled risk-taking was an essential element of their fruitfulness.

The Great Deliverer
(Judges 13:1–25)

*The woman gave birth to a boy and named him
Samson. He grew and the Lord blessed him, and the
Spirit of the Lord began to stir him.*

(Judges 13:24–25)

When most people think of the book of Judges, they think of
Samson. He is its stand-out superhero. Who doesn't get excited
when reading about the way he ripped apart a lion with his bare
hands, the way he beat the Philistines single-handedly armed
only with a jawbone, or the way he tore the gates off a city to
evade capture by his foes? He is the archetypal strongman, the
Hercules of the Bible, but we are about to find out that he was a
spiritual weakling. The writer devotes four chapters to the rule
of the last of these twelve judges – that's more than to any other
judge – because it shouts out the book's conclusion. None of
these twelve men and women is the Great Deliverer our world
truly needs.[1]

Judges 13 emphasizes that Samson had the greatest
potential of all the judges of Israel. We meet the first eleven
judges in adulthood, but we pick up the story of Samson before
he is even conceived. The twelfth judge of Israel is born to
an infertile couple as a God-given miracle, prophesied in two

---

[1] Like its shorter form Noah, the name Manoah means *Rest*. The life of
Samson is meant to stir us to cry out for a far better Great Deliverer to come
from heaven.

separate appearances of the Angel of the Lord.[2] We have never read anything like this in the book of Judges. If there is ever going to be a great deliverer in its pages, then it surely has to be Samson.

That's not all. The Angel stipulates that Samson needs to live a more devoted life to the Lord than any of his predecessors. There is no record that any other judge of Israel took the Nazirite vow that is described in Numbers 6 by observing a special fast for several days or weeks in order to pursue deeper friendship with the Lord. Samson, on the other hand, must live under the Nazirite vow for his entire life. Even his mother must live under the vow while she is pregnant with him.[3] Samson must never drink wine or beer or any other alcoholic drink. He must even stay away from grapes in case they are slightly fermented. Nor must he eat any of the foods that are described as unclean in the Law of Moses. He must never cut his hair. It must hang down to his waist as an outward sign to the people of Israel that their new judge is wholly devoted to the Lord.

Samson is also given an amazing promise from God before he is even conceived. The Angel of the Lord faces up to the earthly facts – *"You are barren and childless"* – but then uses Hebrew perfect tenses to promise literally, *"but you **have conceived** and **have given birth** to a son"*.[4] By now the Philistines have emerged as the greatest remaining enemy of God's people and they have occupied much of the land of Israel.[5] The Lord therefore promises that Samson *"will take the lead in*

---

[2] Manoah's wife is not named, but she is part of a long line of infertile women whose prayers God used to grant them children who would transform the world: Sarah, Rebekah, Rachel, Ruth, Hannah and Elizabeth.

[3] The Angel of the Lord says that the vow applies, not just from birth, but *from his mother's womb*.

[4] Faith is not blind, ignoring the facts. Quite the opposite. It is unbelief that is blind, since it fails to see how much heavenly facts dictate what happens on earth. See Romans 4:17.

[5] Samson came from the tribe of Dan, on the border of Philistia. Dan bore the brunt of this in its early days.

delivering Israel from the hands of the Philistines".[6] The Israelites can start planning their victory celebrations. It looks as though the Great Deliverer of Israel is on his way.[7]

Except he isn't. This chapter ends on a high. Samson is conceived miraculously, just as the Angel of the Lord promised he would be, and he experiences the blessing of the Lord even as a child. Although the writer was quiet about Ibzan, Elon and Abdon's experience of the Holy Spirit, we are told that while Samson was still a teenager, *"the Spirit of the Lord began to stir him."*[8] This chapter describes the great potential that Samson had in the Lord's hands, but the next three chapters will reveal him to be a colossal underachiever. The book of Judges belongs with the "Former Prophets" because, even in this chapter, we see several prophecies about a far greater deliverer than Samson.

First, we are meant to note the many parallels between the birth of Samson, the twelfth judge of Israel, and the birth of Samuel, the fourteenth and final judge of Israel. If we are to believe the tradition in the Jewish Talmud that Samuel wrote the book of Judges, it is even more important that we spot this. Samuel was also born of a barren woman. He also lived his whole life under a Nazirite vow and was dedicated by his mother to the Lord at a young age. Samuel also grew up under the blessing of the Lord and came to know God's Spirit in his

---

[6] The Hebrew text says literally that *"He will begin to save Israel out of the hands of the Philistines."* Even as he makes the promise, the Lord knows that Samson will respond badly and become a massive underachiever.

[7] We saw in the timeline in the chapter "Milk and Honey" that these 40 years were 1160–1120 BC and that Samson was active for the second half of them (16:31). Although technically listed as the twelfth judge of Israel, this means he actually judged Israel in the west *before* Jephthah judged Israel in the east (see 10:7). He was so disobedient that God had to raise up deliverers elsewhere in Israel during his lifetime. His rule is recorded last because it represented rock bottom for the judges, preparing us for the message of 17:6 and 21:25.

[8] The Hebrew word *pā'am* means literally *to disturb* or *to distress* (Genesis 41:8; Daniel 2:1, 3). One of the marks of being filled with the Holy Spirit is that we grow agitated about the spiritual status quo. Calmness is therefore not always a mark of godliness. Anguished tears, prayer and action often are.

early years. Samuel also delivered Israel from the Philistines.[9] In Samuel, we see what Samson might have been had he been willing to obey the Lord.[10]

But we are also meant to spot the many parallels between the birth of Samson and the true Deliverer of Israel. Ultimately, Samuel was an underachiever too. He failed to control his sons, was rejected as a judge by Israel and died with the Philistines still dominating the land. He was the best of Israel's fourteen judges, but he still points towards the true and greater Judge. That's why Luke 1:15 deliberately echoes this chapter when it tells us that an angel promised the infertile Elizabeth that she too would conceive a son who must live his whole life under the Nazirite vow. It's why Luke 1:80 echoes this chapter when it tells us that her son, John the Baptist, was also strengthened as a child by the power of God's Spirit. It's why Jesus even makes a cameo appearance in this chapter, as the Angel of the Lord. The message of the book of Judges is that even the best of humans are humans at best. To enjoy all of God's promises requires faith in a better Deliverer.

This chapter hints several times that the Angel of the Lord is the Son of God in pre-incarnate form. He accepts Manoah's dinner invitation by requesting that a sacrifice be offered to the Lord. When asked his name, he reveals in verse 18 that it is *Pele'*, meaning *Wonderful* – the exact same Hebrew word that is used in Isaiah 9:6 to prophesy that Jesus *"will be called Wonderful".*[11] When Manoah sees the way his visitor ascends to heaven in the flames of his sacrifice, he cries out, *"We are doomed to die! We*

---

[9] 1 Samuel 1:1–20, 24–28; 2:21, 26; 3:1–21; 7:2–17.

[10] The names Samson and Samuel sound superficially similar but actually come from different words in Hebrew. Samson means *Sunshine*, whereas Samuel means *Heard By God*.

[11] *Pele'* can also be translated *Secret*, so Revelation 19:12 is also meant to echo this verse.

have seen God!"[12] His wife is more practical. This theophany means that God has pledged to deliver his people.[13]

So as we read about the twelfth and final judge in the book of Judges, don't miss the mighty message amid the crushing disappointment. Samson failed to be the deliverer he ought to have been but, praise God, he points forward to the coming of the Great Deliverer.

---

[12] Manoah clearly knew Exodus 33:20. Note the contrast between his faith in 13:12 and Zechariah's unbelief in a similar situation in Luke 1:11–20.

[13] Luke 2:40 and 52 are meant to echo Judges 13:24–25. Consider the humility of Jesus, coming to announce the birth of yet another flawed deliverer, trusting in his Father's perfect timing for his own arrival (John 7:6).

Strike One (Judges 14:1–9)

*The Spirit of the Lord came powerfully upon him so
that he tore the lion apart with his bare hands.*

(Judges 14:6)

On a summer's day in 2016, a visitor to Blenheim Palace did
a double-take when walking past a bed of tulips. He was an
antiques specialist and he recognized the ornate carvings on
the coffin-shaped box of marble filled with soil. He excitedly
informed palace officials that it was a Roman sarcophagus
brought back from Italy by the Duke of Marlborough in the
nineteenth century and thrown out in error by one of his
successors. It was worth £300,000 but it was accumulating
moss in the garden like a cheap piece of terracotta. It was the
most expensive flowerpot in history.

At the start of Judges 14, we discover that Samson prized
the promises of God just as poorly. He has been commissioned
to lead sinful Israel back to God, yet he is on his way to Timnah,
the town on the border between Dan and Philistia where the
patriarch Judah had sinful sex with his daughter-in-law, thinking
she was a prostitute serving at the shrine of a Canaanite idol.
The writer wants our hearts to sink with disappointment as
we realize that God's deliverer has set his face towards a town
tainted with shame.[1]

The Lord has promised Samson that he will use him
to deliver Israel from the Philistines, but Samson is more
interested in sleeping with Philistines than slaughtering them.
He spots a pretty Philistine girl and demands his parents get

---

[1] Genesis 38:12–16; Joshua 19:40–43.

her for him. They are horrified. Their son's Nazirite vow was meant to be an expression of his devotion to God, but he is far more governed by his lust than by his Lord. They know better than to confront their unruly son with the many Scriptures that forbid the people of God from marrying nonbelievers.[2] They know that he will not listen to reason. Their only hope is to persuade him to marry an even prettier Israelite. *"Must you go to the uncircumcised Philistines to get a wife?"* Samson refuses to listen to them, replying to his parents literally, *"Get her for me, for she is right in my eyes."* He is determined to walk by sight, not by faith.[3]

The writer expects us to be as horrified as Samson's parents, so he reassures us in verse 4 that the Lord is powerful enough to fulfil his purposes through us even when we disobey him. When we break his commands, we break ourselves against them, but we cannot shatter his purposes for his people. Yes, it appears that Samson's parents waited so long for a child that they indulged and spoiled him. They loved him so much that they destroyed him.[4] Yes, Samson was rude and unruly as a result, but he was not strong enough to thwart God's purposes through his sin.[5]

In verse 5, Samson takes his parents to Timnah with him. The man called to lead Israel back to God is now leading Israelites into a place of shame with him. The Lord decides that it is time to deliver a hefty warning. Samson has taken a Nazirite vow not to drink wine or eat grapes, so he is very foolish to court temptation by taking a shortcut through the vineyards

---

[2] For example, Exodus 34:15–16 and Deuteronomy 7:1–6. We might also add Joshua 23:12–13; Judges 3:5–8; 1 Corinthians 7:39 and 2 Corinthians 6:14–17.

[3] Tragically, he loses his eyes in 16:21. Only when blinded would he learn the lesson of 2 Corinthians 5:7.

[4] Proverbs 19:18 warns us sternly that Samson's parents are by no means alone in doing this.

[5] This should encourage you if you feel deflated by the failures of the judges. If you repent of your own sin and seek the Lord, then you are ahead of Samson when it comes to partnership with God.

of Timnah. As he approaches the vines, a young lion runs out to attack him, a graphic warning about the dangers of playing around with sin. This is Samson's equivalent to what the Lord says to Cain in Genesis 4:7: *"Sin is crouching at your door; it desires to have you, but you must rule over it."* It is his equivalent to what 1 Peter 5:8–9 says to us: *"Your enemy the devil prowls around like a roaring lion looking for someone to devour. Resist him, standing firm in the faith."* If Samson ignores this warning, then he will continue hurtling towards destruction. It will be strike one in Timnah.

In verse 6, the Lord helps Samson in the same way he helps us whenever we are tempted to sin. He grants him supernatural strength to overcome by anointing him with the Holy Spirit. Since Samson rips the lion apart with his bare hands, many people assume he must have been a muscular bodybuilder, but we are told in 16:17 that he was as weak as any other man. This was his spiritual initiation into having supernatural strength to tear apart a lion as easily as a chef preparing tender meat for dinner. Samson had experienced the Holy Spirit from childhood, but this took things to such a new level that the Hebrew text says literally, *"The Spirit of the Lord rushed on him."*[6] As the lion pounced on Samson, so did God's Spirit. The Lord is giving him a choice here: be mastered by the Holy Spirit or by an evil spirit, be overcome by God or by a lion.

Sadly, Samson refuses to repent and turn back to the Lord. He is emboldened by his newfound supernatural strength instead of taking it as a warning. Catching up with his parents, he does not confide in them what has just happened. He knows full well that they will lecture him again about the Angel who appeared to them before he was born. Unable to bear any more talk about God's plan to anoint him with his Spirit to defeat the Philistines, he carries on to Timnah and follows through with

---

[6] This Hebrew word *tsālah* is also used for people being pounced on by the Holy Spirit in Judges 14:19; 15:14; and 1 Samuel 10:6, 10; 11:6; 16:13. It conveys the sense of *coming powerfully* on someone.

his engagement to one of them. In a literal translation of verse 7, Samson persists in what *"seems right in his eyes"*.

In verses 7–9, things therefore go from bad to worse for Samson. *"Some time later"* – in other words, the Lord has given him time to reflect on what happened with the lion – he sets off again to Timnah to get married. Although his Nazirite vow forbids him from going near a dead body (Numbers 6:6), he disappears into the undergrowth to see what is left of the lion. Spotting a bees' nest in the lion's carcass, he defiles himself by scooping out some of its honey. Instead of reflecting on the supernatural strength that makes him oblivious to the pain of bee stings, he lures his unsuspecting parents into eating it with him.[7] The man called to lead Israel back to God leads two Israelites into sin.

It is strike one in Timnah. As we grieve for what might have been for Samson, let's not miss out on what the Lord is also saying to us here. This is God's answer to our question: *Why don't you fill me more with your Holy Spirit?* It isn't because we are too sinful – the example of Samson clears that up for us once and for all. It is because he loves us too much to give us power we can't handle. I have seen my young children crash their little go-kart, so I don't let them drive my seven-seater car. God has seen the way we mishandle the little power that he has given us, so he holds back on more in love. John 3:34 assures us that *"God gives the Spirit without limit"*, so any limits must be on our side. Surrender to God today so that he can entrust you with the full power of the Holy Spirit.

---

[7] The writer emphasizes that Samson scooped out the honey *"with his hands"* rather than using a stick. His supernatural strength makes him reckless rather than repentant.

Strike Two
(Judges 14:10–20)

> *Samson held a feast, as was customary for young men.*
>
> (Judges 14:10)

I became a Christian through the story of Samson. I found myself at a meeting in Germany where somebody preached a sermon from these chapters about the dangers of playing around with sin. I had heard it all before, but I was suddenly convicted. After all, it isn't hard to see how the Lord's warnings to Samson apply to each of us too.

Philistine tradition demanded that Samson hold a seven-day bachelor party before his marriage. The Lord was in this, since it gave him seven more days in which to consider whether it was wise for a man called by God to deliver Israel from the Philistines to be marrying one. It also did more than that. The Hebrew word *mishteh* in verse 10 refers literally to a *drinking-feast*, so holding one would be a violation of his Nazirite vow. The Lord had backed Samson into a corner to deliver a second warning. Unless he nailed his colours to the mast as a devotee of the God of Israel, he would sink even deeper into his rebellion. It was time for him to come clean with his fiancée and with her pagan friends. He could neither share their Philistine customs nor her Philistine bed.

Sadly, we are told in verse 10 that he chose to reject the Lord. "*Samson held a drinking-feast, as was customary for young men."*[1] He didn't come clean with the Philistines. He didn't nail his colours to the mast. He didn't stay true to his Nazirite vow. Instead, he got drunk with a bunch of pagans. Part of the tragedy is that these men aren't even his friends. Samson is such a loner that his Philistine future in-laws take pity on him and press-gang thirty virtual strangers into acting as rent-a-friends. This was a moment for him to come to his senses and to recognize that the honey in the lion's carcass was an invitation for him to die to himself and allow the resurrection power of God to turn his bitter life into something sweeter, but instead of coming to his senses he opts to get drunk senseless instead. He shows his disdain for the Lord by turning his first warning into a silly bet. He challenges his thirty companions to guess the meaning of a riddle: *"Out of the eater, something to eat; out of the strong, something sweet."*

Leaders are seen by the way in which they gather followers. When Ehud and Gideon blew ram's-horn trumpets, the men of Israel rallied to them. When Barak called the northern tribes, they rallied to him too. The elders of Gilead were so impressed with Jephthah that they went and begged him to become their leader. We are therefore meant to spot the striking contrast to this in these chapters. Samson never leads anyone. We can only imagine what the Lord might have done through his life had he learned to lead by the power of the Holy Spirit instead of using his anointing to pursue his own agenda. Instead, even when his future in-laws provide him with a group of ready-made friends, he manages to turn them into enemies within a few short days.

Even now, it isn't too late for Samson to turn back to the Lord. The writer refers three times in these verses to his Philistine fiancée as his *"wife"*, but he has not yet gone through with the wedding. She is only viewed as a wife under Philistine law, which treated a broken engagement as a source of shame

---

[1] This verse is a direct challenge to Christian men today. If we get drunk at bachelor parties just because unbelievers do so, we are just as disobedient as Samson.

for both families, and he is not yet committed to the match before God. The Lord graciously uses Samson's drunken bet to reveal how much danger lies ahead if he goes through with marrying a nonbeliever. She proves Moses and Joshua right in their warnings when she nags and pesters him into doing what he knows is foolish.[2] For all his supposed strength, he allows himself to be manipulated by her cries of *"You hate me! You don't really love me."* He tells her the answer to his riddle and she promptly tells the Philistines. In the dying moments of Samson's bachelor party, they win their drunken bet, turning the whole marriage sour.

Samson is furious. He doesn't merely call his fiancée a cow. He accuses his thirty companions of *ploughing with his heifer* – an angry slur that they must have had sex with her to extract this information. Having already paid the caterers, the girl's father does not want to let the food go to waste so he quickly marries her off to one of the bachelor-party guests instead.[3] Suddenly we realize that the Lord has been sovereign over all of Samson's sin. He is about to use him to strike terror into the hearts of the Philistines. They are about to see the power of the Lord.

Samson has failed to control his lust (14:2), his appetite (14:9), his tongue (14:17a), his fiancée (14:17b) or his temper (14:18). This has put him in an expensive predicament. He owes each of his bachelor-party guests an expensive set of clothes. Suddenly the Holy Spirit pounces on him a second time and empowers him to travel twenty-five miles deep into enemy territory to ambush thirty men in the Philistine city of Ashkelon. Without the Lord, this would have been a suicide mission, but with the Lord he easily overcomes the odds of thirty-to-one. Samson drops their clothes off in Timnah before storming back

---

[2] The Hebrew word *tsūq* in 14:17 means literally *to oppress*. Because he has refused to deliver Israel from the Philistines, as commanded by God, Samson finds himself oppressed by one instead.

[3] Some readers see a contrast here between Samson's unfaithful groomsman and the faithful groomsman of the true and better Samson in John 3:29.

to his parents' home in the territory of Dan. There, as his anger slowly subsides, he has time to reflect on his own riddle. If he surrenders his life to the Lord, he will reap a sweet reward, but if he ignores this second warning it will be strike two in Timnah.

The Lord had commissioned Samson to bring unfaithful Israel back to him. Because he despised his calling, his so-called friends, his fiancée and her father have all been unfaithful to him. Still Samson refuses to repent. The Lord had warned Israel that if they consorted with the enemy it would spell disaster for them. Because Samson failed to listen, his life now lies in tatters. Still he refuses to repent. The Lord had used a lion and the Philistines of Ashkelon to demonstrate what he is able to do through Samson's life if he surrenders it to him. Still he refuses to repent. He decides to go back to Timnah and to press on with his own agenda. He says no to the Lord's second warning.

It is strike two. As the twelfth judge of Israel takes the road back to Timnah, he casts off all sound judgment. He plunges headlong towards his own terrible Judgment Day.

Strike Three
(Judges 15:1–20)

"Don't you realise that the Philistines are rulers over us? What have you done to us?" He answered, "I merely did to them what they did to me."

(Judges 15:11)

In the classic movie *The Bridge on the River Kwai*, Sir Alec Guinness plays a World War Two officer who forgets that the Japanese are his enemy. He becomes obsessed with the idea that he and the other prisoners of war in his labour camp will demonstrate to the Japanese the superiority of British engineering. Never mind the fact that the bridge they build will be used to transport soldiers to fight his own countrymen. Never mind the fact that a team of British commandos have parachuted in to plant explosives along the bridge. He tries to stop them to preserve his feat of engineering, but while doing so he stumbles and falls on the detonator. The bridge is blown sky high, just as a train filled with enemy soldiers tries to cross it. The British officer becomes an accidental hero.

Judges 15 is the Bible's equivalent of *The Bridge on the River Kwai*. Samson has forgotten that God has called him to deliver Israel from the Philistines. Instead, he is still hell-bent on marrying one of them. The Lord therefore unleashes a catalogue of events that result in deliverance for Israel. He turns Samson into an accidental hero too.

In verses 1–3, the Lord sets Samson into conflict with his former fiancée's family. We can tell how much lust drives his actions from the gruff way he greets her father: *"I'm going to my wife's room."* The man under a Nazirite vow to devote himself to the Lord is now salivating at the thought of having sex with a pagan woman.[1] Her father has to break the bad news to him. He has married her off to a member of his bachelor party – would he like to marry her prettier younger sister instead? Samson is so furious that he finally turns on his Philistine fiancée's family.

Verses 3–5 give us a sense of Samson's wasted potential. If he could manage to catch 300 foxes and tie them tail-to-tail in pairs, what could he have done to the Philistines had he obeyed the Lord?[2] He is not thinking of his calling when he fastens torches to each set of tails, lights them and releases the 150 pairs into the fields of the Philistines. He is only thinking of his wounded ego and his ruined wedding plans. Nevertheless, the Lord uses his anger to set him into conflict with the Philistines. When they see that Samson's foxes have destroyed their wheat, their vineyards and their olive groves, they march to his fiancée's house and do the very thing she feared in 14:15. They lock her and her family inside, then they burn the house down over their heads.

In verses 6–8, Samson responds. He instantly forgives his dead fiancée and swears vengeance on her killers. Up until this moment, he has been mainly interested in sleeping with Philistine girls, but now he becomes equally passionate about slaughtering Philistine men. The Hebrew phrase *"he struck them hip and thigh"*, in verse 8, describes a merciless campaign of killing. Since Samson has no intention of obeying his command to deliver Israel from the Philistines, the Lord has made it his personal agenda. God's will is never thwarted. We only get to choose whether or not to embrace it gladly.

Samson has no friends even within his own tribe. When his anger subsides, he does not return to the tribal territory

---

[1] Samson is as naïve in his human relationships as he is in his relationship with the Lord. He thinks that giving his fiancée a goat will be enough to patch up their argument and to get in her bed.

[2] The Hebrew word *shū'āl* means literally *a burrowing animal*. It can be translated as either *fox* or *jackal*.

of Dan. He knows that they will hand him over to his enemies, so he withdraws to a cave all by himself within the territory of Judah. We are meant to pity this lonely figure in the cave of Etam, driven into solitude by his sin and rebellion. We are also meant to wonder what this twelfth judge of Israel might have achieved had he learned first to lead himself, and then to lead others. Samson's name means *Sunshine*, but he lives under a black cloud and fails to attract a single follower. He is nothing like the Sun of Righteousness, who would one day come to be the Great Deliverer of Israel and a light for every nation of the world.[3]

In verses 9–13, the Lord entices the Philistine army into a showdown with Samson. They chase him into the territory of Judah and, instead of defending him, the men of Judah blame him for disturbing the status quo: *"Don't you realise that the Philistines are rulers over us?"* Christians echo them whenever they complain that certain individuals are provoking persecution by living out the Gospel too loudly in their land. Now is the right moment for Samson to proclaim that God has given him a bigger vision for Israel than cowering before the Philistines. Now is the time for him to rally an army and to sweep the Philistines out of the Promised Land. Instead, he behaves like a petulant child, telling the men of Judah that *"I merely did to them what they did to me."* Requiring a more inspiring battle cry than "They started it", the men of Judah tie him up and hand him over to the Philistines to save their own skins. The only concession they give Samson is that they won't kill him themselves. They will let the Philistines have that honour.

The Lord now shouts out a third loud warning to Samson. It is game over for him unless God performs a mighty miracle. Suddenly the Holy Spirit pounces on him for a third time, enabling him to shake off the ropes that bind him. Picking up the jawbone of a dead donkey lying on the ground, he is empowered to wield it like Shamgar and his ox-goad. Using the heavy bone as a club and the

---

[3] Samson's parents may have been inspired by Deborah's words in 5:31. See Malachi 4:2 and John 8:12.

donkey's teeth as a stabbing weapon, he kills 1,000 Philistines. The others drop their swords and spears and run away.

In verses 16–17, Samson responds to this latest miracle. Instead of repenting, he composes a ditty which celebrates his own role in the battle and mentions nothing about the Lord. He then shows how little he cares about heeding this third warning by throwing away the jawbone as something that has no more meaning for him.[4] It is strike three for Samson, and every baseball fan knows that it's three strikes and you're out.

In verses 18–20, the Lord reaches out to Samson. He refuses to accept his disobedience as a final answer. He allows him to become so thirsty in the desert that he thinks he is about to die. In his desperation, Samson finally confesses that *"You have given your servant this great victory."* It is the first record of Samson ever praying, and God responds by opening up a sudden spring of water in the desert.[5] Samson drinks and his strength is revived, along with our hopes that his life may yet end happily.[6] The writer feeds our hopes by telling us at this point in the story that *"Samson led the Israelites for twenty years."*[7] Could it be that these twin miracles will provoke a lasting change within him?

We will find out the answer in the final chapter of Samson's ministry.

---

[4] The men of Judah honour this miracle by naming the Philistine burial mound Ramath Lehi, which means *Jawbone Hill*. Samson, however, ignores the miracle and carries on in his persistent sin.

[5] The Israelites hear about his prayer and name that place En Hakkore, which means *The Caller's Spring*.

[6] Samson had known the Holy Spirit as a young man (13:25). He had been pounced on by the Holy Spirit three times as an adult (14:6, 19; 15:14). This miraculous provision of spring water was therefore an invitation from God to learn to drink deeply from the Holy Spirit (Exodus 17:1–7; John 7:37–39; 1 Corinthians 10:4). Sadly, the Hebrew text states literally that when he drank *"his own spirit returned"*.

[7] This isn't as positive as it sounds. The writer always states this at the end of a judge's life, so placing it here communicates that it is now game over for Samson's ministry. Even the 20 years that he judged are described as *"the days of the Philistines"*.

You're Out
(Judges 16:1–19)

*"If my head were shaved, my strength would leave
me, and I would become as weak as any other man."*
(Judges 16:17)

It's never easy to be a football fan in Gibraltar. With only a few
thousand able-bodied men to choose from, fans are used to
watching their team lose to every European nation. But that
can't have made it any easier on 10th October 2016, when
Christian Benteke scored for Belgium against Gibraltar only
eight seconds after kick-off. It was the fastest goal in FIFA World
Cup history, but it was slow compared to Samson in Judges 16.

At the end of Judges 15, we were left wondering whether
Samson might repent and start serving the Lord. In the very
first verse of Judges 16, however, he outpaces Christian Benteke
to settle that score. We are meant to do a double-take when the
chapter begins with the statement, *"One day Samson went to Gaza,
where he saw a prostitute. He went in to spend the night with her."*
In an instant it is obvious that the Lord's mercy towards him has
fallen on deaf ears. He is back in a Philistine city, drooling over
Philistine women. He is again more focused on sleeping with
their women than on slaughtering their men.[1]

The Lord knows the rules of baseball: it's three strikes and
you're out. Even so, he tries to give a fourth chance to the twelfth
judge of Israel. Proverbs 25:28 warns that *"Like a city whose*

---

[1] There is no standing still spiritually. Whenever we fail to move forwards with
the Lord, we move backwards. In Judges 14, Samson at least tried to marry a
Philistine. Now he pays to have sex with one.

walls are broken through is a person who lacks self-control", so the Lord uses the fortified city of Gaza to teach sinful Samson a lesson in self-control. Midway through the night, Samson grows suspicious that the men of Gaza are planning to kill him. It is too late to evade them, since the city gates are locked, so the Lord performs another mighty miracle to deliver him. He empowers Samson to rip the doorposts of the city gate out of the ground and to carry the gates on his back to the top of the hill that faces Hebron. If you don't know your Bible geography, this will mean very little to you, but Hebron was deep in the territory of Judah thirty-eight miles away! Most people would struggle to walk that distance in a day, but Samson did it carrying the gates of one of the five great cities of the Philistines! The Lord is inviting Samson to imagine his potential if he repents of his fatal lack of self-control.[2]

Sadly, Samson rushes faster than Christian Benteke into the sin that will cost him his life. In verse 4, he falls in love with yet another Philistine girl. She comes from the Valley of Sorek, which means the *Valley of Choice Vines*, but Samson pays no attention to the lesson that the Lord tried to teach him when the lion attacked him by the vineyards of Timnah. He thinks nothing of his Nazirite vow to stay away from grapes in case the slightest trace of wine should cross his lips. Even the fact that Delilah means *Weak* or *Brought Low* does not alert him to the danger. He has learned nothing from his former fiancée. He does not imagine for a moment that Delilah is negotiating behind his back with the Philistine kings over how much she can earn by betraying him.[3]

---

[2] We saw in Joshua 15 that the name Hebron means *Union*. The location of this hill was therefore significant. The Lord is inviting Samson into partnership with him.

[3] *"The rulers of the Philistines"* mentioned seven times in Judges 16 are the kings of the five great Philistine cities: Gaza, Ashdod, Ashkelon, Gath and Ekron. Together they put a bounty of 5,500 shekels of silver on Samson's head. That's 65 kilograms, or 550 times an annual salary (17:10), showing just how much they hated him.

Many readers find it hard to understand how Samson could be so stupid. When Delilah nags and pesters him to know the secret of his strength, he lies that he will be as weak as any other man if tied up with seven fresh bow strings. Since she immediately ties him up and then calls Philistine soldiers out of hiding, why on earth does he carry on his relationship with her?[4] Because persistent sin always breeds complacency, that's why. Samson never dreams he is in any kind of danger.[5] The Philistines can see he is no more muscular than they are and that he must therefore be endued with some kind of supernatural power, but Samson has forgotten this.[6] He actually thinks that he tore apart the lion in his own strength. He genuinely believes that he slaughtered the Philistines at Ashkelon and Lehi through his own power. He doesn't realize that he was only strong enough to lift the gates of Gaza because the Lord anointed him with the Holy Spirit. He toys with Delilah because he feels no sense of danger. He thinks his strength is his own.

When Delilah nags and pesters him a second time, he happily plays along. It's endearing when she talks as if his strength were supernatural – it reminds Samson of his mother. When she betrays him by tying him up with new ropes, it gives him a chance to fight some more hidden Philistines. This is fun. When she pesters him a third time, Samson is emboldened to sail even closer to the wind. Since his mother told him that his strength lay in keeping his Nazirite vow, he points to his hair and tells a modified version of the truth: if Delilah weaves his long hair into a loom, he will become as weak as any other man. When he wakes up to find she has betrayed him to the Philistines,

---

[4] If the Hebrew text of 16:10 truly means *"You have made a fool of me"*, Delilah cannot merely be complaining that he has lied to her. She must be complaining that he made her look an idiot in front of the soldiers.

[5] Samson had seven plaits of long hair so his talk of *seven* bowstrings is closer to the truth than it sounds.

[6] The Philistines clearly see this in 16:5. Delilah clearly sees it too in 16:6 and 15.

he quickly frees himself, but he has come a step closer to death. Although he may think that his mother told old wives' tales, Delilah has more faith in the words of the Angel than he does.

When she pesters him a fourth time, he tells her what the Angel told his parents.[7] He knows that she will probably shave his head, but he has laughed for so long at the warnings of his parents that he doesn't believe it will make any difference. Sadly, his parents are right. This final act of disdain towards his Nazirite vow proves the final nail in the coffin of his ministry.[8] Delilah puts him to sleep on her lap (presumably indicating that he has been drinking heavily) then shaves off the seven plaits of his long hair. At once, verse 19 says *"his strength left him"*. When the Philistine soldiers come out of hiding, Samson is horrified to find that he is powerless to resist arrest by them.

Strike one for Samson had been his refusal to learn the lesson of the lion by the vineyards of Timnah. Instead of viewing it as an invitation to partner with God, he turned it into an excuse for further self-reliance. Strike two had been his failure to take to heart his drunken riddle about the sweetness of dying to his sin. Strike three had been his stubborn refusal to acknowledge the lesson of the jawbone and of the spring water in the desert. Now it was three-strikes-and-out. He was a prisoner of the Philistines. The twelfth judge of Israel hadn't been a great deliverer. He had been a great dunce instead.

---

[7] As in 14:17, the Hebrew word *tsūq* in 16:16 means literally *to oppress*. Having failed to deliver Israel from Philistine oppression, Samson is himself oppressed by a Philistine.

[8] When we are told literally in 16:16 that *"his soul was vexed to death"* by Delilah's nagging, it genuinely was.

Alone (Judges 16:20–21)

He awoke from his sleep and thought, "I'll go out as before and shake myself free." But he did not know that the Lord had left him.

(Judges 16:20)

The Mexican poet Octavio Paz believed that *"Solitude is the profoundest fact of the human condition. Man is the only being who knows he is alone... When he is aware of himself, he is aware of his lack of another – that is, of his solitude."*[1]

Perhaps he is right. Perhaps one of the greatest tragedies of the human condition is our awareness of being alone. If so, then even more tragic is what happens to Samson in Judges 16:20. He is left all alone, even by God, yet is entirely unaware of it.

When Samson awoke from dropping off on Delilah's lap, he had no idea that the Holy Spirit had abandoned him. He had known God's presence from his mother's womb. He had been stirred by God's presence even as a child. He had been empowered by God's presence throughout his adult life, but he never realized God's presence was a person. He had despised the Holy Spirit, attributing his miraculous victories to his own strength, so imagine his despair as the Philistines rushed out of hiding and fell upon him. *"He awoke from his sleep and thought, 'I'll go out as before and shake myself free.' But he did not know that the Lord had left him."* Samson suddenly discovered that he was a weakling without God. He couldn't stop the Philistines from gouging out his eyes to stop him ever fighting them again in the future. He couldn't stop them from dragging him to

---

[1] He wrote this in his famous essay *The Labyrinth of Solitude* (1950).

Gaza and chaining him to a millstone like a common donkey. Empowered by God's Spirit, he had torn that city's gateposts out of the ground, but now he was alone.[2]

When reading passages like this one, we always need to remember that Joshua and Judges were originally listed among the "Former Prophets". Jesus is the true and greater Joshua, who defeats the demonic enemies that stand against us and who leads us to possess all the promises of God. Jesus is also the true and greater Judge that is described in 11:27. He is the true Ruler, the true Rescuer, the true Deliverer. The book of 1 Samuel informs us that Israel had fourteen judges in total, but only twelve judges are mentioned in this book as a prophetic pointer to the twelve Spirit-filled disciples of Jesus.[3] What happened to Samson is meant to speak into Church history and into our own experiences of God today.[4] If Samson was unaware that the Lord had left him, then it ought to provoke an urgent question in our own hearts as we read.

It should make us question how much we value the presence of the Holy Spirit in our own day-to-day lives. David cherished it so deeply that his number-one prayer after sinning with Bathsheba was *"Do not cast me from your presence or take your Holy Spirit from me"* (Psalm 51:11). Do we prize the presence of God's Spirit that much in our churches? How often are they a bit like Samson – devoid of God's power, yet largely unaware of it?

---

[2] It was common practice in the ancient world to mutilate prisoners of war (1:6–7; 1 Samuel 11:2). Samson had done what was right in his own eyes. Blind, he would learn to walk by faith and not by sight.

[3] Samuel 4:18 and 7:15 say literally that Eli and Samuel *judged* Israel. See also 1 Samuel 12:11.

[4] The death of Joshua paved the way for 12 judges to be anointed with the Holy Spirit. The death, resurrection and ascension of Jesus paved the way for 12 apostles (Matthew 19:28; Revelation 21:12–14 and Peter's insistence in Acts 1:15–26 that their number must be restored to 12). We are further taught in Luke 11:13 and Acts 2:16–39 that these 12 apostles paved the way for all of us to be anointed with God's Spirit too.

The seventeenth-century Puritan John Flavel warned that congregations very quickly learn how to replace the presence of the Holy Spirit with other things. He argued that many of our rituals, much of our music and a lot of our leadership has this end in view:

The Christian who goes for a long time without the experience of heart-warming will soon find himself tempted to have his emotions satisfied from earthly things and not, as he ought, from the Spirit of God. The soul is so constituted that it craves fulfilment from things outside itself and will embrace earthly joys for satisfaction when it cannot reach spiritual ones. The believer is in spiritual danger if he allows himself to go for any length of time without tasting the love of Christ and the felt comforts of a Saviour's presence. When Christ ceases to fill the heart with satisfaction our souls will go in silent search of other lovers.[5]

For Samson, the biggest danger was his self-reliance. These verses should make us question whether it may be a danger for us too. The Lord could anoint Samson with his Spirit while on a sinful shortcut through the vineyards of Timnah. He could anoint him with his Spirit while angry at Ashkelon and while sulking at Lehi. But the Lord refused to fill him with his Spirit while full of himself. As he taught Gideon, he will never share his glory with our inflated pride. The nineteenth-century evangelist D. L. Moody taught this to those who wanted to see as many conversions as he did:

I believe firmly, that the moment our hearts are emptied of pride and selfishness and ambition and self-seeking, and everything that is contrary to God's law, the Holy Ghost will come and fill every corner of our hearts; but

---

[5] John Flavel in *The Method of Grace in the Gospel Redemption* (1680).

if we are full of pride and conceit, and ambition and self-seeking, and pleasure and the world, there is no room for the Spirit of God; and I believe many a man is praying to God to fill him when he is full already with something else. Before we pray that God would fill us, I believe we ought to pray Him to empty us. There must be an emptying before there can be a filling.[6]

The twentieth-century Bible teacher Oswald Chambers taught the same. In his daily devotional *My Utmost For His Highest*, he insists that *"Every element of our own self-reliance must be put to death by the power of God. The moment we recognize our complete weakness and our dependence upon Him will be the very moment that the Spirit of God will exhibit His power."*

So let's feel a godly hatred towards the self-reliance that shipwrecked the great potential of Samson's ministry. Let's look to the true Judge of Israel, who cried out from the cross, *"My God, my God, why have you forsaken me?"* so that we need never know the pain of forfeiting God's presence ourselves.[7] The God who keeps on giving will forgive and restore us if we confess to him our disobedience and self-reliance. The issue is not one of whether or not we sin (these dirty dozen judges surely settle that question once and for all) but one of how quickly we repent of our sin and return to partnership with the Lord.

You don't have to suffer with Samson in these verses. You don't have to be alone, abandoned by the Holy Spirit. Confess your apathy, your self-reliance and your disobedience. Tell the Lord that you surrender to obeying his call upon your life today.

The nineteenth-century missionary Hudson Taylor pleads with us:

---

[6] D. L. Moody in his book *Secret Power* (1881).

[7] Matthew 27:46 is the glorious New Testament counterpart to Judges 16:20.

If we were to set ourselves to obey the command of our Lord to the full, we should have such an outpouring of the Spirit, such a Pentecost, as the world has not seen since the Spirit was poured out in Jerusalem. God gives His Spirit, not to those who long for Him, not to those who pray for Him, not to those who desire to be filled always; but He does give His Holy Spirit to them that obey Him.[8]

---

[8] He preached this at a missionary conference in Shanghai, China, on 7th May 1890.

Resurrection Power
(Judges 16:22–31)

But the hair on his head began to grow again after it had been shaved.

(Judges 16:22)

There are a lot of surprising statements in the Bible, but not many that make you do as big a double-take as the praise heaped on Samson in Hebrews 11:32–34.

> *I do not have time to tell about Gideon, Barak, Samson and Jephthah... who through faith conquered kingdoms, administered justice, and gained what was promised... whose weakness was turned to strength.*

215

Those verses make us wonder when exactly Samson expressed faith in the Lord. Was it when he decided to marry a Philistine or when broke his Nazirite vow by eating honey from a carcass? Was it while visiting a prostitute in Gaza or while lying back in the arms of Delilah? Of course, it was none of the above. The writer of Hebrews is talking about the last ten verses of his life story, when he finally surrendered to his calling. In his dying moments, Samson came to faith in God and experienced his resurrection power.

It was only after the Philistines gouged out his eyes that Samson finally began to see. Until that moment, all his thinking had been driven by the sights of earth – a pretty Philistine girl, a glistening mass of honey, a tempting bottle of red wine or the pile of Philistine corpses that persuaded him that he was strong.

He had laughed at what his parents said the Angel of the Lord had prophesied about him. He had acted as if his life belonged to himself and as if the power he felt coursing through his body was his. When the Philistines gouged out his eyes, Samson finally began to see the truth. He looked back on his life and started to see it from the perspective of heaven.

Samson's birth had been a miracle. The Lord had chosen a woman who could not bear children to give birth to his deliverer for Israel.[1] He had promised to empower him through the Holy Spirit, like the other judges, but he had marked him out as having more potential than his predecessors by commanding him to live as a Nazirite for life. His uncut hair and unshaved face were meant to proclaim to the world that he was consecrated to God. Shackled to a millstone in the prison yard in Gaza, Samson scratched his bald head and stroked his smooth chin and faced up to the consequences of a life spent denying this. He had boasted in 15:16 that he made donkeys of the Philistines, but now the Philistines had made a donkey out of him.

Doing donkey work in Gaza helped Samson to look back on his life clearly. He had been a fool to think that, armed only with the jawbone of a donkey, he had managed to kill 1,000 Philistines on his own. He had admitted as much at the time, when he nearly died of thirst after the battle and confessed, *"You have given your servant this great victory."* That was the only occasion in the whole of his life's story that we are ever told that Samson prayed. Now the blind Samson finally saw how stupid he had been to toss away the donkey's jawbone without learning its lesson. It finally dawned on him how foolish he had been to treat deliverance from a lion as a pretext for a riddle instead of as a prompt to repent. His own riddle taunted him as he worked the millstone in the prison yard. *"Out of the eater, something to eat; out of the strong, something sweet."* The answer

---

[1] The miracle marked such a turnaround for her that we also read about her other children in 16:31.

to his riddle had been staring him in the face all his life. If only he were willing to die to his own sinful desires, he would taste the sweet resurrection power of God.

It didn't take a lot of faith for the Lord to rush to Samson's aid. We are told with great excitement in verse 22 that *"The hair on his head began to grow again after it had been shaved."* Yes, Samson had blown it. But no, that was not to be the final word. It is never too late to repent of our sin and start over again with God. Even in his dying moments, Samson would yet have a chance to put his faith in God and fulfil his life's calling.

The Lord used Samson's failure to gather all his enemies together in one room. The kings of the five Philistine cities threw a party to celebrate the capture of their greatest enemy. Together they worshipped the fertility god Dagon and boasted that the fall of Samson had proved once and for all that the gods of the Philistines were stronger than the Lord.[2] As they raised a toast to Dagon in his temple, they got so excited that they ordered the guards to go and fetch Samson. If they could make him perform like a monkey for their party guests, it would bring the house down.

This was the very moment that the Lord had prophesied. He had gathered all the leading Philistines into one place so that Samson could fulfil his divine destiny, even as he died.[3] With a hand on each of the two central pillars that supported the temple, Samson could hear the laughter of every Philistine who had made it on to the guest list for this cruel party.[4] He could tell from their voices that the temple was packed with

[2] Dagon means *Grain God* or *Fish God*. He was depicted as a merman – *"Upward man and downward fish"* (John Milton in *Paradise Lost*, 1.462–463). The Lord would clear up any illusions over his power in 1 Samuel 5.

[3] This is hugely encouraging. It assures us that the Lord is powerful enough to fulfil his purposes even through our sin. See Romans 8:28, or Genesis 38 and Matthew 1:3.

[4] There were 3,000 rank-and-file Philistines on the roof, but the big prize was inside the temple. It appears that almost every ruler, nobleman and army officer was there. Samson could decapitate a nation.

people and that the rooftop was crowded too. Filled with fresh faith in the God who keeps on giving, Samson prays for only the second time in the book of Judges: *"Sovereign Lord, remember me. Please, God, strengthen me just once more, and let me with one blow get revenge on the Philistines for my two eyes... Let me die with the Philistines!"*[5]

Suddenly the Holy Spirit strengthens Samson's arms once more. It only takes one push for him to bring the house down. Through a single moment of faith and a very simple prayer, the Lord turns Samson's failure into victory and fulfils his promises to him.

As Samson dies, betrayed, bound and mocked, with his arms outstretched, he becomes a prophetic pointer to the death of a far greater Judge of Israel. It points the way for us to follow him along the death-and-resurrection pathway that Jesus has hacked out for us. The statement that *"he killed many more when he died than while he lived"* invites us to consider the role that we have to play in the story of God's people too. If we live for ourselves, like Samson, we will remain weak, but if we are willing to die with Jesus and live for God we will be made strong. We will experience the resurrection power of God that Paul describes in Philippians 3:7–11:

> *I consider everything a loss because of the surpassing worth of knowing Christ Jesus my Lord, for whose sake I have lost all things. I consider them garbage, that I may gain Christ... I want to know Christ – yes, to know the power of his resurrection and participation in his sufferings, becoming like him in his death, and so, somehow, attaining to the resurrection from the dead.*

---

[5] This is only Samson's second prayer in four chapters. Like the one in 15:16, it confesses that his strength comes only from the Lord. Humility precedes victory. Spiritual death precedes resurrection power.

The Back of the Book
(Judges 17:1–13)

In those days Israel had no king; everyone did as they saw fit.

(Judges 17:6)

When I was studying Advanced Mathematics at school, my teacher made a schoolboy error. He didn't realize that our textbooks had the answers in the back and, as a class of sixteen-year-olds, we naturally didn't rush to tell him. Every time he set us homework, the entire class got full marks. When you can turn to the back of the book it's pretty easy.

Most readers find the final five chapters of the book of Judges baffling and confusing. That's such a shame, because they are like the back pages of my Advanced Mathematics textbook. They explain for us what the Lord has been trying to say through the lives of the twelve judges in the first sixteen chapters, so let's read them slowly together.

When we resist the urge to skim-read through these final chapters, we find an important answer in 20:27–28: *"In those days the ark of the covenant of God was there, with Phinehas son of Eleazar, the son of Aaron, ministering before it."* That's the same Phinehas we read about in Numbers 25 and Joshua 22, who was a young man when Joshua led the Israelites across the River Jordan. It means that the events recorded in these last five chapters took place within thirty years of the death of Joshua, during the days of Othniel, the first judge of Israel. They are not placed at the end of the book because they happened last, but because they spell out the book's message clearly: God keeps on giving to us even when we sin but, unless we repent, eventually we forfeit everything.

We also find a second answer in 18:1, 17:6, 19:1 and 21:25. Twice we are told that *"In those days Israel had no king"*, and twice that *"In those days Israel had no king; everyone did as they saw fit."* In case we miss the significance of this quadruple repetition, it also serves as the final verse of the book of Judges. The writer clearly wants to shock us with what happened under the twelve judges to persuade us that Israel needs a godly king instead. This makes perfect sense when we read who the Jewish Talmud claims wrote the book of Judges: *"Joshua wrote the book which bears his name and [the last] eight verses of the Pentateuch. Samuel wrote the book which bears his name and the Book of Judges and Ruth."*[1] Samuel had recently anointed a young man from Bethlehem to become king of Israel. That's why he starts these five chapters with what happened to a Levite from that same town to convince his readers that they need the man God has anointed to rule over them.

In 17:1–6, we see the corrosive effect of idolatry on Israel. It doesn't matter that Micah's mother has given him a name that means *Who is Like the Lord?* Her decision to commission a silver idol pollutes everything.[2] It doesn't matter that she tries to bless him in the name of the Lord. The curse she spoke over his thievery still stands. It doesn't matter that she promises to devote her thirteen kilograms of silver to the Lord.[3] The fact that she holds back four-fifths of it proves that her heart has

[1] Baba Bathra 14b, written in c.200 AD as a record of long-standing Jewish oral teaching. We know Samuel was a writer from 1 Samuel 10:25. He dies in 1 Samuel 25:1, so if the writer of the Talmud is correct then somebody else completed 1 and 2 Samuel for him – possibly Nathan or Gad (1 Chronicles 29:29).

[2] The Hebrew text of 17:3, 18:14 and 18:17 can either be translated *"an image overlaid with silver"* or *"a carved image and a cast idol"*. It is unclear whether she commissioned one big idol or two smaller ones.

[3] 1,100 shekels of silver is the same amount offered to Delilah in 16:5. It represents similar folly.

been led astray from him. These verses depict Israel's spiritual confusion and its need for the strong rule of a king.

In 17:7–13, we see how deep this spiritual confusion goes. The Lord had set apart the tribe of Levi to be the priestly tribe that preached his Word and kept the rest of Israel walking in obedience to his Law. This young Levite from David's hometown of Bethlehem therefore represents the best hope of revival for Israel, but he cares more about wandering in search of a fortune than about preaching in search of people's souls.[4] If the nation of Israel hopes to find salvation through its priestly classes, then this listless explorer shows how wrong they are. The writer insists that what Israel needs is a king.[5]

The young Levite ought to have taken one look at Micah's homemade shrine and rebuked him. It didn't matter that his mother had commissioned her silver idol out of a misguided desire to please the Lord.[6] Idolatry was idolatry, as the collection of sundry household gods that soon sprang up around it quickly proved. Nor did it matter that Micah had made a precious *ephod* to clothe his own son to serve as priest for him.[7] Installing an Ephraimite as priest instead of a Levite was strictly forbidden in the Law.[8] The Lord had called the tribe of Levi to study the Law of Moses and to teach the other tribes of Israel the right way to serve him, but this young Levite clearly hasn't done so. One glance at Micah's silver and the comforts of his shrine is all it

---

[4] Numbers 8:23–26 says that all Levite males aged 25–50 were to serve at the Lord's Tabernacle. This Levite had therefore already started wandering from obedience to the Lord before he drifted to the hills of Ephraim.

[5] The Levite is even more sinful than Micah, since his compromise leads Micah to believe he is in good standing with the Lord (17:13). Smooth-talking preachers are guiltier than those they deceive.

[6] Like Jephthah, her ignorance of God's Word makes her devotion fatally misguided (Exodus 20:4–6; Deuteronomy 27:15). It also makes her underestimate the power of her curse on her son (Genesis 27:33).

[7] The Hebrew word *'ēphōd* in 17:5 is the same word used for Gideon's idolatrous royal clothes in 8:27.

[8] Exodus 29:9; Numbers 3:10; 1 Kings 12:31; 13:33–34; Hebrews 5:4.

takes for him to throw away his calling. He takes Micah's money and humours his empty superstition, *"Now I know that the Lord will be good to me, since this Levite has become my priest."*

The Israelites still have faith of sorts in the Lord. Three times in this chapter Micah and his mother refer to him by his covenant name *Yahweh*. They both express fear that the Lord will carry out the curse that Micah's mother has spoken over him. They both betray a latent desire to live in the good of all that God has promised to their nation. They simply don't know how. They are superstitious rather than spiritual. They are deluded rather than devoted. They put their faith in the wrong deliverer from Bethlehem. Their priests and judges are unlikely to lead them back to the Lord. What they need is a king.

The young Levite quickly starts to reap the consequences of his sin. Micah promises to look to him as a spiritual *"father"* (17:10) but soon begins ordering him around like a *"son"* (17:11). Micah also starts to reap the consequences of his idolatry. He ends the chapter in a state of dangerous complacency, having hired a priest to say what he wants to hear and therefore unaware that judgment is about to fall on him in the next chapter.

These answers at the back of the book of Judges explain to us why things went so wrong for Israel during this period. Whenever people do *"what is right in their own eyes"*, it always spells disaster.[9] Only when we submit to the throne of God do we truly enjoy all the blessings of his Promised Land. The New Testament counterpart to the back of the book of Judges is what God speaks over King Jesus on the Mount of Transfiguration:

> *A voice came from the cloud, saying, "This is my Son, whom I have chosen; listen to him."* [10]

---

[9] The traditional translation of 17:6 and 21:25 – *"every man did what was right in his own eyes"* – links back to Samson's sin in 14:3 and 7: *"She is right in my eyes"*.

[10] Luke 9:35. There *was* a king in the period of the judges. It was the Lord himself.

Settlers (Judges 18:1–31)

In those days Israel had no king. And in those days the tribe of the Danites was seeking a place of their own where they might settle.

(Judges 18:1)

If Samuel wrote the book of Judges, he wrote it at a time when the Israelites had settled for the wrong kind of king.[1] They had grown impatient waiting for the messiah the Lord had promised them in the Law of Moses and had pressured Samuel into crowning a man named Saul instead. King Saul looked impressive, but his reign was a total disaster. Perhaps that's why this chapter spells out the dangers of settling for too little in God.

The chapter starts with a splinter group from the tribe of Dan giving up on capturing the land that Joshua has allocated to them.[2] *"In those days the tribe of the Danites was seeking a place of their own where they might settle, because they had not yet come into an inheritance among the tribes of Israel."* We need to read between the lines a little here, since Joshua 19:40–46 says that they were allocated the lush coastland around the port of Joppa. It was highly desirable, but that was precisely the problem. Sea

---

[1] Judges must have been written after the coronation of King Saul (or else it would make no sense to say, *"In those days Israel had no king"*), but before the coronation of David (since Jerusalem was still ruled by the Jebusites – see Judges 1:21 and 2 Samuel 5:6–10). The *captivity of the land* in 18:30 either refers to the horrific events of 1 Samuel 4 or to the Danites losing their city to northern raiders even before the time of Samuel.

[2] Only 600 Danite warriors are mentioned in 18:11 out of 64,400 counted in Numbers 26:42–43. Many of the Danites, such as Samson's family in Judges 13–16, remained in the western coastlands to fight.

Peoples from the island of Crete had landed all along the coast, eventually settling down and becoming better known as the Philistines.[3] This breakaway group of Danites began drifting across the Promised Land because they came to believe their land was unconquerable.[4] They are a picture of what happens whenever we lose faith in the Lord's promises. They give up on the fertile western coastlands of Israel and settle for a single city in the north instead.[5]

If Samuel wrote the book of Judges, then this was hugely important. The Philistines were not just history in his day. Having been defeated by Shamgar (3:3, 31), they had bounced back strongly to harass Israel during the days of Jephthah (10:7). Dealt a severe blow by Samson (13–16), they had staged a major comeback in the days of the thirteenth judge Eli (1 Samuel 4). One of Samuel's primary tasks as the fourteenth and final judge had been to rout them in battle (1 Samuel 7), yet King Saul had thrown that great victory away. The Philistines roamed unchecked under Saul (1 Samuel 13–31), so this chapter warns us that it never ends well for us when we run away from our enemies.[6]

Micah was a settler. He had traded in the God of Israel for a collection of metal idols. He had traded in the presence of the Lord at the Tabernacle at Shiloh for a manmade shrine in his spare bedroom. He had traded in the godly high priest Phinehas for a pay-as-you-go Levite from Bethlehem. He embodies the compromise of Israel under the judges, so note what happens to him. The wandering Danites recognize his priest's Bethlehem

---

[3] Amos 9:7; Jeremiah 47:4. The name *Philistine* simply means *Immigrant* and was a name given to the Sea Peoples by the native Canaanites.

[4] The Danites had already convinced themselves in 1:34 that Amorite chariots made the lowlands untakeable, so it was no big jump to start believing that Philistine spears made the highlands untakeable too.

[5] Joshua 19:47 laments their lack of faith, telling us literally that *"the territory of the Danites was lost to them."*

[6] It was only when Israel was ruled by King David that the Philistines were defeated once and for all.

accent, become curious and discover that he is a spiritual mercenary whose priestly services are for hire.[7] They gazump Micah by making his priest a higher offer. After all, who wouldn't prefer to serve as priest to a tribe than to a single household? To add insult to injury, the Levite steals Micah's ephod and his idols as he leaves. That's what always happens when we settle for false gods and fake religion. They always let you down when you need them most.[8] Micah is left out of pocket and all alone.

The Levite is also a settler. He has turned his back on the calling that God has given him and auctioned off his priestly services to the highest bidder. His eagerness in verse 6 to prophesy to the Danite soldiers whatever he knows they want to hear reveals how little he truly cares about speaking up for the Lord. The ease with which he waves goodbye to his little congregation in the hill country of Ephraim shows how little he truly cares for those he pretends to serve.[9] The Lord therefore judges him for settling for less than he was promised. Although the Danite soldiers promise to make him priest of their tribe, when they bump into the grandson of Moses they quickly decide to give the job to this better candidate instead.[10] So the Levite is

---

[7] They spot that his priest isn't a local in 18:3 because the Ephraimites had a distinctive accent (12:5–6).

[8] We see this clearly in Micah's pathetic cry in 18:24: *"You took the gods I made."* Manmade gods are easily lost and stolen. They can't even save themselves, let alone the fools who follow them.

[9] Church leaders reveal the same mercenary motives whenever they abandon too easily a small congregation to accept an offer from a bigger church elsewhere. When church leaders sell their services for hire, they sin. We cannot serve a salary and a vocation at the same time (Luke 16:13).

[10] 18:30 links with Exodus 2:21–22. *Manasseh* and *Moses* are only one letter different in Hebrew. Most Hebrew manuscripts say Jonathan was the son of *Manasseh*, but the Septuagint translators were convinced the text had been doctored to prevent the name of *Moses* from being sullied by association with his sinful grandson.

left out of pocket and alone too, and as we will see in the next chapter, God's judgment upon him is only just getting started.[11]

If Samuel wrote the book of Judges, this chapter asked some very urgent questions of its original readers. Like the Danites, would fear of the Philistines cause them to settle for less than all the land that God had promised them? Like Micah, would their neglect of the Scriptures cause them to settle for less than the true God of Israel? Like the Levite, would love of money and of an easy life cause them to settle for less than their divine calling? Settlers always suffer loss. Would the readers of Judges remember this and go out, determined to settle for nothing less than their entire Promised Land?

For readers in any generation, this chapter still poses urgent questions. All of us can easily settle for less than God has promised us. Twice the writer warns us that the people of Laish were slaughtered because they were *"at peace and secure... and had no relationship with anyone else"*.[12] If we grow complacent as Christians, forgetting we have an enemy, drifting from active church involvement, we are easy pickings for the Devil.

The writer also warns us that when we flee from troubles, they usually pursue us. The Danites who settled in the far north soon found that life was even harder there than it had been in the western coastlands. Although they renamed their city Dan, they soon grew weary of the long journey south to worship at the Tabernacle, and it soon became a centre for idolatry. As they drifted away from the Lord, their borderland location meant they suffered more frequent enemy raids than any other city.

---

[11] In ancient Hebrew culture, such a betrayal of hospitality was extremely serious. The Danites know this, which is why they put their warriors between their children and the men of Ephraim in 18:21.

[12] 18:7, 27–28. Laish means *Lion* and echoes Moses' prophecy in Deuteronomy 33:22. Its other name was Leshem, meaning *Precious Jewel* (Joshua 19:47).

Settling for less than God had promised didn't make their lives easier. Compromise always makes things harder.[13]

So this chapter ends with God's people needing fresh deliverance from the Lord, not from their enemies this time but from themselves. Their judges, their priests and their tribal leaders have failed to save them. They need God to send his messianic King.

---

[13] Dan was the northernmost city in Israel (20:1). Its promotion of idolatry (1 Kings 12:28–30) fulfilled Jacob's prophecy in Genesis 49:16–17 that Dan would become a snake within Israel.

Newsflash
(Judges 19:1–20:48)

"No. We won't go into any city whose people are not Israelites. We will go on to Gibeah."

(Judges 19:12)

Sometimes a terrible newsflash shocks a nation into some long-overdue soul-searching. Think of the student who was savagely raped in Nottingham, England, in 2011 because nobody was willing to give her the twenty pence she needed for the last bus home. Think of the fifteen-year-old girl in Chicago whose rape was broadcast on Facebook Live in 2017, without any of the viewers calling the police to help her. Think of the photo of a dead Syrian boy, washed up on the beach in Turkey in 2015, that persuaded the nations of Europe to open their borders to thousands of refugees fleeing from the civil war.

That's the kind of newsflash that gripped the nation of Israel a few years after the death of Joshua. The writer of Judges wants it to shock us and convince us that no human judge could ever truly deliver Israel from its sin. For the third time in three chapters, we are reminded that *"In those days Israel had no king."*[1] They need a different kind of Saviour.

Readers of Judges cannot agree on whether the Levite in 19:1–10 is the same man who double-crossed Micah in chapter 18. The writer of Judges never states it explicitly, but there are strong reasons for believing that it is. The population of

---

[1] When people betray the Lord, they soon betray one another too. Micah was betrayed by the Levite, who was betrayed by the Danites. The concubine betrays the Levite, and he betrays her to the mob.

Bethlehem at the time was less than a thousand people, so the chances of two different Levites travelling back and forth from there to the hill country of Ephraim were tiny. These final five chapters hang together as a single story, and in chapter 19 the story hits rock bottom.[2]

It is difficult for modern readers to imagine how sinful the ancient world regarded any betrayal of hospitality. This was a culture where fathers would rather see their own daughters raped than see it happen to a houseguest.[3] The Levite had committed a terrible crime in his culture when he betrayed and robbed a man who had received him into his home. When the Levite's concubine cheated on him, his neighbours must have nodded with approval. *What goes around comes around.* Betrayed by both the Danites and his concubine, in their eyes he was simply getting what he deserved for his crime.

In 19:11–30, the writer therefore shocks his Hebrew readers. The Levite has gone back to Bethlehem to fetch his unfaithful concubine. After finally persuading his reluctant father-in-law to let him return with her to the hill country of Ephraim, he is faced with a choice. He needs to seek protection inside a walled city before night falls, so should he seek refuge in Jerusalem, even though it is inhabited by pagan Jebusites, or should he press on to the Hebrew city of Gibeah, in the tribal lands of Benjamin? When he decides to put his faith in his fellow countrymen, something terrible occurs. The men of Benjamin surround the house to gang-rape the Levite.[4] To save himself he sends his concubine outside to be raped by the mob

---

[2] The deliberate symmetry of these five chapters also identifies them as a single story. The 600 Danites are mirrored by 600 Benjaminites. Micah's corruption of religion is mirrored by Gibeah's corruption of morals.

[3] 19:22–24. See also Genesis 19:4–8.

[4] *Sons of Belial* in 19:22 means literally *sons who will not bear a yoke*. The writer appears to see gay sex and sexual violence as two clear signs that people refuse to submit to God's Word and are hell-bent on doing what is right in their own eyes, regardless of what the Lord says (17:6; 21:25).

while he cowers inside in safety.[5] In the morning, he loads her corpse on his donkey, returns to the hill country of Ephraim, hacks her dead body up into twelve pieces and mails them to the twelve tribes of Israel. The entire nation is appalled at this outrage. *"Such a thing has never been seen or done, not since the day the Israelites came up out of Egypt. Just imagine! We must do something!"*

If Samuel wrote the book of Judges, he is doing something very clever here. You will miss it if you read these chapters too quickly. Bethlehem was the hometown of David and Gibeah was the hometown of Saul, so we are meant to see this as far more than a random act of sexual violence.[6] It is meant to remind readers that King Saul is the son of a depraved city.[7] He can never be the true Deliverer of Israel![8] They need a better king, one like the shepherd-boy that Samuel has just anointed in Bethlehem.

In 20:1–48, the Lord's judgment breaks out against Israel as a whole.[9] The nation descends into its first civil war. The tribe of Benjamin does the unthinkable by defending the sinful city of Gibeah. It decides that blood is thicker than water, unity more

[5] Although the Levite is going to the Tabernacle at Shiloh in 19:18, his persistent compromise has turned him into a monster. He literally *seizes* his concubine and throws her outside by force. He opens the door in the morning, not to go looking for her, but to continue his journey, commanding her gruffly, *"Get up; let's go."*

[6] 1 Samuel 10:26; 11:4; 15:34; 17:58; 20:6; 2 Samuel 21:6; Isaiah 10:29. Gibeah means *Hill*. Centuries later, the Lord would still refer to this event as a low point in Israel's history (Hosea 9:9; 10:9).

[7] The writer makes it clear that this rape was not an isolated sin. Under ancient rules of hospitality, it was outrageous that not a single man of Benjamin had offered to host the Levite when they saw him waiting in the town square. The fact that only an Ephraimite outsider offered him hospitality was a source of shame.

[8] Saul imitates the Levite's action in 1 Samuel 11:6–7 but soon proves he is every bit a man of Gibeah. He would be replaced by a man of Bethlehem who wholeheartedly followed the Lord.

[9] *Dan* was on Israel's northern border (18:28–29), *Beersheba* on its southern border and *Gilead* on its eastern border. See also 1 Samuel 3:20; 2 Samuel 3:10 and 24:2; 1 Chronicles 21:2 and 2 Chronicles 30:5.

precious than God's Law and tolerance the ultimate virtue. The other eleven tribes gather at the Tabernacle to purge this evil from their land, as commanded in Deuteronomy 13:12–18.[10] It is eleven tribes against one, and their soldiers outnumber those of Benjamin fifteen to one, so they feel confident. It ought to be an easy battle for them, yet they lose 40,000 soldiers in their first two attacks on Gibeah. The Lord uses this to bring them face to face with their own shortcomings. Only after they have repented of their own share in Israel's sin does he use them to inflict his judgment on their brothers.

In the third attack, they triumph. There are 45,600 warriors of Benjamin counted in the census of Numbers 26, and this is whittled down to only 600 men by the end of the fighting.[11] Their women and children are also butchered in the slaughter that follows the battle. One of the twelve tribes of Israel is virtually wiped out as a result of its sin.[12]

We still have one chapter left of the book of Judges, but its message is abundantly clear. God's people don't just need saving from their external enemies – they need saving from themselves. We have such a bias towards doing what is right in our own eyes that no human judge or priest or leader can ever truly deliver us. We need God to rescue us by sending an entirely different type of Saviour. Our only hope lies in his messianic King.

NEWSFLASH (JUDGES 19:1–20:48)

---

[10] Bēyth-ēl in 20:18–28 means house of God. It probably refers to the Tabernacle at Shiloh, not the city of Bethel.

[11] 26,700 soldiers mustered in 20:15 minus 25,100 soldiers killed in 20:35 does not equal 600. It appears that 1,000 men of Benjamin had already been killed in the first two days of fighting.

[12] Most of us are shocked by this violent judgment. To help us, the writer uses the Hebrew word hātā' in 20:16 for missing the mark, a word which also means sinning. We have missed the mark so often when it comes to God's commands that we forget how serious sin is and how resolute the Lord is to judge it (Genesis 18:25).

The Great Saviour
(Judges 21:1–25)

In those days Israel had no king; everyone did as they saw fit.

(Judges 21:25)

As he lay dying at the age of eighty-two, the great hymn writer John Newton whispered to a friend, *"My memory is nearly gone, but I remember two things: That I am a great sinner, and that Christ is a great Saviour."*[1] As the book of Judges draws to a close, we are reminded that it is a book which invites us to believe that what John Newton said is true.

The Israelites have amply proven John Newton's first statement. They have repeatedly shown us that the best people are still people at best. Barak trembled instead of trumpeting for battle. Gideon demanded sign after sign before he acted, then commissioned a set of special clothes to honour himself for his victory. Jephthah studied the Scriptures too selectively. Samson didn't study them at all. The men of Benjamin out-sinned the Canaanites and perished just like them. These twenty-one chapters are a catalogue of human sin and failure, so the writer ends the book of Judges by reassuring us that John Newton's second statement is equally true. The tribe of Benjamin deserves nothing but destruction, but the Lord has mercy on them to prove that our great sin is not the end of the story. We have an even greater Saviour.

Only 600 men survive from the entire tribe of Benjamin.

---

[1] See John Pollock's *Amazing Grace: John Newton's Story* (1981).

Not a single woman, child or old man is left – only the 600 warriors that managed to escape from the battlefield. What makes things worse is that the men of the other eleven tribes vowed before the battle that they would never give their daughters in marriage to any man of Benjamin who survived. These 600 survivors have therefore been robbed of any hope of having children to repopulate their tribe. The twelve tribes of Israel have been reduced to eleven. The victors go back from the battlefield to the Tabernacle, not to celebrate, but to grieve and mourn.[2] They plead with the Lord to have mercy on the defeated tribe of Benjamin. Yes, some of them needed to be punished as sex offenders and murderers. Yes, so did the rest for defending instead of judging them for their crime. Yes, they are great sinners, but isn't the Lord an even greater Saviour? Can't mercy triumph over judgment, even now? Can't the book of Judges have a happy ending?

It is almost too good to believe it when the Lord responds that indeed it can. After all that we have read about the sins of Israel, it ought to blow our minds to discover that both of John Newton's statements are equally true. It doesn't matter how great our sin is, Jesus Christ is an even greater Saviour. The writer of Judges points prophetically to him when he says that the Israelites slaughtered offerings and sacrificed them on the altar.

Even while they are repenting, the Israelites start sinning once more. They pray a loaded prayer, *"Why has this happened to Israel?"*, as if accusing the Lord of having been too harsh in his judgment.[3] Instead of waiting for him to reveal his solution to their dilemma, they devise their own solution. They vowed not to *give* their daughters to the men of Benjamin. They didn't say anything about not *stealing* each other's daughters! When

---

[2] As in 20:18 and 26, the Hebrew *bēyth-ēl* probably means *the house of God* – that is, the Tabernacle at Shiloh – rather than the city named Bethel.

[3] The Hebrew word *nāham* in 21:6 and 15 conveys that they *regretted* delivering God's judgment to Benjamin.

they realize that no warriors came to fight from Jabesh Gilead, a city in the territory of Manasseh east of the River Jordan, they hatch a hasty plan. Hadn't the Lord cursed the town of Meroz in Naphtali for its failure to fight in 5:23? Hadn't Gideon punished the Gadite towns of Sukkoth and Peniel for their failure to fight in 8:5–17? Hadn't the people of Jabesh Gilead therefore fallen under a similar curse in 21:5?[4] They slaughter the city and spare only its 400 virgin daughters for the men of Benjamin.[5]

Whenever we act out of our own wisdom instead of waiting for the Lord, we set ourselves up to fail, and so it proves for the eleven tribes of Israel. They need 600 wives for the men of Benjamin, which means they are still 200 short. Instead of waiting for the Lord's solution, they rush into a second quick-and-dirty plan of their own.[6] They inform the men of Benjamin that a festival is taking place to the Lord at his Tabernacle in Shiloh, and they promise to turn a blind eye if they kidnap the unmarried daughters of the pilgrims at the festival. Their first plan was at least defensible from Deuteronomy 13:12–18, but this second plan is entirely sinful.[7] The Lord isn't fooled by their semantics, as if conspiring to kidnap worshippers at the Tabernacle were somehow any less sinful than breaking the vow they made before battle. But this is the book of Judges all over. Even its so-called heroes are revealed to be villains.

---

[4] See Jeremiah 48:10 and Proverbs 18:9, which both teach that failure to resist sin means complicity in sin. Jabesh Gilead would suffer further in 1 Samuel 11, but when it rose up to defend the Lord's honour in 1 Samuel 31:8–13 David would replace its curse with a blessing in 2 Samuel 2:4–7.

[5] The writer is very gracious towards their soldiers, calling them *sons of valour* in the Hebrew text of 21:10 to contrast with the *sons of Belial* in 19:22. Even amid our sinful actions, God can sanctify us.

[6] Note that God says absolutely nothing in this chapter. The Israelites refuse to wait and listen.

[7] We are not told in this chapter that the men of Benjamin repented of their sin, only that the other tribes repented of having dealt so firmly with their sin. The slaughter of chapter 20 hasn't solved anything. Sin has spread across the whole of Israel and it will take more than a human judge to deliver them from it.

But John Newton was right. We are very great sinners, but we have an even greater Saviour. In spite of the sinful way in which they go about it, the Lord blesses the men of Benjamin and allows them to repopulate their tribe. These events took place during the days of Othniel (20:27–28), so Ehud was presumably among their children. Three centuries later, the Lord would use Saul, a man from Gibeah itself, to deliver Israel from the Ammonites in 1 Samuel 11. Perhaps most important of all, the apostle Paul also sprang forth from the sinful tribe of Benjamin.[8] Despite its sin, the Lord salvaged many deliverers from the wreckage of Benjamin. Only Levi and Judah produced more leaders.

That's how the Lord works. Even as the tribes of Israel disband their armies and return home to sin their way through the book of Judges, the Lord is devising a way to bless them in spite of their sin. The final verse of the book speaks of hope as well as judgment: *"In those days Israel had no king; everyone did as they saw fit"*. The writer has made it abundantly clear that Israel does not have it in them to produce a true deliverer. There isn't a sinless tribe, a sinless priest or a sinless judge. But this final verse pledges that God will send his people an altogether different type of Saviour – a messianic King.

The book of Judges has painted an ugly picture of God's people, but we have only half-understood it unless we also see in its pages a beautiful picture of God's Saviour. However great our failures, we can't out-sin the grace of the God who keeps on giving.

The message of the book of Judges is that both dying statements of John Newton are true. *"I remember two things: That I am a great sinner, and that Christ is a great Saviour."*

---

[8] Philippians 3:5. That is why he was originally named *Saul*. He was a proud man of Benjamin.

Ruth:

God's Gift to You

Fruitless (Ruth 1:1–5)

In the days when the judges ruled, there was a famine in the land.

(Ruth 1:1)

The Hebrews weren't always very good at naming different parts of the Bible. The book we know as Deuteronomy they called *Words*. The books we know as 1 and 2 Chronicles they called *Things About Days*. They grouped the book of Ruth, not alongside Joshua and Judges among the "Former Prophets", but in an appendix of books at end of the Old Testament that they unimaginatively named *The Additional Writings*. That's a terrible title, but it's a helpful insight. The book of Ruth was written as a supplement to Judges.[1]

The Jewish Talmud backs this up by claiming that the prophet Samuel wrote the book of Ruth to be read alongside Judges.[2] It is also backed up by the way its first verse refers to *"Bethlehem in Judah"*, a phrase used only six times in the Bible – twice in Judges 17, twice in Judges 19, here in Ruth and once in 1 Samuel 17:12. Many readers miss it, but *Bethlehem* is named more times in Judges, Ruth, and 1 and 2 Samuel than in the rest

---

[1] The four sections of the Hebrew Old Testament are the "Torah", the "Former Prophets", the "Latter Prophets" and the "Additional Writings". The fourth section of leftovers mingles wisdom literature with history.

[2] Baba Bathra 14b. Ruth complements Judges just as Chronicles complements Samuel and Kings. Ruth was written after Saul became king (since 1:1 treats *"the days when the judges ruled"* as history) but before David succeeded him (since 4:22 calls Jesse the father of *David*, not of *King David*). It was therefore written roughly at the same time as Judges, and its events took place three generations before the birth of David, in c.1120 BC.

of the Bible put together, binding those books tightly together.[3] In the book of Judges, the writer hints that a new king of Israel will arise from Bethlehem, but in the book of Ruth he names that king and explains how he will finally come. Ruth ends with a dramatic unveiling of the messiah. The final word of Ruth is *David*.

The book of Ruth isn't just more personal about Israel's new king. It is also much more personal about what that king means for the reader. Judges described the highs and lows of a nation across three centuries, whereas Ruth describes the highs and lows of one particular family in a town in Judah. Judges declares that God keeps on giving to sinners in general, whereas Ruth invites us to believe he will keep on giving specifically to us. The book of Judges is a war story, whereas the book of Ruth is a romance. The Lord uses it to woo us to believe that his promises are made to us personally.

The book of Ruth begins with a married couple named Elimelek and Naomi. They ought to have everything going for them. They are Ephrathites, descendants of the first Hebrew family to settle in Bethlehem. Elimelek's name means *My God Is King*, suggesting that his parents understood the principle that permeates the book of Judges. Naomi's name means *My Pleasant Girl* or *My Delight*, suggesting that her life is very joyful and fruitful.

But it isn't. It isn't at all. The opening verse of the book describes how Elimelek and Naomi are caught up in the sin and judgment of the book of Judges. Bethlehem means *House of Bread* and its fertile fields were meant to be the breadbasket of Israel, yet we are told that *"there was famine in the land"*. Ephrath, the other name for Bethlehem, means *Fruitful* yet its fields become so fruitless that eventually Elimelek and Naomi feel forced to abandon the Promised Land. They give up on the

---

Israelite Dream and set up home in the pagan land of Moab. They cross the River Jordan in the opposite direction to Joshua.

Their two sons were evidently ill from birth. The names Mahlon and Kilion mean *Sickly* and *Wasting Away*. They marry forbidden Moabite women yet neither of them manages to produce an heir in almost ten years of marriage. Elimelek dies and is buried in foreign soil, far away from the Promised Land. Mahlon and Kilion die shortly after their father. Naomi is left all alone with her foreign daughters-in-law. She finds herself utterly fruitless and bereft of hope, a haunting example of God's judgment on his sinful people.

The book of Ruth starts where the book of Judges left off: with sinful Israelites hitting rock bottom. Although it sounds depressing, the Lord starts here so that he can paint a vivid picture of how he draws sinful people back to himself. It shows what we are to do if we want him to help us at a time when most people have turned their backs on him.

First, we are to recognize that the Lord is still in control. One of the most striking contrasts between Judges and Ruth is that the shorter book speaks very sparingly about God. The characters in the book refer to him, but the narrator rarely does. He stops himself from doing so to open our eyes to how much the Lord is doing all around us, undetected in the background. One of the best examples of this is when the narrator says literally in 2:3 that Ruth *"happened by chance"* to end up in the fields of Boaz. This book stirs our faith to believe that the Lord is fully in control of the events in our own lives too.

Second, we are to recognize that our periods of fruitlessness come from the Lord. When things get tough for us personally, it doesn't mean God's promises have failed. When a town whose two names meant *House of Bread* and *Fruitfulness* became a famine-stricken wasteland, it didn't indicate that the Lord had given up on it. It indicated that he had a far greater gift to give it, and that he was determined to drive Naomi to her knees so that he could grant something far better than bread to Bethlehem in response to her prayers. Had Naomi not given up on the fields of Judah, she would never have converted a Moabite woman. Had the barns of Bethlehem been full, she would never have brought home the true Bread of Life to one of its mangers.[4]

Third, we are to recognize that, if we repent and keep placing our faith in the Lord's promises, periods of decline can lead into periods of revival. Naomi sinned by chasing after Moab as a manmade solution to Israel's problems.[5] She brought down God's judgment on herself by marrying her sons to forbidden Moabite women.[6] She isn't exaggerating when she laments in verse 13 that *"the Lord's hand has turned against me!"* She is being spiritually perceptive. But no matter how great our sins, they are never greater than our Saviour. Things look pretty bleak in these first five verses, but it only takes a mustard seed of faith to quickly turn around the fortunes of Naomi's family.

So if you feel fruitless, don't despair. Instead be encouraged. The Lord may well be trying to drive you to your knees so that he can bless you with a new type of fruitfulness that is far better.[7] Stay in the place where he has put you, cry out for him to help you and then wait patiently for the God who keeps on giving to make you genuinely fruitful.

---

[4] Matthew 1:5; 2:1–8; Luke 2:1–12; John 6:35, 48–51.

[5] There is no record of Elimelek and Naomi actually praying in these opening verses. Whenever Christians or churches chase manmade alternatives to prayer, it always results in spiritual death for them.

[6] Numbers 25:1–3; Deuteronomy 23:2–6; Nehemiah 13:1–3, 23–27.

[7] God used Rachel and Hannah's barrenness to make them pray hard for the birth of Joseph, the saviour-son of Jacob, and for the birth of Samuel, the saviour-judge of Israel (Genesis 30:1, 22–24; 1 Samuel 1).

*When Naomi heard in Moab that the Lord had come
to the aid of his people by providing food for them,
she and her daughters-in-law prepared to return
home.*

(Ruth 1:6)

Many readers draw a parallel between Naomi in Ruth 1 and the Prodigal Son in Luke 15. In the famous parable of Jesus, the young man also leaves the Promised Land to seek his fortune in a far-off foreign land. He grieves his father just as much as Naomi grieved the Lord when she took idolatrous foreign women as wives for her two Hebrew sons. Like Naomi in the land of Moab, the young man finally comes to his senses when his raging hunger reminds him of happier times back in the Promised Land. Verse 6 marks a turning point for Naomi: *"When Naomi heard in Moab that the Lord had come to the aid of his people by providing food for them, she and her daughters-in-law prepared to return home."*

The writer wants us to see this as a moment of repentance for Naomi. The Hebrew word he uses here for food is *lehem*, which means literally *bread*. She isn't merely going back to Bethlehem in the land of Judah; she is renewing her faith in the Lord to feed her in the *House of Bread*. As she sends her Moabite daughters-in-law back to their parents, she blesses them twice in the name of Yahweh, the God of Israel: *"May the Lord show you kindness… May the Lord grant that each of you will find rest in the home of another husband."* Like the Prodigal Son in the parable, she sets off back down the road in trepidation, hoping to find forgiveness and a fresh start with the Lord.

If Naomi reminds us of the Prodigal Son, her daughters-in-law remind us of the two sons in another parable of Jesus.[1] In Matthew 21:28–32, one son says yes to serving his father but later changes his mind. His brother says no to serving his father but later repents and decides to serve him after all. Kilion's widow is named Orpah, meaning *Gorgeous*, and the legal declaration in 4:9 says she was married to Naomi's firstborn.[2] She is like the son who says yes to helping his father in the parable. She weeps as loudly as Ruth in verse 9 and choruses with her in verse 10 that *"We will go back with you to your people."* But she doesn't follow through on her profession of faith in Naomi and her God. When her mother-in-law points out that she has no more sons for her to marry, Orpah's faith begins to falter.[3] When Naomi worries that *"The Lord's hand has turned against me!"*, Orpah thinks it is his final word. She goes back to her parents and their pagan gods.

Ruth means *Friend*, and she is more faithful to Naomi than her sister-in-law. She does not merely promise to go back to the Promised Land with her. She is so determined to make this choice that she renounces her parents, her nation and her idols to side squarely with Naomi and her God. This is massive, because throughout the Old Testament Moab is an archenemy of Israel. Yet Ruth uses the covenant name Yahweh, which we translate into English as the Lord, to insist that she now views

---

[1] We are meant to see this scene as a Gospel picture. It doesn't matter how much we profess to follow Jesus; what matters is whether we actually do. Orpah held back from giving up her old life and lost everything. Ruth died to her old life to know God and gained everything. See Matthew 16:24–25.

[2] Orpah literally means *Neck* but we can tell from Song of Songs 4:4 that to the ancient world that meant *Gorgeous*. Ruth 4:10 says that she was Kilion's widow and Ruth Mahlon's widow.

[3] The Lord commanded Hebrew men to take care of an older brother's widow by marrying her instead (Deuteronomy 25:5–10; Genesis 38:1–11). This concept of "levirate marriage" is important later on in Ruth.

herself as an Israelite: *"Where you go I will go, and where you stay I will stay. Your people will be my people and your God my God. Where you die I will die, and there I will be buried. May the Lord deal with me, be it ever so severely, if even death separates you and me."*[4] This is one of the most memorable scenes in the book of Ruth, as two women make two very different choices.

We have already noted the theme that runs through Joshua and Judges of women having greater faith in God's promises than their men. Aksah is more eager than Othniel to ensure that their family gets its full allocation of land. The daughters of Zelophehad are more eager than half the tribesmen of Manasseh to gain a full allocation of land west of the Jordan. Deborah needs to mother Barak and the other tribal leaders into challenging the status quo. While Barak dithers, Jael kills a Canaanite with a tent peg. So Ruth joins the long line of women in these three books who have more faith than the men around them that the God of Israel is the God who keeps on giving.

Note the way the writer presents Ruth's courageous choice as more than simple loyalty to her mother-in-law.[5] He presents it as a conversion from serving Chemosh, the god of Moab, to serving the Lord God of Israel – *your God will be my God.*[6] He presents it as a desire to be numbered among the people of the Lord and not among the pagans – *your people will be my people.* He presents it as a longing to live and die in the Promised Land – *where you die I will die, and there I will be buried.* At a time when the men of Israel were abandoning the Lord, giving up on the Promised Land and running after pagan idols, Ruth abandons her pagan idols, gives up on her homeland and runs after the

---

[4] Used throughout the Old Testament, this was a deadly serious oath in Hebrew. It means, *May the Lord strike me down with every weapon in his arsenal if my actions fail to match my words.*

[5] The Hebrew word translated *determined* in 1:18 is *'āmats*, which means literally *to be bold* or *brave*.

[6] Numbers 21:29; 1 Kings 11:7; 2 Kings 23:13. Chemosh demanded human sacrifice (2 Kings 3:26–27).

Lord! He is so delighted with her faith that he commissioned a book of the Bible to be written about her.

Meanwhile, news spreads like wildfire across Bethlehem that its Prodigal Daughter has returned. The young man in the parable has a speech rehearsed in his head: *"Father, I have sinned against heaven and against you. I am no longer worthy to be called your son; make me like one of your hired servants."* Naomi's speech is far less repentant. She points a finger at God for her troubles: *"The Lord's hand has turned against me!"* Instead of facing up to the sin she committed when she abandoned the Promised Land and took pagan wives for her sons, she tells the women of Bethlehem, *"Don't call me Naomi [which means My Pleasant One]. Call me Mara [which means Bitter], because the Almighty has made my life very bitter. I went away full, but the Lord has brought me back empty. Why call me Naomi?"* The Prodigal Daughter has returned to Bethlehem, but she has not yet returned to the Lord. Her final words in this chapter are a complaint rather than a confession: *"The Lord has afflicted me; the Almighty has brought misfortune upon me."*[7]

Instead of getting angry at her lack of repentance and faith, in his mercy and compassion the Lord starts to unfold a series of events that will draw Naomi back to himself. He finds two things he can work with. First, she just called him *"the Lord"* and *"the Almighty"*, so she has a bit more faith in him than she pretends. Second, the pagan convert who has come back with her from Moab has a more radical faith than her mother-in-law. He will use these things to teach the Prodigal Daughter that he is the God who keeps on giving. The chapter ends with words of hope: the barley harvest is beginning. Naomi's empty life is about to be filled.[8]

---

[7] Naomi accuses him literally of *doing evil* to her in 1:21. Her claim that she went away from Bethlehem full is ridiculous – she left Bethlehem because there was a famine and her stomach was empty!

[8] The barley harvest began in Israel in late March or early April. Spring has sprung for Naomi.

The Outsider (Ruth 2:1–18)

"Why have I found such favour in your eyes that you notice me – a foreigner?"

(Ruth 2:10)

When the Paris newspaper *Le Monde* compiled a list of the hundred greatest books of the twentieth century, the list was topped by the Albert Camus classic *The Outsider*. That's how Ruth felt as she set foot for the first time in Naomi's hometown of Bethlehem.

For a start, Ruth was a woman in a male-dominated world. We can tell that from verses 9 and 22, which hint that a woman found out alone in the fields was likely to be sexually assaulted.[1] We can also tell it by looking at a list of the books of the Bible. Thirty-eight books contain the name of a man in their title. Only two contain the name of a woman.

Ruth was also an outsider by race. She wasn't just a foreigner. She was a hated Moabite, the result of Lot's drunken incest with his daughter. She came from a nation which worshipped idols that demanded infant sacrifice, and which had once sent its women to seduce the Hebrew men away from their wives to worship those bloodthirsty idols too. Because of her nation's depravity, Ruth and any children she bore would be banned to the tenth generation from coming anywhere near the Lord's Tabernacle at Shiloh. She belonged to a race that had tried to steal the Promised Land from Israel in the days of Ehud, so she knows that the gossips of Bethlehem don't want her living there

---

[1] What happened in Judges 19 wasn't a one-off. Sexual assault was clearly rife in the days of the judges.

now. The writer emphasizes her sense of rejection by referring to her as *"Ruth the Moabite"* at both the start and the end of this chapter. She is a complete outsider to the promises of God.[2]

One of the big themes of the book of Ruth is that God loves to call outsiders in from the cold. What she lacked in ethnic pedigree she made up for in faith.

She had really meant it when she swore to Naomi on the road back to Bethlehem that she was renouncing the gods of Moab to become a worshipper of the Lord. This was a time when most Israelites neglected the Scriptures, so note how eagerly Ruth grabs hold of one of the promises in the Law of Moses. In Leviticus and Deuteronomy, the Lord had forbidden harvesters from going back over the fields to gather any crops they missed the first time around. These and any gleanings dropped by the harvesters were to be left as scraps for the widows and foreigners who went out scavenging behind them.[3] For those of us who are used to a welfare state, it doesn't sound like much of a promise, but Ruth grabbed hold of it with both hands. It was a back-breaking and humiliating task, but she works hard from morning to evening, taking only one short rest in the shade.

Ruth also meant it on the road back to Bethlehem when she renounced the land of Moab for the Promised Land. Having sworn to Naomi that she will be buried in Israelite soil, she now finds her salvation in the fruit of the land that Joshua conquered. There is a reason why Jewish communities around the world still read the book of Ruth aloud at their early harvest festival, known to Christians as Pentecost. The book of Ruth is as much about the Promised Land as Joshua and Judges. Ruth loves it more than do most Israelites.[4]

---

[2] Genesis 19:30–38; Numbers 25:1–4; Deuteronomy 23:2–6.

[3] Leviticus 19:9–10; 23:22; Deuteronomy 24:19–22. It wasn't exactly a handout, but this provision in the Law ensured that outsiders had a way into Israel's harvests and didn't need to starve.

[4] Ruth does not view hard work in the fields as somehow beneath her. Without insisting that her mother-in-law pull her weight by helping too, she sees it as an

Ruth also meant it on the road back to Bethlehem when she declared that she now viewed herself as part of God's people. The Hebrew word for the *grace* of God is *hēn*, so it's significant that Ruth uses this word in verses 2, 10 and 13 to describe her search for *grace* or *favour* among the Israelites. At a time when most of them are giving up on their national faith, Ruth places all hope of salvation in God's promises to his people.

The writer begins in this way to unveil the Lord's plan to bring this outsider in from the cold. He starts by teasing us, saying literally in verse 3 that *it happened by chance* that she ended up in the fields of Boaz. A similar Hebrew phrase is used in 1 Samuel 6:9, where it is translated *"it happened to us by chance"*.[5] It is a tongue-in-cheek statement, like the one in Acts 17:17 that says Paul's strategy for converting the city of Athens was to reason *"in the market-place day by day with those who happened to be there"*. The writer provokes us to recognize that there is no such thing as coincidences, only God-incidences. He wants to teach us that, through events all around us, God is constantly calling outsiders home.[6]

The Lord accomplishes this through the man who owns the fields where she is foraging. Note how much their first meeting identifies Ruth as an outsider. When Boaz enquires about her background, it comes twice in a single sentence: *"She is the Moabite who came back from Moab with Naomi."* When he expresses unexpected kindness towards her, it comes a third time in her reply: *"Why have I found such favour in your eyes that you notice me – a foreigner?"*[7] The writer wants us to see this as a personal invitation. It doesn't matter where you've been, it

honour to reap the fruit of Israel's soil.

[5] This is another clue that the writer of Judges and Ruth also wrote much of 1 Samuel.

[6] 2 Samuel 14:14 says God *"devises ways so that a banished person does not remain banished from him"*.

[7] There is no sense of entitlement in Ruth's voice. That chases away God's blessing. Because she humbles herself, Boaz invites her to dinner and feeds her so well that she even takes home a doggy bag to Naomi.

doesn't matter what you've done and it doesn't matter who you are. The God who keeps on giving loves to welcome outsiders in from the cold.

The best Ruth imagines she can hope for from the Lord is some leftover corn. But he does more than fill her basket with produce. He introduces her to a person. Boaz reaches out to the migrant worker in his fields as *"my daughter"*, providing her with free water and a team of bodyguards. Although she works tirelessly in his fields, don't miss Naomi's surprise when she returns home with thirteen kilograms of barley. The older woman recognizes that no worker could ever gather that much in their own strength. Ruth has clearly been helped by a man who embodies the lavish generosity of the Lord.

So be encouraged when Boaz tells Ruth that the Lord loves to bring outsiders home. Treat his words as a personal promise to you: *"May you be richly rewarded by the Lord, the God of Israel, under whose wings you have come to take refuge."* Be encouraged that the God who welcomed Rahab out of the ruins of Jericho, who welcomed the Gibeonites out of the slaughter of Canaan, and who welcomed Jael out from among the nomadic allies of Israel's enemies – the Lord God, who keeps on giving to his people throughout Joshua and Judges – now reaches out to you personally and welcomes you as one of his own.

> *"That man is our close relative; he is one of our guardian-redeemers."*
>
> (Ruth 2:20)

Boaz is an anomaly within the pages of Joshua, Judges and Ruth. He is a man of faultless character. As we have seen in these three books, such men are few and far between.

Joshua served the Lord wholeheartedly, but he failed to check the small print before signing a peace treaty and forgot to raise up a successor. Othniel grew lazy, Gideon grew proud, Jephthah sacrificed his daughter and Samson was a colossal underachiever. Boaz is the only man we meet in the pages of these three books of the Bible who appears to be flawless. It's that way for a reason. We are meant to regard him as a prophetic pointer to the perfect Judge who would one day come and bring salvation to Israel.

It helps if we understand a bit about the Law of Moses here. One of its clearest prophecies about the Great Deliverer surrounds the Hebrew word *gō'ēl*, which means *guardian-redeemer*. It is a noun that comes from the Hebrew verb God uses in Exodus 6:6 to describe his longing to redeem Israel from the hands of their harsh slave-masters in Egypt. In the stipulations of the Law, it reveals his desire to keep on giving to his people. If an Israelite fell on such hard times that he lost his share in the Promised Land, then his closest relative was to act as his *gō'ēl* by buying back his land for him (Leviticus 25:25). If the Israelite fell still further and was forced to sell himself into slavery, then that close relative was to act as his *gō'ēl* again by paying the redemption price to set him free (Leviticus 25:47–49). If the Israelite were murdered, his close relative was to act as his *gō'ēl* by hunting down his killer and enforcing the death penalty prescribed by the Law (Joshua 20:5). His *gō'ēl* was to be both his "*guardian-redeemer*" and his "*avenger of blood*".

The Law of Moses also commanded that the *gō'ēl* perform another duty, and this is one of the great themes of the book of Ruth.[1] If an Israelite died without children, the Law commanded his close relative to marry his widow and have a son with her to preserve the dead man's lineage in Israel. This ensured that his family would not die out and lose its share in the Promised Land (Deuteronomy 25:5–6), but it came at a heavy price. If the dead man owned property or was owed debts, it was advantageous for the *gō'ēl* to fulfil his duties as guardian-redeemer and avenger of blood (Numbers 5:6–8). But if the *gō'ēl* was rich and the widow was poor then it was very costly, since their son would bear the dead man's name yet have a claim to inherit the property of the *gō'ēl* (Ruth 4:6).

Enough of the lecture in law. In verse 20, we see this theory in practice. The only thing that surprises Naomi more than the thirteen kilograms of barley Ruth has managed to gather in a single day is the name of the man in whose fields she has gathered it. Boaz is a *gō'ēl* to her family. Suddenly she sees the hand of God behind what was described, tongue-in-cheek, as a coincidence in verse 3. Suddenly Naomi dares to hope that the Lord might yet restore her fortunes. Boaz is one of the men that God's Law calls to act as a guardian-redeemer to Elimelek and Mahlon's widows in their hour of need.

That's why Boaz is presented as the only squeaky-clean Israelite in these three books of the Bible. It is because the Lord himself pledges to act as a *gō'ēl* to his people in Job 19:25, Psalm

---

[1] The Hebrew words *gō'ēl (redeemer)*, *ge'ullāh (redemption)* and *gā'al (to redeem)* occur 23 times in Ruth.

19:14 and Proverbs 23:11. Boaz is a prophetic pointer to Jesus, the great Redeemer. His kindness speaks of the God who keeps on giving, even when we sin against him.

Boaz means *In Him Lies Strength*. He is described literally in verse 1 as *"a mighty man of valour"*. Although the nation of Israel has largely rejected the Lord and run off after idols, Boaz greets his workers with the blessing, *"The Lord be with you!"* and encourages them to reply, *"The Lord bless you!"* While many men in Israel think nothing of sexually assaulting women (or even men, in the case of Gibeah), Boaz treats with impeccable virtue the beautiful yet vulnerable foreigner who has come to work in his fields.[2] We are meant to see the righteousness of Jesus in the way he acts towards her.

We are also meant to see the unquenchable love that Jesus extends towards sinners. When Boaz discovers that the beautiful woman who has caught his eye is a foreigner, he does not reject her. He invites her to drink from his water jars during the day and to feast at his table in the evening. He lavishes mercy on her, even commanding his harvesters to harvest badly so that she can return home with extra barley. Instead of rejecting her as an outsider, he becomes the saviour who brings her in from the cold.

It is hard to know how much prophetic detail the Lord inspired in this chapter. Take for example verse 14, where Boaz tells Ruth to *"Come over here. Have some bread and dip it in the wine vinegar."* That's an odd piece of detail to throw into what is quite a punchy story. Surely it's enough simply to tell us that Boaz invited Ruth to dinner? Why emphasize that bread and wine are on the menu? Could it be an ancient precursor to the moment when Jesus explained the significance of the bread and wine at the Last Supper? *"This is my body given for you... This cup*

---

[2] Ruth 2:9 and 22 reflect the dangers of living in the nation described in Judges 19:22.

is the new covenant in my blood, which is poured out for you."[3] As Boaz invites Ruth in from the cold, he points forward to a greater Redeemer.

This is not going to be a marriage of equals. Boaz addresses Ruth as *"my daughter"*, not sister, because she is significantly younger than he is.[4] The final verse of the chapter also reminds us that being a foreign migrant worker also places her at a huge disadvantage. Her spell as a pauper in the fields of Boaz can only last for the three months of the barley and wheat harvests, from late March through to early June. After that, she is back on her own. Ruth has nothing to offer Boaz other than her faith in the God of Israel, but Boaz finds this faith gloriously attractive:

> *"I've been told all about what you have done for your mother-in-law since the death of your husband – how you left your father and mother and your homeland and came to live with a people you did not know before. May the Lord repay you for what you have done. May you be richly rewarded by the Lord, the God of Israel, under whose wings you have come to take refuge."*

May you be richly rewarded for your faith too, as you see a better Guardian-Redeemer in these verses than Boaz. May you be rewarded as you treat the book of Ruth as God's personal invitation to you. May you be rewarded as you put your faith in better bread and wine than those given to Ruth by Boaz. May you enjoy discovering that, in Jesus of Nazareth, the Lord has given you a far better *gō'ēl* who welcomes you back home.

---

[3] Luke 22:19–20. Although we are speculating, Psalm 110 and Hebrews 7 are clearer that the *"bread and wine"* offered by Melchizedek to Abraham in Genesis 14:18–20 prophesied about Jesus' body and blood.

[4] 2:8 hints at a big age gap; 3:10 states it explicitly.

It's Your Move (Ruth 3:1–9)

"Spread the corner of your garment over me, since you are a guardian-redeemer of our family."

(Ruth 3:9)

In March 2014, three students from New York State University bought a beaten-up sofa at a Salvation Army store. Taking it home to their apartment, they noticed it was strangely lumpy. Unzipping one of the arms, they found an envelope hidden inside containing $4,000. When they hurriedly unzipped the other arm and the cushions, they discovered several more. Altogether their $20 charity-store sofa yielded $40,800.

The students were honest. Finding an address on one of the envelopes, they drove to the house that had donated the sofa to the Salvation Army. It belonged to a ninety-one-year-old woman, whose daughter found the couch uncomfortable and decided to throw it away, completely unaware that her ageing mother had hidden her life savings inside.[1]

Tragically, many people treat God's promise of redemption a little like that daughter. They treat it like a shabby couch instead of as the offer of a lifetime. They settle for something far less than the Promised Land God wants to give them. Some people disbelieve the Gospel message, complaining that it sounds too good to be true. Other people believe it but do little about it. That's why the message of Ruth 3 is: *It's your move.*

Three months have passed since Ruth met Boaz for the

---

[1] This story and the quote at the end of the chapter were reported in the British newspaper *The Guardian* on 16th May 2014. The grateful woman gave the honest students $1,000 as a reward.

first time. The final verse of chapter 2 informs us that the barley and wheat harvests have now come in. Boaz has not made any formal move to rescue the two widows from their poverty. He has looked into the legal situation and discovered that it isn't his place to take the initiative. Besides, he wants Ruth to choose him as her guardian-redeemer because she truly loves him, not just because she is poor and he is rich and single. Boaz reflects the way that Jesus refuses to force us to accept his sacrifice for us. He waits for Ruth to ask him to save her.

In verses 1–6, Naomi tells Ruth that it is now or never. Boaz is winnowing the last of the harvest on his threshing-floor. In ancient Israel, after grain had been separated from the stalk by crushing it with a thick-toothed threshing-board, it was thrown into the air so that the chaff would blow away and only the edible part would fall back to ground. The key point here is that this was one of the final actions of the harvest season. Once it was completed, harvest-time was over. If Ruth did not act quickly to lay hold of the redemption God was offering her, then her days in the sunshine with Boaz would come to an abrupt end. There is a time for hearing and considering the Gospel, but there also comes a time for making a speedy and definite decision.[2]

Ruth does as her mother-in-law tells her.[3] Instead of resisting her Gospel cajoling, she swallows her pride, takes a bath, puts on her best clothes and slaps on some perfume.[4] It is going to be hard enough for a foreign pauper to reach out to a rich Israelite, without the smell of three months' labour in the harvest fields filling the evening air.

---

[2] Naomi uses a Hebrew perfect tense in 3:2 to point out that Ruth *has been working* in the fields. Now harvest is over. If Ruth fails to lay hold of her redeemer now, she is likely to end up dying a pauper.

[3] We are meant to spot a deliberate contrast here between *"everyone did as they saw fit"* (Judges 17:6; 21:25) and *"she did everything her mother-in-law told her to do"* (Ruth 3:6).

[4] Ruth corrects the misuse of 1 Peter 3:1–6 to forbid women from wearing fine clothes, jewellery, make-up and perfume. Pursuit of inner beauty does not mean neglect of outer beauty. Dowdiness is not godliness.

Boaz has been celebrating the end of a successful harvest with his workers. Eventually he lies down at the far end of the grain pile (no farmer would leave his pile unguarded for robbers to snatch in the night) and quickly drops off into a contented sleep. There is a time for praying and a time for acting, and Ruth knows the difference between the two. Remembering the words of Boaz to her in 2:12, she makes it clear to him that she expects him to be the agent of the Lord's redemption towards her. Boaz had blessed her, *"May you be richly rewarded by the Lord, the God of Israel, under whose wings you have come to take refuge"*, so Ruth decides to take refuge under the end of his blanket. She does not see her prayers as a reason to hold back from asking Boaz to redeem her. She sees them as a springboard to help her reach the handle on this great door of opportunity.

Boaz awakes with a start. He can't see in the dark who is tugging at his bedclothes. It's time for Ruth to make her move, and she uses the right Hebrew word to make it. The word translated *"corner of your garment"* in 3:9 is *kānāph*, the same word that Boaz used in 2:12 to describe salvation coming out from under the Lord's *wings*. It is the same word that is used in Malachi 4:2 to prophesy that healing redemption will flow out from the *wings* of the coming Messiah. Little grasping the full importance of the prophetic picture she is painting, Ruth begs Boaz, *"Spread the corner of your garment over me, since you are a guardian-redeemer of our family."*

Boaz has been waiting for three months for Ruth to make a move of faith towards him. He instantly promises to help her and even tries to make her feel better about having needed to come begging at his bedside. Ruth can surely not be fooled when he expresses his surprise that she has chosen to direct her love towards him instead of one of the younger Israelite men who are closer to her own age. She cannot truly think that she, a foreign widow and a pauper, is doing anyone a favour by her willingness to marry the rich Boaz. Even so, the writer uses the generosity of Ruth's *gō'ēl* to encourage us that if we make a move of faith towards Jesus, he will always make several moves of kindness back to us.

Boaz reveals to Ruth that he has spent the past three months doing his legal homework. He has discovered that he is not the only guardian-redeemer of her family. There is another man, who is more closely related to Naomi's dead husband Elimelek than he is. A reluctant saviour might have used this as an excuse to wash his hands of Ruth's dilemma, but not Boaz. He pledges to do all he can to marry Ruth in the morning, sending her back home with a generous gift of barley in lieu of an engagement ring.

"We put it all on a bed," revealed the New York students who bought the battered sofa at the Salvation Army store. *"We laid it all out and started counting. And we were screaming. In the morning, our neighbours were like, 'We thought you won the lottery!'"*

We have won something far better than the lottery. These verses prophesy to us that we have won the affections of God's Son. He eagerly desires to be our Guardian-Redeemer. So let's respond with greater excitement than those students. Jesus says: *It's your move.*

The Avengers Assemble
(Ruth 3:10–4:12)

So the guardian-redeemer said to Boaz, "Buy it yourself." And he removed his sandal.

(Ruth 4:8)

In the first half of this chapter, it is Ruth's move. In the second half and in the whole of chapter 4, Boaz is in the driving seat instead. The minute she asks him to become her guardian-redeemer, he flies into action. He is determined to marry her that day.

Few readers stop to wonder how life must have felt for Boaz before Ruth came down to his threshing-floor. They married young in the ancient world, but Ruth must have been aged around thirty.[1] That meant Boaz was aged over forty, so how many times must he have cried out to the Lord for a wife during that time? How many times must he have shouted angrily at the night sky and asked why the God of Israel had provided a wife for his friends but not for him? Suddenly he realizes that God's delays are often God's blessings. The Lord had the perfect wife waiting for him all along, but he wanted to give him far more than just a marriage. Boaz can smell destiny in the early morning air.

Lesser men might have been concerned for their own reputation. If news got out that a woman had come down to the threshing-floor and slipped under his blanket, the tongues would start wagging across Bethlehem. Boaz doesn't care.

---

[1] We are not told explicitly in 1:1–5 that Ruth and Mahlon were married for the whole ten years that Naomi lived in Moab, but the implication is that they were married for the bulk of that time.

He knows that he will lay his reputation on the line for Ruth anyway later on that day.[2] He treats her with absolute purity, allowing her to sleep at his feet all night and then sending her back home before the harvesters wake up on the other side of the threshing-floor. Naomi takes a look at the shawl full of barley that she has brought home, and she quizzes Ruth carefully. She assures her daughter-in-law that it's now time for Boaz to take the wheel. She is confident that *"The man will not rest until the matter is settled today."*[3]

Boaz rushes from the threshing-floor to Bethlehem.[4] Forget the rallying cry of the Marvel comic-book superheroes: this is the real moment when the avengers assemble. Boaz waits until he sees his rival walking through the town gate, then he lays hold of ten of the town elders. He demands that they pass judgment on the two of them.[5] Which *gō'ēl*, which *avenger of blood*, which *guardian-redeemer* will be permitted to step into the shoes of Elimelek and his two dead sons? Until now the rival suitor has not expressed any interest in helping revive the fortunes of his dead relative, but when he learns that it might earn him a cheap piece of land he is suddenly interested after all. Boaz saw that one coming. He has spent the past three months doing his legal homework, which is why he called ten of the elders of Bethlehem to witness this conversation. He points out to his rival that the land is cheap for a reason. Whoever purchases it

[2] The Hebrew phrase used to describe Ruth in 3:11 also describes the *"wife of noble character"* in Proverbs 31:10. It is the female equivalent of the Hebrew phrase that describes Boaz as *"a man of standing"* in 2:1. He is confident that no one would believe any gossip spread about them.

[3] All four chapters of Ruth end on a cliff-hanger: *It's harvest-time… Harvest is nearly over… It will end with a marriage… That marriage will result in King David.*

[4] We might have expected 3:15 to say that Ruth left and *she* went back to town. However, the most reliable Hebrew texts say that *he* went into town. Boaz was so eager to marry Ruth that he rushed into Bethlehem.

[5] Although some English translations have Boaz call the man *"my friend"*, he actually addresses him in Hebrew as *"such a one"*. That's not very friendly, betraying his eagerness to overcome this rival.

must also marry Ruth and count the first son born to them as if he were the son of her dead first husband Mahlon. Acquiring Elimelek's land will produce a child that has a claim to inherit the rival suitor's estate in the dead man's name. Redemption always carries a hefty price tag.

What Boaz is discussing here in front of the elders of Bethlehem is known as "levirate marriage". It was commanded in the Law of Moses for the same reason that the daughters of Zelophehad were to be counted among the clans of Manasseh. The Lord had promised an inheritance to the people of Israel and it matters to him how much we care about inheriting our Promised Land. The stipulations concerning levirate marriage in Deuteronomy 25:5–10 were extremely strict in this regard. They insisted that if a close relative refused to marry his brother's widow and count their first son as his brother's heir he was to be shamed before his Israelite neighbours. If the elders of the city were unable to convince him to step into his dead brother's shoes, they were to take off one of his own shoes and spit in his face for despising his brother's family line. His own family would forever be labelled "The Family of the Unsandalled" in memory of his sin.[6]

To the relief of Boaz, the other potential guardian-redeemer isn't willing to rescue Elimelek's family from their poverty. It doesn't matter that Ruth is beautiful or that her dead husband and father-in-law are about to lose their share in the Promised Land. The rival is thinking only of himself. He does not wait for the elders to rip his sandal from his foot. He gladly takes it off and hands it to Boaz. Better to be given a derogatory nickname than to risk losing his estate to a child that bears another man's name.

The decision to become Ruth's guardian-redeemer is every bit as costly for Boaz. He is a landowner too, so he is in just as

---

[6] There is a similar stipulation in the *Nuzi Tablets*, legal texts from the Akkadian Empire (*c.* fifteenth century BC). It expressed a refusal to step into a dead man's shoes and a conceding of that right to someone else.

much danger as his rival. He has been waiting for decades to find a woman who will bear him an heir, so marrying Ruth is not to his advantage either. What's more, he knows that she was married to Mahlon without producing any children, so she may well be infertile. Even if she does bear him children, the words of Deuteronomy 23:2–3 must be echoing in his head: "No one born of a forbidden marriage nor any of their descendants may enter the assembly of the Lord, not even in the tenth generation. No Ammonite or Moabite or any of their descendants may enter the assembly of the Lord, not even in the tenth generation." In no way is this a profitable match for Boaz.

Nevertheless, his mind is made up. He will lay down his life to become Ruth's redeemer. He used a Hebrew perfect tense in 3:13 to promise her, *"I have redeemed you"*, and he is true to his word. Without giving his rival any time for second thoughts, he declares in Hebrew legal-speak that he is buying Elimelek's land, marrying Ruth and counting their first son together as the heir of Elimelek and Mahlon, not his own heir. Once again, Boaz acts as a prophetic pointer to a greater Redeemer who threw away his own life to pay the price of our redemption with his blood. Jesus is the God who keeps on giving.

In Hebrews 12:1–2, the New Testament encourages us to picture ourselves in this scene. We are Ruth, Jesus is Boaz and Christians throughout the centuries are the elders of Bethlehem. We ought to rush gladly into the arms of our Redeemer. *"Therefore, since we are surrounded by such a great cloud of witnesses, let us throw off everything that hinders and the sin that so easily entangles... fixing our eyes on Jesus, the pioneer and perfecter of faith. For the joy that was set before him he endured the cross, scorning its shame."*

Surprise Ending
(Ruth 4:11–22)

The women living there said, "Naomi has a son!" And they named him Obed. He was the father of Jesse, the father of David.

(Ruth 4:17)

Nobody saw this ending coming. Not Naomi, not Ruth, not Boaz and not us. Nobody expected the story to end this way. Nobody, that is, except the God who keeps on giving.

Naomi expected to die alone. It was nice that one of her daughters-in-law had followed her back to Bethlehem but, with no more sons to take the place of Ruth's dead husband, it wouldn't stop her husband's family line from dying out in Israel. She expected to die a pauper's death, ignored by any guardian-redeemer. After all, who would jeopardize their own estate to help a washed-up old widow and a foreign migrant worker?

So the book of Ruth has a surprise ending for Naomi. The Lord exceeds her wildest dreams in these final verses of the drama. Read the words of the women of Bethlehem slowly. They see Boaz as *her* guardian-redeemer, rather than Ruth's, since he stepped in to restore the fortunes of Elimelek's family. They see the baby that is born as *her* child because he is the fruit of a levirate marriage. They crowd around the little baby Obed and declare excitedly that *"Naomi has a son!"* Under Hebrew law, he is not counted as the child of Boaz, but as the son of Mahlon and the grandson of Elimelek. The book of Ruth begins with Naomi watching the three men she loves die. It ends with her delighting in the resurrection power of the God who keeps on giving.

Ruth had her own private fears. She expected to be overlooked by the single men of Israel. After all, why choose a second-hand foreigner when there were so many virgin Israelite women to choose from? Who in their right mind would choose to exclude their children from the Tabernacle by marrying a Moabite? Even if she found a man who was willing to take her in, Ruth had another fear. She had been married to Mahlon for several years without managing to conceive a child. She was probably infertile. The writer hints at this when he tells us in verse 13 that *"the Lord enabled her to conceive"*. This is one of only two occasions in the entire book that the narrator speaks explicitly about God's action, so it is meant to denote that she belonged to that long line of women in the Bible who were initially infertile: Sarah, Rebekah, Rachel and the mothers of Samson and Samuel. Ruth feared she would never hold a baby in her arms.

That's why these final verses contain a surprise ending for Ruth. The Lord responds to the blessing that the elders of Bethlehem spoke over Boaz in verses 11–12: *"May the Lord make the woman who is coming into your home like Rachel and Leah... May your family be like that of Perez, whom Tamar bore to Judah."*[1] Like the infertile Rachel and the twice-widowed Tamar, the Lord enables her to conceive a baby that will play a vital role in the unfolding history of Israel. The book of Ruth ends with the safe birth of her baby Obed, which means *Servant*. She has brought forth for Israel an obedient servant of the Lord.

Boaz did not expect the story to end this way either. As an unmarried man in his forties, he must have looked around at all his married friends and wondered whether the Lord would leave him on the shelf forever. Even when he met and fell in love with Ruth, he knew that their match would not be like those of his friends. Their first child together would not be counted as

---

[1] Perez was conceived in Genesis 38 when Judah unwittingly performed his levirate duty to his dead son's widow, yet he was counted as the son of Judah. This blessing asks God to safeguard the name of Boaz too.

his, but as Elimelek and Mahlon's. It can't have been easy for him to hear the women of Bethlehem hail his newborn baby as Naomi's son and for them to name the baby without him.[2] It must have hurt when they reminded her in front of him that he was legally a guardian-redeemer: he had sacrificed his paternity rights for the sake of another. Boaz expected to cuddle this baby but not to be known as his father.

These final verses therefore contain a surprise ending for Boaz too. He discovers that the God who keeps on giving is the God of death and resurrection. The Lord is delighted that Boaz was willing to sacrifice his own name to preserve that of Elimelek and Mahlon. He therefore responds to the blessing spoken over him by the elders of Bethlehem in verses 11–12: *"May you have standing in Ephrathah and be famous in Bethlehem... May your family be like that of Perez, whom Tamar bore to Judah."*[3] Yes, Obed will be counted as the heir of Elimelek and Mahlon when it comes to inheriting the Promised Land of Israel, but God has promised his people something far bigger than 8,000 square miles of land in the Middle East. Obed was counted as the child of Elimelek in the land registry of Israel, but he is counted as the child of Boaz in the family tree of the Messiah. Note whose name appears in the family tree at the end of the story: *"Salmon the father of Boaz, Boaz the father of Obed, Obed the father of Jesse, and Jesse the father of David."*[4]

So the book of Ruth has a surprise ending for us all. When this book began by telling us that its events took place during the days of the judges, we did not expect its love story to provide the Lord's solution to the greatest problem of that period: *"In those days Israel had no king; everyone did as they saw fit."* When

---

[2] The verb in 4:17 is a feminine plural. Naomi and her friends named the baby, not Boaz.

[3] Ephrathah was the old name for Bethlehem in the days when Rachel was buried there (Genesis 35:16–20; Micah 5:2).

[4] This is a very abbreviated family tree, since David was born in c.1040 BC, over 800 years after Perez!

the book began with three dead men from the tribe of Judah, we did not expect their family to fulfil God's great promise to their tribe in Genesis 49:10: *"The sceptre will not depart from Judah, nor the ruler's staff from between his feet, until he to whom it belongs shall come and the obedience of the nations shall be his."* We did not expect the last word of the book of Ruth to be *David*, but of course the writer did. He has been preparing this surprise ending from the very start. He has brought the three books of Joshua, Judges and Ruth to their perfect conclusion.

The big theme of the book of Judges was that God keeps on giving to sinners. When the family tree at the end of Ruth is extended at the start of Matthew's gospel, we discover just how much this is true. There is Tamar, who played the prostitute with Judah to conceive Perez. There is Rahab, who played the prostitute with lots of men in Jericho. There are Boaz and Ruth, the ageing Hebrew bachelor and the Moabite widow. There is King David, not excluded from the Tabernacle by the stipulations of Deuteronomy 23, but invited to build a new Tabernacle on Mount Zion by the lavish grace of God. The Lord decrees that Ruth will not corrupt the children of Boaz with the idols of Moab. Like Jesus touching lepers, the infection will work the other way around! The Lord purified Ruth and her children so that they could play a key role in his plan to bless Israel.[5]

The extended family tree in Matthew's gospel keeps on going, way past David, to the birth of Jesus, the true Messiah who was born to their family in Bethlehem eleven centuries later. That would have surprised even the writer of the book of Ruth. Even he gets to share in this surprise ending inspired by the God who keeps on giving.

---

[5] These stipulations were still in force centuries later in Nehemiah 13:1–3, but Boaz and Ruth's family acted as a prophetic promise of their being undone through the blood of Jesus (Isaiah 56:3–7; Hebrews 2:11).

Conclusion: The God Who Keeps on Giving

Then Boaz announced to the elders and all the people, "Today you are witnesses... Today you are witnesses!"

(Ruth 4:9–10)

For the first 1,000 years of Church history there was pretty much only one Church. You were either part of it or you were not, end of story. That's one of the reasons why the Christian Gospel spread so rapidly in the first few centuries. There was one message, one baptism and one people of God. Despite fierce persecution, the Church emerged victorious, as in the days of Joshua. Even the idols of the mighty Roman Empire fell.

But the Church grew corrupt and complacent. It became more like the book of Judges. People's hearts turned to the world instead of worship, towards money instead of mission, and to the pursuit of human plans instead of the promises of God. As in the days of Abimelek, God's people began to forget that there is only one true King, one true Saviour, one true Deliverer and one true Redeemer. They provoked the Lord to judgment. Vast swathes of the Christian world fell, either to Islam or to worldliness and apathy. In 1054, the Church split in two: Catholic in the West and Orthodox in the East.

From time to time, the Lord raised up leaders to refocus them on Jesus as their King. Monks such as Benedict and Dominic and Francis of Assisi called people to withdraw to find intimacy with him. Theologians such as Anselm and Thomas Aquinas and Thomas à Kempis helped people to rediscover many of the promises in his Word. Missionaries such as Patrick and Cyril and Ramón Llull reminded the Church that many nations had yet to hear the Good News about him. Much of the time, however, it was a lot like the book of Judges. Christians largely learned to live with the way things were.

In 1517, the Church splintered even further. After the Reformation, there were no longer two churches. There were now dozens: Lutherans, Anglicans, Anabaptists, Baptists, Presbyterians, Episcopalians and just about every shade in between. Some of this was positive. Gospel truths that had lain hidden for centuries were rediscovered, and millions of Europeans were saved from nominal Christianity into a genuine knowledge of Christ as Lord. Missionaries were sent to all the other continents of the world. Many were martyred and many more died of diseases, but slowly people from Africa and Asia and the Americas came to accept Jesus as their Lord. There were many moments of triumph, but there were also long periods of disobedience and decline.

The twentieth century saw the greatest changes in Church history. Some were positive. More people surrendered their lives to Jesus in Africa, Asia and South America in that century than in all the previous centuries combined. Churches rediscovered that part of the Promised Land they had been given was a daily experience of the Holy Spirit's power. Pentecostalism became one of the fastest-growing movements in Church history. Advances in technology enabled Gospel preachers to reach millions at a time.

At the same time, the Church splintered further. In 1900, there were a few dozen denominations, almost all of them split by differences in theology. By 2000, there were over 20,000 different groups of churches all around the world, divided more often by personalities and preferences of style than on theological grounds. Disunity became the norm, yet few believers even viewed this as abnormal. Never before had the

Church looked so much like the book of Judges: *"Israel had no king; everyone did as they saw fit."*

As we end our journey through Joshua, Judges and Ruth, we need to recognize that the message of these three books is still hugely relevant for our own day. They culminate with Boaz issuing a solemn charge to the elders and people of Bethlehem, *"Today you are witnesses... Today you are witnesses!"* Boaz could just as easily be issuing that solemn charge to us. Together we have witnessed how the Lord led the people of Israel for 300 years. We desperately need to respond to what we have seen.

We need to respond to what **Joshua 1–12** says about the vast scale of **God's gift to his people**. We mustn't settle for the lowest-common-denominator Christianity that quickly descends on our churches whenever we focus too much on what we have been saved *from* and not enough on what we have been saved *for*. We mustn't squat in the hallway of our salvation, when Jesus wants to lead us into all the rooms of the palace of Christianity. We must follow him over the River Jordan to possess our Promise Land.[1]

We also need to respond to what **Joshua 13–24** says about the full extent of **God's gift to each of us**. We mustn't become passive about the promises he has given us personally. We need to learn to trace the contours of the specific land that he has allocated to us. The Devil knows he is defeated. He is in damage-limitation mode. He hopes to trick you into thinking that pockets of your Promised Land are unwinnable. He hopes to lure you into compromise with sin. Don't listen to him. Stand up to him. Go and get your land!

At our stage in Church history, it is particularly crucial that we respond to what **Judges** says about **God's gift to sinners**. Looking at the condition of the Church today, it's easy to get depressed, so we need to remember what God did through the

---

[1] God saves us to enjoy *him* (Exodus 19:4), to enjoy *freedom* (Leviticus 26:13), to enjoy *his blessing* (Deuteronomy 4:20) and to enjoy *your Promised Land* (Leviticus 25:38). Anything less is sub-Christian.

dirty dozen judges of Israel. If we devote ourselves to Jesus as our true King, doing whatever he tells us rather than what seems good in our own eyes, we will see the Church restored to purity, unity and revival. The judges blew ram's-horn trumpets as prophetic pointers to the blood of Jesus. We have the real thing. The judges had occasional experiences of the Holy Spirit strengthening them for victory. We have the promise of Pentecost every day. We are given power to live out Revelation 12:11: *"They triumphed over him by the blood of the Lamb and by the word of their testimony; they did not love their lives so much as to shrink from death."*

So let's respond to the way the book of **Ruth** makes all of this personal. How will you respond to **God's gift to you**? Whatever your situation, you have a Guardian-Redeemer who is loving enough and powerful enough to transform it in a day. You may not know the end of your life's story, but you do know its final word. It isn't just *David*, like the book of Ruth. It's something far better than Boaz, Ruth or Naomi ever knew. It's *Jesus*.

Studying Joshua, Judges and Ruth together, you have witnessed God's people floundering for 300 years as they waited for God's King to come. Since you live on the other side of that King's arrival, live in the good of his words: *"The kingdom of God has come upon you... The kingdom of God is in your midst... Seek his kingdom.... Do not be afraid, little flock, for your Father has been pleased to give you the kingdom."*[2]

The God who keeps on giving has now given you his King. Don't settle for anything less than his Promised Land.

---

[2] Luke 11:20; 12:31–32; 17:21.

STRAIGHT TO THE HEART SERIES

TITLES AVAILABLE: OLD TESTAMENT

ISBN 978 0 85721 001 2

ISBN 978 0 85721 056 2

ISBN 978 0 85721 252 8

ISBN 978 0 85721 428 7

ISBN 978 0 85721 426 3

ISBN 978 0 85721 754 7

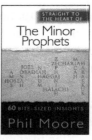

ISBN 978 0 85721 837 7

STRAIGHT TO THE HEART SERIES

TITLES AVAILABLE: NEW TESTAMENT

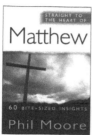

ISBN 978 1 85424 988 3

ISBN 978 0 85721 642 7

ISBN 978 0 85721 799 8

ISBN 978 0 85721 253 5

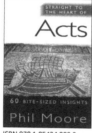

ISBN 978 1 85424 989 0

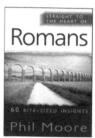

ISBN 978 0 85721 057 9

ISBN 978 0 85721 002 9

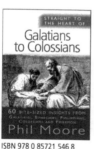

ISBN 978 0 85721 546 8

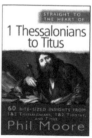

ISBN 978 0 85721 548 2

ISBN 978 0 85721 668 7

ISBN 978 0 85721 756 1

ISBN 978 1 85424 990 6

OTHER TITLES FROM PHIL MOORE:

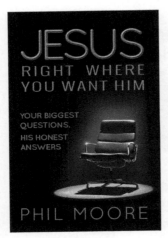

ISBN 978 0 85721 677 9

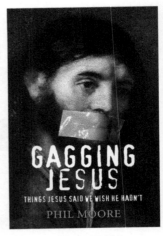

ISBN 978 0 85721 453 9

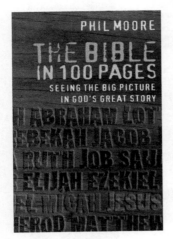

ISBN 978 0 85721 551 2

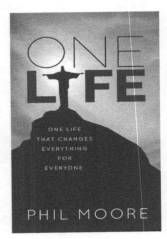

ISBN 978 0 85721 801 8

Lightning Source UK Ltd.
Milton Keynes UK
UKHW020806300819
348855UK00007B/89/P